Electrifying the Rural American West

Electrifying the Rural American West

Stories of Power, People, and Place

LEAH S. GLASER

University of Nebraska Press
Lincoln and London

© 2009 by the Board of Regents
of the University of Nebraska.
All rights reserved. Manufactured
in the United States of America. ∞

Library of Congress
Cataloging-in-Publication Data
Glaser, Leah S.
Electrifying the rural American
West: stories of power, people,
and place / Leah S. Glaser.
p. cm.
Includes bibliographical
references and index.
ISBN 978-0-8032-2219-9
(cloth: alk. paper)
1. Rural electrification—West
(U.S.)—History. 2. Electric
utilities—West (U.S.)—
History. I. Title.
HD9688.U53W345 2009
333.793'2—dc22
2009014811

Set in Scala.
Designed by A. Shahan.

Contents

Illustrations

Acknowledgments

This book is dedicated to the memory of Dr. Noel J. Stowe, 1942–2008.

Many people have contributed to the evolution and final completion of this book. I appreciate all of the help offered by so many of those rural Arizonans affiliated with the case study communities in this study. I am most grateful to those who shared their stories and memories with me through formal interviews. I am indebted to the Max Millett Family Fund, the Charles Redd Center for Western Studies, and the Associated Students of Arizona State University for their financial support while I conducted fieldwork for this project as a dissertation. I would also like to express my gratitude to Central Connecticut State University's School of Arts and Sciences for providing funding for the book's index through the Dean's Research Initiative. And a thank-you to editors Heather Lundine, Elizabeth Demers, and Gary Dunham, who took an interest in my topic and shepherded my dissertation into a book contract.

I credit several other men and women with helping me collect a vast amount of information and source materials within and outside of traditional archives. Wayne Crane of the Sulphur Springs Valley Electric Cooperative and Tim Brown of the Arizona Electric Power Cooperative provided invaluable aid and assistance since the inception of this work as a seminar paper topic years ago. It was largely because of their openness and friendliness that I decided to pursue this topic. I also want to recognize Jim Donahue of the Grand Canyon State Electric Cooperative, Nelson Peck of the Graham County Electric Cooperative Association, Edres Barney of the Eastern Arizona Museum and Historical Society, and Raydene Cluff of the Graham County Historical Society as exceptionally useful resources. I will not forget the generosity of the Sloans for opening their home to me during my trip to Willcox. Marian Garsha and the staff at the Navopache Electric Cooperative welcomed me into their office and gave me wonderful suggestions about interviewees. Raymond Endfield went out of his way to meet and speak with me about Navopache as well. Randall Medicine Bear, Marlene Tsosie, Walter Wolf, and Malcolm Dalton of the Navajo Tribal Utility Authority (NTUA) showed amazing generosity in sharing their time and resources to help me. The NTUA also provided my accommodations at the Navajo Nation Inn. Peterson Zah, Martin Link, and Bruce Gjeltema also gave me useful advice and exhibited enthusiasm for telling the NTUA's story.

Special thanks to Noel J. Stowe and Jannelle Warren-Findley, who served as academic and career mentors in my field of Public History and taught me to connect history to the present. Peter Iverson and Robert Trennert provided a foundation in the history of the American West and offered valuable comments on my work. David Nye's books on electrical history all served as great inspiration, and his encouragement to look at this topic on the American West, and particularly Native American reservations, helped inspire me to embark on this research. I want to thank the participants in the Clements Center for Southwest Studies Symposium on Indians and Energy—James F. Brooks, Benedict Columbi, Don Fixico, Brian Frehner, Andrew Needham, Colleen O'Neill, Dailan Long, Dana Powell, Sherry L. Smith, Rebecca Tsosie, and Garrit Voggesser—for their comments on a related work that really helped focus this one. Brian Cannon had valuable comments on this manuscript, as did Jay Brigham, who spent many hours reading through all of its permutations. Jay knew more about this topic than almost anyone else, and I owe him countless free lunches for the many conversations and e-mails that helped me focus my ideas.

Finally, I simply would not have completed this project without the support of amazing friends, my colleagues at Arizona State University and Central Connecticut State University, and my family. Special thanks go to my parents, Rochelle and John Glaser, and parents-in-law, Mary Alice and Gary Amerman. They have all listened to my frustrations for years and continued to love and support me through my most difficult moments. And of course, I owe my sanity and happiness since the inception of this research in graduate school to Steve Amerman, my husband, editor, colleague, and best friend. He and our children, Meredith Hope and Benjamin Ellis, have provided me with an atmosphere of encouragement, patience, warmth, humor, and much-needed balance.

Abbreviations

AAA Agricultural Adjustment Administration
AES Agricultural Extension Service
APA Arizona Power Authority
APS Arizona Public Service
BIA Bureau of Indian Affairs
GCEC Graham County Electric Cooperative
IRA Indian Reorganization Act
NTUA Navajo Tribal Utility Authority
OIA Office of Indian Affairs
PWA Public Works Administration
REA Rural Electrification Administration
SRP Salt River Project
SSVEC Sulphur Springs Valley Electric Cooperative
TVA Tennessee Valley Authority

Glossary of Electrical Terms

current: the flow of electricity.

electrification: the act of electrifying, the building of electrical infrastructure, or the distribution and use of electrical power.

load: the amount of current supplied by a source of electrical power and carried by an electrical system. Also refers to the various factors that may cause stress on an electrical system or on a tower or pole, which include electrical voltage, physical pull, wind pressure, climate, and market demand. This may include the variations of use over a twenty-four-hour day. Utilities calculate load in kilowatts.

kilowatt (kw): a unit of electrical power equal to 1,000 watts.

kilowatt-hour (kwh): the unit of electrical energy generated or used equal to one kilowatt acting for one hour. A kilowatt-hour measures the quantity of power consumed per hour and charged to each customer accordingly. For example, in 1938 lights and small appliances operated at about 30 kwh a month, a refrigerator at 50 kwh, a range at 150 kwh, and a water pump at 10–25 kwh.

voltage: the force of a current; a volt is the unit of measurement.

watt: a unit of measurement used to determine electrical power consumption. Today, an average table lamp uses 60–75 watts, while a large appliance like a refrigerator may require 600–1000 watts. Such appliance and household energy requirements have grown as new technologies have required more energy.

Electrifying the Rural American West

Introduction

"A Blessed Way of Life"

As the year 2000 approached, fanfare and doomsday predictions simultaneously accompanied the arrival of the new millennium and a post-industrial age. Yet, the preeminent technology of the last century's industrial era continues to loom large. A few minutes after four o'clock in the afternoon on August 14, 2003, when a regional blackout paralyzed eight northeastern states and two Canadian cities, no one in the northeastern United States could doubt the importance of electricity in twenty-first-century America. Computers shut down, trains and subways stopped moving, gas pumps stopped working, and food spoiled by the ton.

Until the lights go out, most Americans take their unrestricted access to electricity for granted, never pausing to consider its profound impact on their daily lives. The novelty of candles and lanterns placate many of us for a few hours, after which we assume bulbs will flutter back on and we will merely have to run around the house resetting the blinking clocks. As exhibited during the blackout of 2003, lengthier power outages cripple the economy and severely compromise the lives of many Americans, regardless of socioeconomic and ethnic background.

This failure of the northeastern regional power grid continued an ongoing twenty-first-century crisis that began across the country in the far West. In 2000 and 2001, shortages of electrical energy in California forced rolling blackouts. Utilities borrowed power from neighboring Washington and Oregon, consumers were fielding the expensive wholesale electrical power prices set by private companies like Enron, and the nightly news anchors speculated over California's economic future and the possible national impact of the events. The widespread interruption of electrical service and manipulation of the power market marked a national crisis. When a reporter asked if newly elected President George W. Bush would advocate energy conservation as a response, White House spokesman Ari Fleischer replied that high energy use constituted part of America's "blessed" way of life.[1] Other political leaders agreed, referring to electricity as "industrial oxygen" and the "flagship of the American economy." They echoed President Franklin D. Roosevelt, who said, "Electricity is no longer a luxury, it is a definite necessity."[2] Americans have advocated building electrical distribution lines as a primary tool for extending our values of freedom and democracy, whether to regions like rural America in 1933 or the Middle East in 2003.[3] Electrical lines may connect communities to all kinds of power sources, but local characteristics have determined the nature of electricity's role in different communities.

Equity and Electricity in America

Is electricity, by the nature of its production, distribution, and use, different from other commodities? Do the principles of social equality, democracy, and distributive justice apply? Does competition ensure the affordable delivery of electrical power to everyone?[4] The brownouts and the blackout at the turn of this century spotlighted Americans' socioeconomic dependence on electricity. Electrical power and its wide distribution historically played a vital role in stabilizing America's diverse communities and bringing them, for better or worse, into the industrial era. Americans wielded electrical power to transform, augment, unite, divide, or sustain social, cultural, and economic lives across communities and geographic regions. As the homestead acts and railroad accelerated American settlement after the Civil War, electrical power systems, with their elaborate and extensive infrastructure of substations, wires, towers, and poles, soon followed and spread westward across America's cultural landscapes as one of the industrial era's most prominent symbols of progress, power, and a modern lifestyle.[5] Government agents encouraged these ideas through large federal programs that reached into diverse rural communities across the country to homogenize and assimilate them through urban technologies. Since the 1920s, most Americans have considered electricity essential to living a modern American life, and the production and distribution of electrical power continues to be a controversial political issue that challenges values of free enterprise.

Eight years before the financial crisis of 2008, the electrical industry imploded. The Enron scandal reintroduced a nationwide debate on the regulation, production, distribution, and consumption of electricity.[6] A jury's conviction of Enron CEOs Jeff Skilling and Ken Lay on numerous fraud and conspiracy charges in 2006 generated article after article trying to make sense of the disaster that was the Enron scandal. Most writers tended to focus on the company's leaders as symbols of corporate greed and corruption: modern-day robber barons whose crimes led to the indictment of other high-profile CEOs. For many, the convictions seemed to close a sordid chapter in American business history. Yet others astutely observed that Enron's legacy raised questions about the company's business philosophy and its practices associated with government regulation of energy, particularly for electrical power. Columnists speculated about how this twenty-first-century company had changed the way American corporations conducted their business since before the Great Depression, subjecting any product or service, even electricity, to the open market.

As the fastest-growing energy company in the 1990s, Enron served as a leading advocate in the drive to deregulate the electric industry. Enron "was going to replace sclerotic government regulation with Adam Smith's invisible (and efficient) hand of the free market," observed Allan Sloan of *Newsweek*.[7] But as Harvard professor William Hogan argued, "markets only work when they are carefully regulated, not controlled by private companies."[8]

Deregulation severs the ties between utilities and local communities, divides electrical systems among various parties, and separates the functions of power generation, transmission, and distribution. This leaves no assurance that all Americans will have access to electrical power when they want or need it.[9] It may still be too early to assess the short- and long-term effects of deregulation on consumers, but the decision to deregulate marked a profound change in how Americans have viewed electrical power since the Great Depression, when the New Deal created a new activist role for government.

As California's energy crisis escalated, the Energy Information Administration (an independent agency within the U.S. Department of Energy) authored a far less publicized but startling report revealing gross violations of democratic equality and distributive justice. The March 2000 report disclosed that more than 14 percent of Native American households on reservations lacked access to electricity, compared to 1.4 percent of non-Natives. In addition, Native Americans paid the highest electrical rates in proportion to their income, while consuming the least energy per household. The report cited the tribes of the West, and particularly those in Arizona, as having the greatest problems accessing electricity. Hydroelectric dams, coal deposits, oil, and uranium mines have made many Native American reservations regional centers of power production, but communities like the Navajo Nation have the highest percentage of unelectrified homes in the country (37 percent).[10] The findings suggest links between what the government determines as an acceptable standard of living in America and the accessibility, distribution, and use of electrical power (a sequence hereafter referred to as "electrification").

The Department of Energy report illustrates the sharp divide between California and its neighboring western communities in their access to and use of industrial-age technology. Chronologically, western expansion and community building coincided with industrialization and the emergence of the electrical industry, yet few scholars have examined the interaction of these historical processes and explored electrification in the American West.[11] Historian Richard Lowitt indicated that the production of hydroelectricity, especially after the New Deal, essentially broke the West away from its "colonial" status to the industrial East. In 1989, historian David Nye asked others to acknowledge electricity along with the railroad as a technology that transformed the region's settlement.[12] Yet the disparity of its distribution and use poses a challenge to historical notions of a democratic lifestyle, economy, and culture.

With the decision of many states across the West and the nation to deregulate the electrical industry by opening electrical power production, and possibly distribution, up to free-market competition, the importance of equal access to electrical power and modern technologies has become increasingly relevant. Congress held hearings in 1998 and 1999 to determine the impact of deregulation on some of the country's most economically vulnerable communities: those in rural areas. Witnesses like Glenn English of the National Rural Electric Cooperative Association warned politicians that the high costs of rural service would "overwhelm the competitive benefit" and asked that flexibility be maintained in any federal legislation to account for local or regional differences.[13] These events indicate a need to review the history of regulation within the electrical industry. Who has controlled the process of electrification and its impact? What influence has government oversight had on providing access to and encouraging the use of technology across the nation's diverse communities and regions?

A Historical Review of Electricity in the American West

Throughout the twentieth century and even today, reformers and government officials have argued that those who gained access to the new technology became part of an emerging modern, industrial era in America. In the years following the Civil War, technological innovation, the rise of big business, immigration, urbanization, and the massive trans-Mississippi migrations in and around the American West transformed the United States from an agrarian nation into an industrial one. Technological innovations and mechanization spawned new economic structures, fueled new types of corporations, created new aesthetics, and inspired new ways of thinking, living, and working. Historians have long characterized this period as the Gilded Age, a phrase coined by Mark Twain to indicate an era of excess. The emergence of political movements like Populism and Progressivism, which emerged largely out of the southern and western regions to challenge and reform the power shifts of the industrial age, indicated that not all Americans shared in the wealth of the era. Decades earlier, socialist theorist Karl Marx characterized technology as "a weapon in the struggle between classes." Under laissez-faire capitalism, private parties determined who received the benefits of urban, modern technology and when. Marx advocated public control of technology in order to eliminate economic competition and ensure equal access to technology across class lines.[14]

The public regulation of utilities and other urban services was a prominent political issue in the early twentieth century. Some historians have enlisted the phrase "power wars" to describe the highly charged political debates over who should control the distribution of electricity in America during the 1920s and 1930s. Since the Great Depression, state and federal governments have maintained a strong regulatory hand in the electrical market by determining who has access to power lines and how much consumers pay for its delivery. Under the assumption that building reliable electrical systems necessitated the formation of natural monopolies, the 1935 Public Utility Holding Company Act granted state and federal governments the power to regulate utilities in the interest of consumers and to established a type of "regulatory compact."[15] In an effort to encourage environmental responsibility and alternative energy, the 1978 Public Utility Regulatory Policies Act opened up wholesale power competition for industrial customers and paved the road for retail competition.

Mark Rose and Jay Brigham have specifically explored electrification in communities throughout the early twentieth century, emphasizing the importance of localism in the electrification process.[16] Literature about local electrification efforts outside major urban centers has primarily revolved around the New Deal's Rural Electrification Administration (REA), which provided loans and guidance to rural communities to build electrical systems when investor-owned utilities considered such communities unprofitable. Most studies about the REA have taken a broad agency overview or focus on the Southeast or the Midwest. Others have also claimed that the REA had less impact in the West than in other regions, based largely on the idea that hydroelectricity and irrigation presumably already made electricity more available to farmers.[17] Yet, as historians of the region attest, the West deserves examination specific to its own historiography, history, and geography.

At the 1893 World's Fair in Chicago, Frederick Jackson Turner, arguably the most influential interpreter of the American West, linked the West with the values of technological progress and equality in his famous thesis on the "significance of the frontier."[18] Referred to as "The White City," the Chicago exposition featured fantastic displays of electricity to celebrate the idea of technology as progress and as America's future. Still Manifest Destiny and Thomas Jefferson's dreams of an agrarian nation continued to penetrate the hearts and minds of millions of eighteenth- and nineteenth-century Americans, including Turner. According to the essay, the self-sufficient yeoman farmer had embodied the cherished republican values of independence, equality, and democratic opportunity. As long as the western regions offered "free land," Turner argued, America could remain democratic and farmers would continue to preserve and transplant those yeoman traits on the frontier as they "progressed"—politically, culturally, and geographically—across the Great Plains, the Rocky Mountains, and the southwestern deserts to the Pacific Ocean. However, Turner argued that the 1890 census revealed (at least statistically) that the frontier had "closed." The plow, the railroad, electricity, and other products of industrialization had encouraged so many settlements that the new demographics threatened to end Jefferson's pastoral ideal and America's rural tradition, even in its western lands.

In his classic work *The Machine in the Garden*, Leo Marx recognized the complexity of interpreting the modern American West in strictly rural, agrarian terms.[19] Many historians of recent years even argue that the West has become more urban than rural since the nineteenth century. "Cities do more than tie together open spaces and isolated individuals of the American West," claims Carl Abbott in *The Metropolitan Frontier*. "They also link the continental space into national and international systems for the exchange of people, products and ideas."[20]

As others departed from writing about the West as only a rural place, some historians initiated discussions about the state of the rural West in the twentieth century.[21] Technological infrastructure had connected people living on farms and in isolated towns to urban dwellers. Technologies like electricity broke down traditional rural community networks and created new relationships. While rural residents moved en masse to the cities, urbanites also migrated into rural communities to escape the city. When they got there, they demanded urban services.[22]

The fluidity with which people moved (and move) between

"rural" and "urban" residences opens the definitions of those terms to wide interpretation. And electricity further complicates the matter. The U.S. Census Bureau historically identified a rural community by population density (less than 2,500 people), but one might consider cultural attributes as well. In 1960 a government study of rural life in America observed: "The industrial society in which we live is urban through and through, especially in the United States, where the farmer is a businessman who keeps a sharp eye on domestic and world markets, applies scientific methods in seeding and feeding, owns a car and a television set, and has his wife and daughter dressed according to the latest fashion. Ecologically speaking, the American farmer does not live in a city, yet his ways are citified. He is of the city even though he is not in the city."[23]

Adopting this view, the arrival of modern technology like electricity—and more recently cable, computers, and the Internet—in rural areas in many ways "urbanized" them by providing miners, ranchers, farmworkers, and Native Americans access to urban information, services, and living standards. To a significant degree, such technologies accelerate the disappearance of a distinct landscape and lifestyle between cities and their surrounding hinterlands. Technology's impact on a community was and is complex. This study follows the view advanced by Hal Barron that rural areas became "urbanized" only to the extent that rural people used similar technologies and services. They did not wholly adopt urban values and cultural practices.[24] One can question whether the impact of electricity upon rural communities was progressive, beneficial, appropriate, or even detrimental to particular rural communities, but those communities largely determined the need for, access to, and use of electrical power.

Considering the historiography of both the American West and technology raises interesting questions for examining electrification and its role in redefining the rural community and lifestyle. Many of the "New Western Historians" have assailed Turner's notions of "progress" when it came to white settlement of the region and instead emphasized how diverse groups responded to that settlement. And likewise, recent historians of technology have placed less emphasis on stories of "progress" and the assumption that technology alone, irrespective of political or social influences, inevitably drives change in people's lives (a notion known as technological determinism). Rather, signature works in both fields undermined the notion of progress, Manifest Destiny, and determinism by arguing that building technological systems to support white settlements reflected political hegemony. Donald Worster's argument in *Rivers of Empire* focused on the idea that oligarchic men of means built large irrigation systems in the West to encourage settlement, urban growth, and economic development unsustainable by the region's environmental realities. Likewise, Thomas Hughes points out in *Networks of Power* that although technological systems may have defined a nation, these systems involved people as well as technology.[25]

Engaging histories explore the complex social process of electrification, in which people manipulate new technology to continue old practices. Recent scholars have shifted examination from the "inventors" to the users. People ultimately decided how to incorporate electricity into existing social patterns and landscapes. When the new technologies of the industrial age began to emerge, a technologically literate elite hoped to guide social change in a rapidly changing era. Race, class, gender, and rural status further marginalized certain groups from "insider" status. Early-twentieth-century progressive reformers believed that access to technology was a key factor separating rural people from their urban counterparts.[26]

As America entered the industrial era, urban life threatened to overwhelm the nation's cherished rural heritage. Urban progressive reformers convinced legislators that plumbing, refrigeration, sanitation, and electricity made it more desirable to remain in rural areas. They also argued that the "democratization" of electrical service would contribute to sacred values of equality by extending urban tools and services to rural people.[27]

Ronald Kline, a historian specializing in technology, presents further evidence that both the media and reformers increasingly associated "the inferiority of rural life" with the lack of electrical power. The reformers of the Country Life Movement (c. 1900–1920) believed that access to and proper use of new technology would improve rural lives. True social democracy would only occur with equal access to technology, and the reformers' ideas would have a large influence on government policies toward rural America. However, Kline argues that rural communities did not wholeheartedly embrace urban infrastructure and technologies as the reformers hoped. Rather, a "contested interaction between producers and consumers" determined the impact of new "urbanizing technologies," including electricity. Like many New Western historians, Kline stresses the idea that various groups exercised agency and resistance in the face of the changes others imposed, often controlling the impact of a particular technology on their lives. Rural people were active in incorporating the new technology into "existing cultural patterns."[28]

Similarly, social, political, and economic factors determined the electrification process. Kline's view of consumerism complements that of Lizabeth Cohen, who writes that various socioeconomic traditions and constructions of gender determined the influence of various new technologies, consumer goods, and appliances in the home. Other scholars, such as Ronald Tobey, Jay Brigham, and Mark Rose, stress that politics played a large part in the mass adoption and use of technology. Such literature suggests useful models with which to examine electrification within the context of the history and demography specific to the rural American West and Southwest.[29]

Historians of the American West have long argued that place

and landscape have dictated the region's unique history and development. In his classic work *The Great Plains*, Walter Prescott Webb introduced the view that "culture grew from place" and that the environment of the West—"its geology, climate, and landforms—differs fundamentally from the East." Aridity and flat, treeless expanses of land shaped all the creatures and societies that have inhabited this environment. Webb's critics argue that he placed too much emphasis on environmental forces and failed to account for cultural maintenance and the power of humans to shape their environment.[30]

As with other products of the built environment, the development of large energy systems was a confluence of cultural choices transmuted into legal mandates. Political ideas and federal programs encouraged electrification, modernization, and industrialization. If urban infrastructure contributes to an understanding of municipal development, as many public and local historians have attested, then surely that same infrastructure in rural regions would contribute to an understanding of those communities.[31] Electrical power systems physically connected traditionally independent rural communities with transmission and distribution lines, creating new technologically defined regions. The wires that eventually crossed rural farms, mountains, valleys, and ranges linked isolated settlements and brought them new tools, appliances, and electrical lighting.

Place, landscape, race, class, and gender typical of the American West complicate traditional discussions of rural electrification. Overcoming economic, cultural, and physical barriers, formerly isolated settlements developed ties to a wider regional culture and economy, often extending beyond politically defined borders. But rural communities maintained their sense of identity and place by accessing electricity in ways that allowed them to integrate these changes on their own terms. In consideration of all this scholarship, this study examines the electrification process as an intrinsically local one involving change, adaptation, and community organization and reorganization.[32] Communities designed electrical systems specific to their local and regional needs. In other words, technology is physically and functionally a product of a place and its people.

Rural consumers of various ethnic and cultural backgrounds may not have responded all that differently to electricity's new challenges and opportunities, but the experiences of various groups are highly relevant if those differences influenced the scope of a region's electrification, as seen in areas dominated by a single group such as Native Americans.[33] David Rich Lewis observes that "rural sociologists seem more interested in the experience of rural blacks or women than in Indians," when "in many ways their situation parallels that of the larger rural West."[34] However, local factors such as geography, historical experiences, culture, economic conditions, and legal status ensured that the electrification process would follow a path specific to Native American communities, among the poorest and most rural in the West. Like other groups, Native Americans had a nuanced response to electrification and the industrial values it introduced, but for Native communities such changes would present greater challenges than they would for non-Native communities.[35]

Rather than isolate ethnic communities into separate works, this book emphasizes the diverse experiences of a multicultural West within a shared rural experience and setting.[36] Eastern Arizona serves as a useful region for exploring how modern forces brought discrete, detached, and diverse communities together to share new cultural platforms.

Arizona as Case Study

Driving across eastern Arizona, one cannot help but notice that power lines and telephone poles are often the only man-made structures for miles. Sometimes they run alongside the road and stretch out for miles into the horizon, at other times they disappear into the forests or mountains, and often they lead to isolated homes or whole villages. While it may not represent the experience of rural electrification for all places, eastern Arizona holds several characteristics that can at least partially describe most areas of the rural American West. The state's rural population is historically ethnically diverse, its predominantly arid landscape varies from desert valleys to mountains of forest, much of the land is federally owned, and the state owes its development to federal land and water programs.

First, geography is one factor that precipitates or inhibits rural electrification, and eastern Arizona's landscape offers tremendous geographic diversity representative of the American West. While the flat, open desert has encouraged the outward expansion of cities, Arizona's dramatic and extreme rural landscapes of high mountain peaks, desert valleys, and deep canyons determine the degree of isolation and contact for different communities. While most of the state is known for its aridity, other parts are quite lush. The availability of natural and federal resources, access to political power, and communal or cooperative organization reshaped traditional rural lifestyles.[37]

Second, the state would not have claimed its prominent place in the Sun Belt today without electricity. Hollywood's classic Westerns still use Arizona's rough and expansive desert setting to evoke visions of solitude and independence that reinforce a rural agrarian and ranching mythology. However, beginning in the 1870s and 1880s American migrants brought industrial tools west to help them make a home in an unfamiliar terrain then known as Arizona Territory. Their settlement of Arizona as both a territory and a state chronologically coincides with the development of the electrical industry.

The introduction of utilities and services into Arizona towns like Tucson and Phoenix mirrored the national trend of urban development. Arizona's state constitution, written in 1912 during an era when exploitative business practices were of great con-

Map 1. The state of Arizona, highlighting areas of study.

Source: Data compiled from the Salt River Project and the Arizona Department of Transportation.

cern, included stipulations about utility regulation. The document's authors created the Arizona Corporation Commission to regulate utilities and protect consumers.

Arizona and other states of the far West rivaled the Northeast in rural electrification largely due to water storage and irrigation activities. Hydroelectricity provided an ample source for power in many western states. Advances in long-distance transmission opened new markets located miles from dam sites. Dominated by arid, desert lands, irrigation, and water control, the West relied upon its streams for agricultural and economic development. Electricity could efficiently exploit watershed and groundwater sources with pumps. Electricity could extract precious minerals, the state's most valuable economic resources. The 1911 construction of Roosevelt Dam in central Arizona not only provided ample water for irrigation to the Salt River valley but placed hydropower production and delivery under the government's jurisdiction. As the beneficiary of one of the Bureau of Reclamation's first hydroelectric programs, the Salt River Project, Arizona provided the raw materials of cotton and copper for consumption and processing throughout industrial America during the early twentieth century. Largely due to the dam, Arizona became one of the country's leading states in rural electrification by 1935, with 5,900 of its farms, nearly 30 percent, receiving central station service. In comparison, less than 5 percent of the farms in the South had electrified.[38]

Thirty-two companies, four municipal systems, eight associations and power districts, and five Bureau of Reclamation or U.S. Indian Service projects operated utility systems in Arizona. Fourteen private companies delivered to mining operations, lumber companies, and three railroad companies. Several small power plants served shops, farms, and homes.[39] This achievement, however, is misleading, because the communities receiving electrical power were usually located near the state's most populated agricultural settlements, like those around Phoenix,

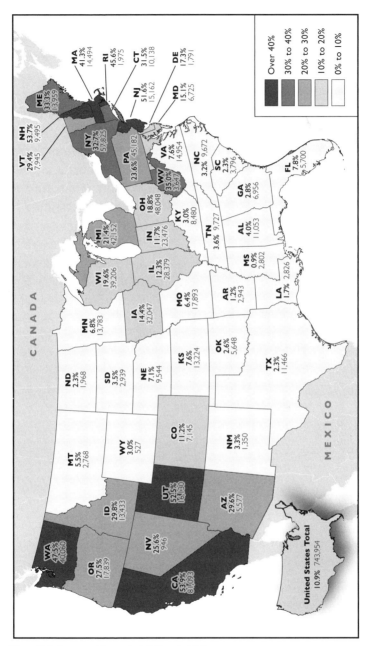

Map 2. U.S. farms receiving central-station electricity, 1935.
Source: Rural Electrification News 1, no. 7 (1936): 16.

and mining towns like Globe or Bisbee where electrical service remained profitable. Those areas with low population density, often with large ethnic diversity, would need to look for additional resources.

Thus the diversity of the rural population is the third reason that eastern Arizona can be considered representative of other areas of the West. When the United States took control of the area under the Treaty of Guadalupe-Hidalgo in 1848 and the 1852 Gadsden Purchase, the territory was already home to Mexicans citizens and Native American tribes. From 1910 to 1930 the census considered 88.2 percent of Arizona's rural residents non-white, as compared to 14.4 percent of the nation.[40] Because of the expense of building power lines to a limited market, people living outside concentrated settlements of all ethnic backgrounds had little hope of accessing electricity. Before the 1930s, primarily major population centers like Phoenix and Tucson received the bulk of their hydroelectric power from large Bureau of Reclamation projects.

Beyond the Rural Electrification Administration

With the aid of New Deal programs, many rural communities took the initiative and constructed electrical distribution systems. Like many of the New Deal's early social programs, the REA did not benefit all groups equally and was not a panacea for rural electrification. Regardless of the REA's promises and many success stories, obtaining an REA loan was a lengthy, complicated, bureaucratic, and often prohibitive procedure for even the most deserving communities. It was also one that required community cooperation, cohesion, persistence, and common goals. Through the U.S. Department of Agriculture's Agricultural Extension Service, county agricultural agents joined state agencies in encouraging the electrification process at the local level as well.[41] Lastly, for many communities, and particularly for those discussed here, the REA is only a small part of larger and more complex stories about the challenges of electrification that continue well past the New Deal and into the postwar period.

This book is therefore not a history of electrical technology or of a single agency. It will not repeat previous work about the impact of electricity on individual homes and farms, which was obviously profound nationwide. Rather, it is a social history of electrification within particular historical and regional settings. Because electrical distribution systems emerged from existing places, geography naturally lends itself to a particular way of telling the story of rural electrification in Arizona. A focus on a particular place and setting highlights the issue of who (beyond the categories of "rural" and "urban") had access to electricity. Change "did not occur for everyone at the same pace nor to the same degree."[42] Ultimately, electrification and its impact depended upon a combination of local factors, including location, population density, culture, housing type and degree of home ownership, an area's economic and demographic makeup, and community action. When these factors denied communities electricity, people were left behind in an industrial era where electrified homes increasingly became a standard for modern living.[43]

Finally, the study of specific regions also reflects the relatively recent scholarship involving cultural landscapes, an interdisciplinary field that examines the interaction of people with places, particularly within those spaces from which inhabitants "derive some part of their shared identity and meaning."[44] A "regional community bound by kinship as well as economy" offers not only an interpretive framework but also an organizational structure.[45] Regional communities do not always conform to political boundaries, and likewise electrical service areas did not always stop at state or reservation boundary lines. Power lines created vast new regional networks.[46]

The three demographically and geographically representative regions examined here do not wholly reflect the complex history of electrification in the American West or even Arizona. Rather, they embody different concepts of "the rural West" in economy, culture, and landscape as defined by Douglas Hurt: "agricultural, small town, and reservation."[47] Readers will recognize similarities of experience among populations, and these are just as important to recognize as the differences.

The chapters that follow describe three rural Arizona communities before, during, and after electrification. The first, in southeastern Arizona, is a largely white desert farming and ranching community; the second is an ethnically diverse company town in the mountains; and the third is a region dominated by Native lands. The discussions are arranged chronologically, following the order of regional electrification. This sequence advances an overall narrative that describes the process of rural electrification across different populations, ending with the seemingly most dramatic example of local power and adaptation in a predominantly Native American region.

The accessibility, distribution, and incorporation of electricity into rural Arizona reflected local characteristics. Each region's traditions foreshadowed the role of an emerging electrical system, one that linked individual communities, altered the area's economy, and introduced selective urban amenities into homes. Reformers and government agencies may have argued that electrification would offer equality and a better, even "blessed," way of life to rural areas, but rural Arizonans of diverse cultural and geographic backgrounds resisted homogeneity and urbanization. Although they were consumers of electricity, they also thought beyond consumerism to pursue power for local needs. They enlisted electricity to exploit the land's natural resources, to create economic opportunity and stability, and so to preserve existing rural communities within an emerging twentieth-century industrial society. Together their stories reveal the challenges of connecting to power, one that might be fruitfully compared to areas throughout the American West and perhaps beyond America as well.

1

Empowering Agrarian Dreams

The Cooperative Model in Southeastern Arizona

The arid, hot desert climate and seasonal crops of southeastern Arizona forced residents to be creative about food preservation. In lieu of refrigeration, rural women employed a variety of solutions that contributed to traditional customs of food preparation and diet. Many people dripped a pan of water over a screened wooden box to keep its contents cool. Some, particularly women of Mexican heritage, practiced alternative methods as well.

Rosalia Salazar and Esperanza Montoya recalled how their families canned jellies and preserves. They also dried fruit, chilies, and meat on wooden planks or steel wire, covering them with cheesecloth to protect the food from insects. Potatoes and carrots stayed fresh in burlap bags stored in the shade. Salazar's mother prevented meat from spoiling by frying it up, rendering its fat, and storing the meat in large cans. These techniques produced many traditional foods, including carne seca, carne adobada, carne asada, chili con carne, quesadillas, tortillas, soup, rice pudding, and even fried chicken on a wood stove. European Americans similarly dried their meat into jerky.

Women of both cultures recalled the time-consuming and labor-intensive activities of ironing and doing laundry. To his daughters, Epimenio Salazar would recite the proverb "It is not a sin to be poor, but to be dirty, heaven forbid!" In addition, Mexican families like the Salazars washed and ironed for the non-Mexican settlers who found the chores too burdensome.

First, the family would gather wood for a large fire to boil water, which they would need to haul up from the river. They boiled the clothes, scrubbed them against a ribbed board, and rinsed everything twice.

Such rigorous treatment was rough on fabrics, making ironing out wrinkles even more necessary than it might be today. Like many other rural families, the Salazars heated a heavy cast iron on the stove. The iron would get so hot that one had to hold the handle with a rag or risk a severe burn. A housewife's pride, claimed Cherrel Batty Weech of the Gila River valley, was a husband wearing a wrinkle-free shirt, even in the field. Weech recalls that her mother hated ironing by the hot stove in the summer heat so much that her family purchased a gas-powered iron in addition to other gas or kerosene appliances (a refrigerator and washer). However, she feared the safety and reliability of gas-powered motors. Besides, they created chores for children like Weech, who had to fill the lamps and tanks every week. The worst, complained Lillie Harrington of Cochise, was chopping and hauling the wood for the stove and fireplace.[1]

The laborious, pre-industrial domestic chores of rural women like Weech, Salazar, and Montoya inspired the national effort of rural electrification. These women elicited enormous sympathy from reformers, regardless of a 1923 study which concluded that 92 percent of farm women nationwide found pride in their work, generally enjoyed rural culture, and resented the Country Life Movement's suggestion that they lived like drudges.[2] Still, the options for lighting or heating a home without electrical power often proved hazardous. One had to continually trim the wicks of kerosene lamps, and wood stoves could, and often did, cause fires. As cities gained access to electrical lights and appliances, the domestic duties of rural homemakers became increasingly different from those of their urban counterparts.

However, when the REA's chief administrator, John Carmody,

received an application from Cochise County on December 14, 1937, the document did not stress the growing discrepancies between the domestic labor of Montoya, Salazar, and Weech and their urban counterparts. Instead, it argued that, unlike many pending applications, the primary purpose of the Cochise project would be for irrigation pumping, and the service area's high rural population ensured heavy use. County Agent A. Mark Bliss explained: "This means that not only would the occupants of the district be benefited through the availability of the electricity to add to home comforts and conveniences, but that their economic situation would be greatly improved and a large potential wealth would be added to the county, state, and nation."[3]

REA cooperatives brought so-called modern conveniences to rural homemakers across the country, but electricity had an additional (and arguably more significant) impact on arid areas like southeastern Arizona. It transformed a cultural and economic region historically dominated by ranching and transitory settlement into a new, technologically defined one of rich agricultural potential. An electrical system integrated two counties (Graham and Cochise) while it connected communities in southeastern Arizona's Sulphur Springs, Gila River, San Simon, and San Pedro valleys. Yet the process also required local leadership, negotiation, persistence, and community cooperation to realize the traditional settlement goals and values of Arizona's southeastern region and its homesteading communities.

Unlike Phoenix and the surrounding Salt River valley of central Arizona, the southeastern portion of the state remained almost entirely rural throughout the twentieth century. According to the census, mining towns such as Bisbee, Douglas, and Clifton constituted the area's few population centers, and even Clifton numbered less than three thousand. However many settlers looked to the region for its vast expanses of land rather than for mineral extraction. Southeastern Arizona's early history reveals the separate traditions and shared practices that settlers of European and Mexican heritage in rural areas established as they struggled to make historically arid land profitable for farming without the aid of electricity.

Searching for the Agrarian Dream in Southeastern Arizona

Southeastern Arizona hardly reflects Thomas Jefferson's image of an agrarian nation. Home to the infamous Earp brothers of Tombstone and the Apache heroes Cochise and Geronimo, southeastern Arizona boasts some of the most classic Wild West tales. Apache conflicts with the United States military throughout the nineteenth century are legendary. The stories surrounding the Cochise stronghold in the Chiricahua Mountains remain among the most dramatic examples of Native resistance to white settlement. The majority of southeastern Arizona's population were settlers of European and Mexican descent. Almost a third of them were foreign-born. Spanish speakers had begun settling in the area now known as southern Arizona as early as the eighteenth century and first established an agrarian presence in the area. After the Mexican-American War (1846–48), many of the large landowners with Spanish grants lost their lands to new American laws and settlement. The area's earliest roads connected several army posts where American soldiers guarded settlers against Native American attacks. Due to the violence, settlers of Mexican and non-Mexican heritage lived close together. This proximity encouraged social and cultural integration through intermarriage and joint business ventures.

The inhabitants of the San Carlos Apache Indian Reservation constituted less than 10 percent of the Graham County population at the time the government established it in 1871. Native Americans remained less than 1 percent of Cochise County's population for nearly a century, clustered around the border town of Douglas. By 1950, Hispanics and other Mexican migrants made up about 32 percent of Cochise County and 16–20 percent of Graham County; however, land records indicate dispersed settlement of Spanish-surnamed landowners. The few Mexican communities in clusters concentrated enough to geographically define a community were located in or near urban areas and labor camps associated with mining or farming.[4]

The capture of Chiricahua Apache Geronimo in 1886 heralded a new era of overwhelmingly white American homesteading, made up of settlers largely from the Midwest and of Mormon and Protestant backgrounds. These migrants clustered into various settlements and formed a new cultural region with values and traditions in opposition to those of the Apaches, utilizing industrial-era technology to settle, irrigate, and cultivate the land. Their community structures and collective goals for the land provided the seeds for electrification in the near future. Yet the region itself offered great challenges for the water-dependent settlement of the independent yeoman farmer.[5]

Throughout the nineteenth century and into the twentieth, mining and farming contributed to the development of southeastern Arizona, but an unstable cattle industry served as the primary economic activity. Cattle ranching in the region dates back to the seventeenth century, when Jesuit missionaries established cattle herds among the Tohono O'odham and Akimel O'odham communities (called Papago and Pima, respectively, by the Spanish). Spanish ranching families along the Santa Cruz and San Pedro rivers raised cattle beginning in the mid-eighteenth century. After independence in 1821, the Mexican government approved an estimated 63,681 acres of land grants, but ongoing conflicts with Apaches caused many would-be ranchers to abandon their efforts until the Americans arrived in the 1860s.[6]

Through public land distribution and administration, the U.S. government has managed, supported, and promoted land improvements across the American West, regardless of environmental conditions. Once surveyors divided Arizona Territory in accordance with the grid system that originated with the

Northwest Ordinance, individuals took advantage of the 1862 Homestead Act and rushed to claim their 160 acres of public land. The Homestead Act essentially distributed free property to anyone who would apply for and "improve" it by building a home and cultivating crops. According to the act, Mexican Americans who had resided in southeastern Arizona for years were "squatting" on what was technically federal land following the Mexican-American War. By the 1870s they bucked efforts of whites to dispossess them of their long-held land by becoming some of the first Americans to either purchase federal land or homestead. By 1890, Mexican Americans owned nearly a fourth of the formerly federal land in Cochise County. Settlers with Spanish surnames claimed 13–15 percent of the county's homesteads before 1900, although this proportion fell to 1 or 2 percent by the early twentieth century.[7]

Several migrants from Sonora and Chihuahua joined the Pueblo Viejo community in the upper Gila River valley to establish farms and ranches, but the area attracted those of European descent as well. U.S. Army colonel Henry Clay Hooker began the well-known Sierra Bonita Ranch, and the Riggs family settled on the western edge of the Chiricahua Mountains, where they established relationships with the nearby Apaches. German immigrant Isadore Solomon established Solomonville by the 1870s. Homesteaders of both European and Mexican heritage (as represented by the Montoya and Salazar families) likewise claimed settlement in Aravaipa Canyon. The canyon's resources provided families with opportunities in ranching, small-scale farming, and eventually zinc mining as early as the 1860s. Considered a refuge and fortress to nineteenth-century Apaches, the canyon remained a camping and foraging area for Apaches living on the reservation.

The 1880 arrival of the Southern Pacific Railroad in Willcox attracted more ranchers of both European and Mexican descent. All of the area cattlemen drove their stock to the town, which rivaled Tucson as one of the country's largest cattle-shipping centers. They established large ranches up and down the Sulphur Springs valley (named for its sulphur-rich springs) in 1883 and 1884. During the next two years, overgrazing began to limit the land's productivity. Drought compounded the problems, particularly when followed by heavy rains that washed away loose topsoil. Following such ecological calamities, grass would never again grow to its former height of one to two feet. Herd sizes diminished as ranchers moved cattle across state borders to graze.[8]

In spite of the ranchers' troubles, homesteaders sought to use the land in the region for raising crops. The territory seemed an ideal place to realize the dream of the independent yeoman farmer when it opened up to Americans in the middle of the nineteenth century. Much of the area's topography ranged from level desert valleys to high peaks like Mount Graham (10,720 feet). A variety of soil textures ensured diverse agricultural possibilities. When combined with steady rainfall, the upper Gila River with its tributaries of Aravaipa and San Simon creeks provided for a relatively high and stable water table, although during droughts the water table (which measures the distance of water from the earth's surface) could drop significantly.[9] Like so many other settlers of this period, they had faith in technology. They rationalized that "rain followed the plow" as they surged into arid lands to establish farms. New scientific and technological methods such as irrigation and dry farming promoted the expanding nation's long-coveted cultural value of landownership.

But in reality, the climate and geography of southeastern Arizona offered mixed opportunities for settlers to realize agrarian dreams. Surrounded by several mountain ranges, the Sulphur Springs valley stretches across the southwestern section of Graham County and through Cochise County to the Mexican border. Even today, the region is both arid and semi-arid. It simultaneously boasts rich, fertile soil and mild temperatures. Precipitation is variable, with years of heavy rains followed by severe drought. The northern part of the valley, near Willcox, has no exterior drainage; the water drains into the Willcox Playa, evaporates, or is absorbed by vegetation.

Fortunately, groundwater historically was fairly close to the surface and settlers could pump it up from the ground by hand. This attracted hundreds of determined farmers searching for a place to sink wells and raise crops in an economical manner. Sinking artesian wells deep enough would create enough pressure from underground water draining off of a higher plain to force the water upward. Because of this pressure, artesian wells required no outside power source to make irrigation pumping possible. In 1875 the territorial legislature offered a reward for the first artesian well in southeastern Arizona to pump water up from the ground. No one met the challenge until May 12, 1883, when W. H. Sanderson sunk a well thirty-eight feet deep and six inches in diameter with a flow of 40,000–50,000 gallons per day. Heavy rainfall in 1888 and 1889 revived optimism in the area and filled the dry washes for several months, prompting ranchers to use mechanized wells for retrieving water. The private Chiricahua Cattle Company operated a steam pump and installed windmills in other parts of the range.

The region continued to attract hopeful homesteaders from the Midwest, only to repeatedly disappoint them when years of prosperity were followed by extended drought. Statistics for precipitation and irrigated acreage between 1910 and 1935 reveal an unstable environment for cultivation as the amount of irrigated acreage in Cochise County continuously rose and fell. In anticipation of the possibility that the Bureau of Reclamation would establish an irrigation project or create a district that would benefit from one, settlers claimed land five to twenty miles southeast of Willcox. Further south, in the Sulphur Springs, San Simon, and San Pedro valleys, farms along the rivers proved that crop cultivation was more unpredictable than anticipated. Extending to the foothills of the Dos Cabezas and Chiricahua mountain ranges, the area known as the Kansas Settlement (named for the home state of a majority of its Euro-American residents) bloomed into a fertile farming community from 1908 to 1909. At the same time, others settled northwest of town in the Stewart District, a farming community that received water from shallow aquifers located further west. The 160 acres designated in the 1862 Homestead Act proved insufficient for successful farming or grazing in the unpredictable area, yet Congress continued to reinforce the belief that farming was an individual effort.

The Desert Land Act of 1877 allowed settlers to claim up to 640 acres, and Congress followed with more land-distribution legislation, including the Enlarged Homestead Act of 1909, which allowed settlers to double their claim to 320 acres of public land, and the 1916 Stockraising Homestead Act, under which people could claim up to 640 acres for grazing. But even the increased amount of property did not promote successful subsistence farming in Sulphur Springs valley. Boosters began to promote the area's health benefits and climate rather than its agricultural promise. Limited land base coupled with the light rains repeatedly spelled failure.[10]

By the end of the nineteenth century, several settlers in the Sulphur Springs and Gila River valleys had begun forming communal or cooperatively based organizations to help find solutions to the area's water and stock problems. Followers of the Church of Jesus Christ of Latter-Day Saints had successfully irrigated the Gila River valley as early as the 1880s. Also known as Mormons, these migrants differed from other Anglo-American settlers because they shared the region's limited water sources with one another.[11]

Others also soon realized that surviving rural life in southern Arizona required reliance on neighbors with common interests. Stock and cattle growers associations from Willcox played an active part in promoting cattlemen interests as well as support-

ing members during times of drought and low grasses by foraging crops for emergency feeding. When federal oversight of the
area's grazing lands limited land use in Cochise and Graham
counties, ranchers continued to successfully negotiate their grazing rights to state and national officials through local communally operated organizations such as the Cochise County Stock
Growers' Association (later the Cochise-Graham Cattle Growers'
Association). By 1916 the General Land Office (today known
as the Bureau of Land Management) transferred much of the
land to state jurisdiction, and new laws ended the environmentally impractical open-grazing policy with fencing regulations.
Mutual water companies irrigated 30,000 out of 57,257 acres
along the Gila River valley over the next few years. And by the
1930s, 11 percent of Cochise County farms engaged in cooperative marketing. While this number may not sound significant,
less than 5 percent of farms in the rest of the state engaged in
such activity.[12]

The federally sponsored Agricultural Extension Service (AES)
built upon these collective activities and offered settlers aid amid
their struggles. Researchers from the University of Arizona, a
state land-grant college, administered programs through the
Agricultural Experiment Station out of Tucson. Created by the
Smith-Lever Act in 1914, the AES responded to the pressures of
the Country Life Movement, which sought to bring the living
standards of rural people closer to those of their urban counterparts. Both the AES and the Country Life Commission, created
under Theodore Roosevelt in 1908, operated under the philosophy that, with proper guidance, farmers could improve their
luck on the farm as well as their standard of living.[13]

AES agents on the county level worked with farmers and ranchers to establish farm bureaus as well as marketing and production cooperatives to support them through difficult times. The
cooperative idea was similar to other the other types of rural organizations the settlers had formed in the past. Members own

and operate their cooperative and elect a board of directors who in turn hires a general manager to establish a staff. In most cases, each member gets only one vote regardless of the amount of service he or she receives. All of a cooperative's profits are allocated back to individuals based upon consumption.[14]

In addition to organization, AES also promoted alternative farming techniques. The agency administered an experimental dry farm in the Sulphur Springs valley that Arizona's territorial legislature established in 1912. The dry-farm movement originally developed during a rainy cycle on the Great Plains and had since moved westward. The dry-farming technique instructed people to plant seeds according to the soil's water supply in an effort to minimize water loss and soil erosion. This method conceivably encouraged the cultivation of crops suited to arid conditions, such as corn, wheat, and alfalfa. Unfortunately, while dry farming had proven at least moderately successful as a technique in places with more than fifteen inches of annual rainfall, the Sulphur Springs valley received an average of just over twelve inches between 1912 and 1924. By 1925, AES's own studies showed some success in growing alfalfa and beans but indicated the limited promise of dry farming in the valley. Extension agents encouraged residents to supplement with or convert to poultry or cattle-raising farms. Lacking the means to grow enough field crops to make a profit, many abandoned their farms.[15]

Those who remained looked to studies of irrigation pumping and concluded that almost any crop could be grown in the valley with a sufficient water supply. Many in the Gila and Sulphur Springs valleys managed to retrieve steady supplies of water from shallow wells through gravity irrigation. However, groundwater supplies never met their needs and high expectations. Ill-equipped to adequately use and maintain pumping equipment, settlers abandoned more than 75 percent of the pumping plants and 66 percent the farms by the 1920s. Some ranchers and farmers experimented briefly with solar equipment, but the wells with windmill pumps or small gas engines (which drew 310–2,000 gallons of water per minute) remained the most popular methods. A few large internal-combustion engines used fuel oil, but by the 1930s these machines were fifteen to twenty-five years old. Often very noisy and unreliable, they usually failed to sustain enough power to run nonstop for twenty-four hours. Frequent breakdowns and high repair and operating costs hampered the expansion of agriculture in the once promising Sulphur Springs valley, where only newer communities like Elfrida and McNeal with larger homesteads showed real agricultural success.[16]

Rural residents in the region had long viewed a central station power plant like those in nearby towns as the solution to their agricultural problems. However, the cost of such large pumping plants was beyond the means of most rural residents. Meanwhile, neighboring towns were beginning to enjoy varying degrees of electricity in their homes and businesses.

Electricity Comes to the Desert, but Not to the Farm

While the rural residents of Cochise County struggled to find economic independence in agriculture, ambitious individuals, entrepreneurs, small private enterprises, and municipalities began delivering central station service to the neighboring mining and railroad towns through self-contained, freestanding generators. These small, privately owned utility services targeted both industrial and domestic markets, but they lacked the technology, money, and generating power to extend their services beyond a local vicinity and customer base. Often, larger private companies moved into the service area to take over the growing demands of these small, independent systems. The origins of electricity in several towns illustrate this trend.

The Willcox Lighting, Pumping, and Ice Company introduced southeastern Arizona's first steam power plant on July 4, 1899, and literally inaugurated electrical power in town with bells and whistles blowing "like they meant business." The electric plant added to the town's claims of an "up-to-date" lifestyle with an ice plant. The local newspaper predicted that such advances would mean "a great boon to the housewife" and bring down insurance rates to the delight of area businessmen. "The mere existence of this magnificent compact in any community," the paper claimed, "would inspire confidence and pride in its public-spirited citizens." Unfortunately for Willcox's boosters, the town had a difficult time sustaining electrical use, because few customers could afford to pay the required power rates. Owners dejectedly sold the machinery to buyers in Mexico, leaving Willcox to wait another twenty-four years for electrical services to return. In the early 1930s, the Southern Arizona Public Service Company absorbed the town into its system.[17] Other municipal systems suffered a similar fate. As mineral production began to decline, electrical power offered faltering mining towns across the state an alternative future in industrial development. Bisbee, Tombstone, and Douglas boasted their own utility systems, and in the 1920s the operators of the Dos Cabezas Mining District introduced a new power plant to the flourishing mine.

Unfortunately, local industries did not always guarantee power to the homes of their workers. The closest electrified house to the predominantly Mexican labor community of Dos Cabezas was located in the nearby settlement of Mascot and belonged to the mine superintendent. Worker housing at Klondyke's zinc mines also lacked electrical service. Those employees fortunate enough to live near the mill site enjoyed electricity, except on weekends when the mill shut down. During that time, residents used kerosene and gas lamps to supplement butane heating and cooking.

Both Mexican and European settlers living beyond the mining communities of southeastern Arizona accepted the lack of electricity in the home as part of the rural way of life. Most lived in houses insulated from the hot weather, often made of adobe. Others constructed homes with lumber from local saguaro cactus ribs or tree trunks, and at least one family hauled in concrete. They enlisted their traditions of food preservation and arduous chores described earlier.[18]

Rural traditions were part of rural life, and throughout the 1930s it was difficult for companies to convince many urban customers to invest in expensive appliances that assured high electrical use. While a lightbulb only required 25 to 60 watts, a refrigerator would use 500 to 1000 watts, or more. Most rural people still lived too far from one another to qualify for power from major investor-owned companies, which claimed that while residents might need lighting, they would not consume enough electricity to provide a large enough electrical demand on the system.

Inexpensive electrical service required that power production be consistent with power consumption. With high electrical use as a necessary factor in lowering rates, power was extremely expensive in sparsely populated areas of Arizona. Profit-minded utilities considered the cost of constructing distribution lines too high given the amount of electricity such sparsely populated areas were likely to consume. Utilities labeled providing electricity under such circumstances "infeasible," leaving rural populations with few options for affordable and accessible electrical power.

Power-driven irrigation promised a higher and more balanced electrical load. Unfortunately, farmers irrigated seasonally, and such use did not ensure the consistency required for an electrical system to operate efficiently year-round. A 1934 study on Arizona power needs concluded that "any great industrial or agricultural expansion will demand a corresponding domestic expansion as the two go hand in hand."[19] Domestic use of electricity appealed to many Arizonans, especially women, but it would be hard for them to rely on the power production from individually owned electrical systems, as most of these enterprises could not sustain themselves economically. Smaller rural communities likewise lacked the funding, the equipment, and even the expertise of their urban counterparts to launch infrastructure projects independent of county or state support.[20] Still, communities continued to try to access electrical services.

As their parents had done with irrigation, the next generation of Mormons spearheaded the introduction of utility service into the upper Sulphur Springs valley in Graham County to build upon the communities their parents founded. In October 1910, several residents of Pima constructed an electrified house in which to hold their town meetings. The following year, amateur electrician David Weech wired his home and attached a small electric plant to his gristmill. The plant lit the community center located above his grocery store, which shone brightly on stormy days and early winter evenings. The Weech plant allowed residents of Pima to enjoy silent movies at a local theater through an electrical projector. Weech's activities attracted interest from neighbors, and he soon developed his own small utility service by stringing wires to several neighboring businesses. To meet the town's growing demand, Weech moved his mill and electrical plant to the railroad depot, where he delivered power for residents from dusk until ten o'clock at night. Aides cranked the engines in order to ignite the fuel each day, but twenty-four hours of service was not practical. When it was time to shut down the engine, Weech blinked the lights to warn his customers that they had about five minutes to get to bed or light a kerosene lamp. Increasingly, customers demanded longer hours beyond the capacity of the little Pima plant. The neighboring San Simon Electric Light and Power Company incorporated in 1925, but it too provided power to only a few residential and commercial customers. Meanwhile, the Arizona General Utilities Company increased its plant capacity and extended its central station lines west through the local distribution systems of Safford, Thatcher, Central, and Solomonville to join Weech's homemade system in Pima. Then, in the mid-1930s, the Arizona Edison Electric Company swallowed up the entire service area.[21]

Private, investor-owned companies like Arizona Edison took advantage of the struggling small utilities and began to acquire the electrical systems of the local towns and settlements across southeastern Arizona as early as the 1880s. They merged the start-up systems into regional monopolies or holding companies. These local utilities refused to offer service outside a certain radius, citing technological limitations. Long-distance electrical transmission was not successful until the turn of the century. After that, companies claimed it would be economically infeasible to build such lines from their power plants out to rural areas. Between 1916 and 1921, several individuals purchased expensive generating plants to run their farms, but over thirty unincorporated communities in southeastern Arizona remained without central station electrical power. In 1923 only 5.9 percent of Arizona's nearly ten thousand farms reported having either gas or electric lights, below the 7 percent reported nationwide. Even in 1934, individual plants provided only 3 percent of the county's farms with electrical service, while the local, private utility served only 19 percent of them with central station service.[22]

Arizona's rural residents remained part of a nationwide struggle to receive affordable electrical and communications technology through means other than the state's largest utility companies. Frustrated by what some viewed as a conspiracy to keep them from affording electricity, many farmers refused to pay the costs and continued to purchase and individually operate expensive and dangerous gas generators.[23] The nation's economic crisis in the 1930s only highlighted their lack of reliable, affordable, and accessible electricity.

The Great Depression Brings a New Deal

While the agricultural and mineral economies in southeastern Arizona had been volatile for decades, the stock market crash in 1929 and the ensuing Depression exacerbated the problems. The price of silver and copper fell, and managers decided to slow mineral extraction to save expenses. When the mining activity at centers like Globe, Miami, Clifton, and Morenci stopped, the small farming communities in the Gila River valley lost the primary markets for their crops. In addition, years of unregulated public land acquisition created serious overgrazing and soil erosion problems that further devastated local economies. Even many of the descendants of original Mormon settlers abandoned their land and moved out of the state. However, the Taylor Grazing Act in 1934 reversed previous land policies of "open use to all." It aimed to stop overgrazing across the West through "restrictive use and management" and allowed stockmen to expand onto adjacent lands. The act no longer required settlers to homestead selected parcels of the public domain; instead, they could purchase up to 760 acres of isolated or vacant tracts of public domain at public auction through the district land office. The money would be used for range improvements. Before anyone could fully test this new legislation as a solution to southeastern Arizona's economic woes, a prolonged drought devastated the cattle industry. The New Deal's Agricultural Adjustment Administration (AAA) initiated an emergency cattle reduction program, but the rains and high cattle prices would not soon return.[24]

As the nation's financial crisis, coupled with drought conditions, threatened to destroy southeastern Arizona's economy, New Deal policy makers drafted federal legislation for relief that targeted rural Americans and their farming practices. New government agencies included the AAA, the REA, the Soil Conservation Service, the Farmer's Home Administration, the Tennessee Valley Authority (TVA), and the Public Works Administration (PWA). At the same time, rural Arizona's vast public landholdings (forests, military bases, and Native American reservations) also attracted federal money. The PWA funded the construction of several irrigation and hydroelectric systems, especially on federal lands and Native American reservations.

Federal agencies such as TVA and REA recognized the importance of electrical power in boosting the nation's crippled industrial economy. Arizona's utilities were not unique in the monopolistic manner in which they operated and consolidated systems. Debates raged across the country over whether electricity should be publicly or privately operated. In the 1920s, Congress had begun to address the corporate practices of private utilities and their exorbitant rates. The stock market crash accelerated the demise of several large holding companies, since utilities led the stock market in speculative trading. To prevent their reemergence, Congress passed the Public Utility Holding Company Act (PUHCA) in 1935. Also known as the Wheeler-Rayburn Bill, PUHCA assumed that electricity was different from other commodities and products. The legislation launched more than fifty years of federal regulation to control the cost of electrical power, to the distress of private interests and other advocates of free market competition.

At the same time, the federal government took steps to further ensure widespread access to electrical power. Based upon the highly successful TVA, the 1935 Rural Electrification Act would be particularly important to improving the southeastern Arizona's regional economies by offering an alternative to private or municipal utilities. According to Morris Cooke, the first administrator of the REA, the agency's goal was total "area coverage." As evidenced in southeastern Arizona, even if private utilities did serve rural areas, they usually delivered only to the most lucrative customers; as a result, power lines rarely extended far beyond large population centers or irrigation districts. In a letter to Cooke, Nebraska senator George W. Norris urged the REA to "take into consideration the supply of electricity to as many rural homes as possible and not leave large gaps in the system of unsupplied [sic] communities." Cook agreed, responding to Norris that President Roosevelt recognized rural electrification as an "essential part of the large National problem of rehabilitating American agriculture and equalizing between city and country opportunities, the conveniences and comforts of life. A decent American standard of living for the millions living in rural areas is impossible without electric power."[25]

Strengthening rural Arizona's agricultural economy through electrification seemed a smart way to ensure the state's economic future in the light of a burgeoning mining industry. When evaluating Arizona's power situation in 1942, the Federal Power Commission stated, "Not only can electricity make the physical environment of the farm home more healthful, cheerful, and livable but also through making possible a higher efficiency of production, it can strengthen one of our country's strongest bastions of economic democracy—the independent farmer who operates his own family-sized farm."[26] But unless new efforts could ensure a stable water supply, present and prospective farmers would abandon their land as they had in years past. The farm bureaus of Graham and Cochise counties agreed, but they would have to traverse the minefield of the "power war."

Federal intervention in the form of reclamation projects, PUHCA, and the REA exacerbated the "power war" politics over who should control the delivery of electricity in rural Arizona. Cooke offered to process Arizona's REA requests through his own office, but the goals of the new agency introduced considerable political conflict with existing private and public utilities over the issue of service area. Private, or investor-owned, utilities continually opposed the establishment of REA projects, but at least in some regions the REA ultimately maneuvered around the political battle lines of private and public power competition by falling firmly into neither category. REA systems allowed local and communal (not public) ownership while ensuring that system operators targeted local needs at an affordable cost. Despite efforts to encourage grassroots development, the REA granted its first loans in Arizona to preexisting institutions like the Salt River Valley Water Users Association (SRVWUA) that could carry out REA objectives of area coverage. The San Carlos Irrigation and Drainage District in Pinal County beat SRVWUA to securing the REA loan in Arizona in August 1936.[27]

With Arizona's first REA loans going to private companies and preestablished irrigation districts, those living outside these service areas had to wait. For southeastern Arizona, the REA program offered more than lifestyle improvement or social homogeneity; it meant economic revitalization of the region's rich soil and land base. Such a task would require its traditional rural communities to abandon the idea of independent farming and individual plant or pump ownership. Rather, they would have to build upon institutions of communal and regional cooperation and insist that the federal program meet their region's specific agricultural needs. They would need to jump through economic and legal hurdles to qualify for a loan through a rigorous application process that favored preestablished agricultural districts or communities promising high domestic loads.

The Sulphur Springs Valley Electric Cooperative

By the late 1930s, about 35 percent of Cochise County was privately owned agricultural land, mostly individual holdings located across the valley floors of the region's drainage basins. Years of struggling to farm in the southeastern Arizona valley had resulted in strong communal relationships through farming associations and partnerships with AES agricultural agents. Soon after passage of the Rural Electrification Act in 1935, Graham County farmers urged their county agricultural agent, Steve Owens, to request a loan. They hoped to construct an electrical distribution system to serve ninety farms and a handful of villages along the upper Sulphur Springs and Gila River valleys with central station service. The Graham County farmers applied as a cooperative organization. Unfortunately, without claiming membership in a federal irrigation district or reclamation project like those located in central Arizona, the group faced challenges for securing the loan.[28]

As of April 1939, the REA had allotted funds to four electrical projects in the state, but none of the borrowers had been legally defined as a cooperative. The agency had only offered loans for line extensions to existing corporate entities, electrical or irrigation districts, municipalities, or farming groups. Arizona's laws on cooperatives in general and defining the roles and regulations for an electrical cooperative specifically were vague. Potential applicants therefore faced the challenge of clarifying their legal status for the purpose of a loan.[29]

Even after overcoming legal issues, economics remained a significant obstacle to an REA loan. Before loaning money, REA appraisers evaluated a system's feasibility by considering a variety of factors specific to the characteristics of each locale. These factors included the availability of a source from which to purchase wholesale power, land use, terrain, electrical infrastructure, and electric rates.

Like the many other Arizona applicants before them, the applicants for Graham County's cooperative could only ensure the approval of their project if it could secure enough users to guarantee a stable, year-round electrical load and a reliable source of electrical power. Its chief competitor for users, the Arizona General Utilities Company, which owned the nearest power plant, challenged the fledgling project by surveying the most populated districts listed in the cooperative's application. The private utility, which had refused to deliver power outside Safford before the creation of the REA, now sought agency funding to serve only the more profitable customers in the area. This willingness of private companies to agree to serve only the highest power users in a service area was so common that REA members nationwide would refer to such a maneuver as "skimming the cream."[30]

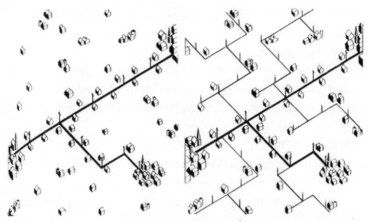

Fig. 1. "Skimming the cream" (*left*) versus area coverage (*right*). Originally published in "Why Area Coverage?" *Rural Electrification News*, November 1944, 3.

The privately owned and operated Southern Arizona Public Utilities Corporation had similarly excluded individual rural farmers and ranchers of Cochise County from power delivery. Like the Graham County applicants, Cochise County farmers saw electrical pumping as the solution to strengthening and stabilizing southeastern Arizona's cattle and agricultural industries in the San Simon and Sulphur Springs valleys.[31] Yet in spite of the government's long-standing rhetorical support for agrarian life, the case of Sulphur Springs valley reveals how the issue of domestic use overshadowed irrigation pumping whenever the government assessed a system's potential electrical load and feasibility. The REA supported the mechanization of the farm and the agrarian ideal, but much of the marketing supported domestic use to raise the living standards of rural Americans. Even so, Cochise County farmers looked to the REA to fund an electrical system to power irrigation pumps.

In the spring of 1937, the Cochise County Farm Bureau requested a visit from REA engineer George de Long to explain the program to local farmers. After a two-day inspection tour of the area, de Long offered Sulphur Springs valley applicants several suggestions for submitting a successful application. He described Cochise County's terrain as an ideal setting for rural power lines with sporadically irrigated sections situated within predominantly uninhabited areas (135 square miles of land to four hundred homes). Aside from some curved roads, the landscape was conducive for line construction and the soil soft enough for digging holes for poles. Dispersed mesquite trees and level plains covered with grass sod presented few physical obstacles. However, the project needed to encourage domestic power use and to supplement the high cost of irrigation pumping. Furthermore, he strongly urged residents to think about expanding their project, possibly to other counties, to increase the electrical load. On May 6, 1937, sixty-eight residents gathered at Willcox High School to listen to another REA representative explain the concept of cooperative organization.[32]

Residents of Sulphur Springs valley submitted an application to the REA that November, but the process proved far slower than they expected. Nearly a year later, in September 1938, the REA granted $100,000 to project "Arizona 14 Cochise" with two provisions. First, the applicants needed to incorporate as a cooperative in Arizona for temporary recognition. County Agent A. Mark Bliss moved to organize a corporation outside of the Farm Bureau to sponsor the REA loan. Eight representatives from the county's local farming towns of Willcox, Cochise, Elfrida, and McNeal met to incorporate the Sulphur Springs Valley Electric Cooperative (SSVEC) on October 18, 1938. On November 21, representatives of various districts in the Sulphur Springs valley elected officers to consider and act upon applications for membership and to adopt a corporate seal.[33]

For the second provision, REA instructed the new cooperative to begin preliminary customer surveys that might predict the use and need for electricity in the region. As integral components to feasibility studies, these surveys recorded the size and location of farms and estimated pumping costs. They also asked about the use of appliances, including lights, refrigerators, and ranges.[34] As the REA's Morris Cooke professed, "The more irons, refrigerators, heaters, and other appliances that are in use, the greater is the quantity of electric energy required. Thus, a large load build-up in the home translates into better service at less cost."[35] Thus, a viable electrical system meant for pumping was predicated on convincing enough people to use electricity in the home.

Because the REA reflected the philosophies of the Country Life reformers, the agency placed immense emphasis on domestic use. The REA magazine *Rural Electrification News* claimed that electricity would rescue a rural woman from her life of drudgery. Articles went so far to predict that once a home became electrified, a woman's work would be "more like play."[36] Since Cochise County claimed up to 21 percent of its homesteaders as women, the region seemed to be a ripe market for REA's promotions, but some residents doubted the promises or simply resisted change. Many older rural people remained skeptical of new devices in the home, or even feared the new technology. One woman reportedly believed that the current would kill off her chickens and refused to even consider electrical power. Other people opted out of the cooperative because of the five-dollar membership fee. Lack of education about and experience with the new machines and domestic appliances that challenged the ways of the region's traditional rural communities may have also contributed to a reluctance to use electricity. Since electricity did not immediately solve or improve every aspect of farm labor, many saw little point in purchasing the frequently unreliable heavy equipment for what would be only limited work relief.[37] Perhaps even more significantly, new appliances would replace the time-honored cultural and economic traditions of food preservation and clothes washing.

In other parts of Arizona, however, the REA had already witnessed successful electrical systems reap the benefits of power-driven irrigation and domestic use at the same time. The REA's 1937 annual report estimated that of the state's 575 REA members, about half of the farmers on irrigation projects owned refrigerators and 30 percent cooked on electric ranges. This was far above the national average. "Electric power," the agency's 1937 annual report continued, "is making it possible for Arizona farmers to reclaim and put under cultivation many acres of arid land, by providing an economical method of irrigation. Among the first to take power from the new REA lines were farmers wishing to operate irrigation pumps."[38] Yet even while boasting these claims, the southeastern Arizona cooperative had to fight to convince the government to support a project where domestic use was secondary to the agricultural economy.

The REA's preoccupation with increasing domestic load caused the Sulphur Springs valley community great frustration. When the agency's Examining Division argued that the project's two hundred customers for 135 miles of line fell below the desired average of two persons per mile (and preferably three), Bliss echoed common complaints about the process for estimating use. Customers wanted to know the cost of the power before they pledged to use it. He predicted that countless more people would no doubt consider purchasing land, developing farms, and installing irrigation wells, but only if they were guaranteed an electrical project that offered low-cost power.[39] Fellow Arizonan and electric cooperative member Violet Irving articulated a common frustration with REA's evaluation process: "Well for heaven's sake, anybody with experience knows that a feasibility survey is the biggest piece of stuff in the world, because nobody knows what they're going to use until they have it to use."[40]

Prioritizing economic development over domestic use prolonged Cochise County's application approval process. The REA repeatedly questioned groundwater levels and how long the applicants might be able to depend upon a reliable water supply in arid southern Arizona. Furthermore, irrigation pumping not only required more investment in each customer than normal electrical service requirements, but the REA would have to invest that money without a guarantee of a large return from crop values. These high costs would put the project into severe debt, rendering the cooperative unable to pay back their loan.

As government officials urged Cochise residents to focus on a project geared primarily to domestic use, the cooperative continued its argument that irrigation was a profitable way to farm in the arid American Southwest. Residents fully expected to bear the high cost of pumping equipment in exchange for continuing to pay the high fuel cost of oil, gas, and diesel motors. With regard to the groundwater supply, Bliss cited the nineteen-page REA application and accompanying reports from the Extension Service of the University of Arizona that attributed the sinking water table to abnormal rainfall patterns. The Extension Service and farm bureaus maintained that rural people understood that the desert held a limited water supply. In anticipation of rising state development concerns, soil surveys regularly assessed areas for good soil and shallow water in order to target loans, such as those from the Farm Security Administration, to the most deserving areas. Besides, development would contribute to power loads, and, the agencies argued, any serious depletion of the water supply would take many years. Furthermore, the area was too remote from other irrigation districts to interfere with other water supplies, so state regulations were barely a concern. Refuting the REA's objections one by one, Bliss argued that the only thing preventing the Sulphur Springs valley from agricultural success was the agency's complicated procedure for assessing a project's use and cost.[41]

Despite the carefully worded pleas, difficulty in identifying an affordable source from which to purchase wholesale power compounded the application's weaknesses. The larger local utilities Southern Arizona Public Service Company and Southern Arizona Edison Company expressed interest but never made the cooperative an offer. The possibility of absorbing the Willcox power plant also arose, but its engines were in need of repair. Consolidation with nearby electrical systems, as suggested by Agent de Long, would provide the solution to both the problems of building membership and of obtaining an energy source by creating the "basis for the most comprehensive electrical development of the entire southeastern Arizona."[42] Thus, the proposed service territory encompassed most of the major irrigated farming and ranching districts in the Sulphur Springs valley. Plans to extend across the Gila River to serve Solomonville, Pima, and even parts of the San Carlos Apache Reservation aimed to provide additional access to hydroelectricity generated at the Coolidge Dam on the Gila River (part of Bureau of Reclamation's development of the Colorado River). At last, on May 19, 1939, the local newspaper's headline blared: "Valley Electrification Program Allotted $488,000.00 by National Administration: Allotment Covers $120,000 for Construction of Generating Plant at Wilcox and $368,000 for construction of lines. Is First Project of this kind in Arizona to get official O.K. from National Administration. Will Mean Much for Cochise and Graham Counties."[43]

Finally, construction of southeastern Arizona's electrical system could begin. The REA was initially involved heavily in the cooperative's activities and decisions, including one to use a natural gas plant at McNeal rather than the one at Willcox. REA officials also approved of the cooperative's choices of engineers and a general manager. Once REA engineers mapped the legal description of the line, the cooperative engineers designed it, purchased material, and solicited bids for power line materials and construction. A California company secured the contract for SSVEC's line construction, but local labor crews began the on-site line construction work in September 1939. From then on, the local cooperative ultimately ran its electrical projects in accordance with REA-specified construction standards and procedures. The REA acted as a banker who oversaw operations in

Fig. 2. Linemen raising distribution poles in Sulphur Springs valley, c. 1942. Courtesy of Sulphur Springs Valley Electric Cooperative, Willcox, Arizona.

order to protect his or her investment by ensuring the applicant organization could pay back its loan at 2 percent interest in quarterly payments.[44]

Then, just when it seemed electrical power was imminent, the securing of rights-of-way and easements again slowed the process. The majority of potential consumers eagerly granted verbal permission for power lines to cross their property, so few formal land exchanges took place. It often took time to contact owners who had abandoned their property in dry years. In a few cases, people denied the cooperative permission to place poles on their land. Some did not want power lines across their property because they would have to plow around the poles, while others still wished to investigate the cost and financing of electrical equipment and sought guarantees that there would be enough electrical power for pumping. Signed cooperative members often failed to mail back easement forms they received months before. As a result, line routes could change, and consumers who thought they would have been close enough to get power (such as those in the Kansas Settlement) were now too far from the line to secure service. Engineering crews completed most of the survey work for the project by the end of 1939.[45]

For rural people who had been waiting for power, the sight of workers finally digging holes and setting the power line was thrilling. Regarding their aesthetic value, one resident commented that it was "only a benefit to urban people to have beautification, everyone else was just glad to see it." Workers often provided a day's entertainment. Another woman recalled having been "tickled to death" when they started to set the poles. "Don't those poles look pretty?" her grandmother remarked.[46]

At long last, on October 20, 1940, the cooperative's secretary, Mrs. C. M. Byrd, threw a switch at the dedication ceremony for the gas-powered plant in McNeal. Almost five thousand people were in attendance, including Governor Robert Taylor Jones. In a continuous effort to build load, the fair that followed exhibited electric pumps, water heaters, stoves, and several other appliances with the full support of the REA. Local mining companies sponsored a barbecue.[47] A couple of months later, the SSVEC sponsored a contest for the best Christmas lights decoration. The winner received free electrical service for the month of December.[48] Customers looked forward to low costs and reliable power. As Double Adobe's J. H. Cunningham, whose house was the first to get the power, expressed in the *HiLiner* newsletter, "Electrification will be the making of this valley. There's no doubt it will induce more investments. In time the Sulphur Springs Valley will become one of the major farming areas of the state."[49] Mabel Brown recalled the domestic reaction: "How grand it was. The children and I couldn't stop admiring all the

Fig. 3. Mrs. C. M. Byrd flips the switch to power ssvec's first plant, 1940. Courtesy of Sulphur Springs Valley Electric Cooperative, Willcox, Arizona.

lights. We had ice from our Frigidaire refrigerator, and wonder of wonders, an electric stove. Then a jet pump to furnish water. We couldn't be happier. We even had an outside light at the front and back doors."[50]

The Obstacles and Opportunities of War

The Sulphur Springs Valley Electric Cooperative made tremendous progress in its first year. The number of pumps rose from nine to seventy-two, and electrical pump use rose by more than ten times. (The cooperative privately purchased most of the pumps under a group contract, and the REA supervised installation.) This trend was true for household equipment as well; average household use doubled each month.[51] But when Japanese bombers flew over Pearl Harbor on December 7, 1941, World

Fig. 4. SSVEC's first general manager, Mike Bennett, observes an electrical irrigation pump, c. 1942. Courtesy of Sulphur Springs Valley Electric Cooperative, Willcox, Arizona.

War II temporarily derailed the growth of SSVEC and other REA cooperatives by suspending the use of materials normally used for construction, such as copper, and funneling them toward the war effort. Congress passed new legislation to push through the rural electrification program. The REA itself encouraged its cooperatives to act as "agencies of community mobilization." The SSVEC joined cooperatives across the country in blackout drills and energy conservation efforts.[52]

In the years leading up to and during the war, Arizona's electrical power requirements had grown exponentially and the state had fallen behind its goals for electrification in only a decade. New industries and military bases found the climate and open spaces especially appealing. Larger populations, both urban and rural, raised many new issues for Arizona's electrical industry.

The supply of electricity continued to fluctuate, and power costs remained the third highest in the nation. The statewide power survey conducted in 1942 cited cheap power as "a key to the state's future." The SSVEC overcame some of the wartime constraints by absorbing the local electrical distribution systems of Willcox, Benson, and Saint David in 1943. However, competition for energy hindered the cooperative's further power acquisition. The increased number of military personnel at Fort Huachuca in the San Pedro valley promised a significant domestic load beyond the capabilities of the base's diesel plant. The SSVEC searched for more power generation and turned to hydroelectric possibilities on the Colorado River.[53]

Anticipation of cheap hydroelectric power via the Colorado River provided a possible solution to southeastern Arizona's needs. Since the 1920s, Congress and several states had discussed a plan to harness the energy of the mighty Colorado River through several federally financed dams. The needs of the REA cooperatives in southeastern Arizona helped convince legislators to support a new state agency in 1944 over the protests of private companies known to some as "The Power Trust of Arizona." The primary purpose of the state's new three-member Arizona Power Authority (APA) would be to oversee the delivery of Colorado River power to areas of the state at affordable rates. Both the Federal Power Commission and the REA aided the APA in evaluating power needs in Arizona and, for the first time, federal and state agencies tried to coordinate electrical service and develop a comprehensive transmission system. The goals included devising a plan to deliver electricity to portions of the state without service.[54]

This did not mean, however, that the APA prioritized rural interests. Arizona's cooperatives fought for a piece of the Colorado River power supply. Electrical cooperatives had joined the public power cause, but they formed political lobbying groups and refused to support APA activities unless they received significant allocations of hydroelectric power from the lower Colorado River via Arizona's Davis and Parker dams. The ssvec finally received Colorado River power through the APA for its new plant at Cochise in 1948. It remained the cooperative's primary energy source until 1961. In anticipation of receiving the Colorado River power, fourteen additional Arizona communities discussed forming electrical cooperatives.[55]

Since World War II, the population and potential service area of Graham County had grown large enough to form a new, local cooperative. Following V-J Day in August 1945, long-denied cooperatives including ssvec had made ambitious plans to build extensions to awaiting customers. But as ssvec's service area grew, physical and communication barriers made it increasingly difficult to coordinate daily operations and activities across land barriers like Aravaipa Canyon. Based upon the portion of the county that the cooperative served, REA's analysts predicted that central station service to parts of Graham County would encourage additional electrical pumps, thus ensuring even higher agricultural production for all. The towns and the Gila River valley were still the most densely settled areas in the region. Since the beginning of World War II, individual property, usually from 10,000 to 100,000 acres. had grown on average another 4,200 acres, and farm size had increased by an average of twenty-six acres. Demands for foods, fats, and fibers had steadily increased farm incomes.

Electricity could help boost production in rural industries other than farming. Tourism and recreational enterprises would increase domestic load on a seasonal basis to various summer cottages on Mount Graham near Safford. Graham County's long, hot summers and mild winters proved attractive to "sufferers of respiratory maladies." Part-time residents also leased lots from the U.S. Forest Service. Central station power could also energize zinc and lead mining, lumbering on Mount Graham, and possibly textile mills, dehydrating plants, and diesel-run cotton gins.[56]

Empowering Agrarian Dreams 53

Disputes with the Safford-based Arizona General Utilities Company hindered progress in Graham County. The SSVEC delivered only to the southern part of Graham County, while the private utility covered residents of Safford, Thatcher, and Pima in the Gila River valley. Walter A. Batty led the cooperative's effort to take over Safford's municipal system and secure its power plant. When the Arizona General Utilities Company offered to sell these lines, the company stipulated that it would do so only if a new, local cooperative would take them over.[57]

The REA's appraisal report estimated that a new cooperative could serve more than 93 percent of the residents, with irrigation pumping remaining a priority. Variable rainfall and years of abnormal drought had limited the number of farms over the decade and shortened the growing season, forcing farmers to use gravity irrigation. Half of the farmers in Graham County specialized in beef or cotton, but the average farm diversified with cotton, alfalfa, barley, and wheat. Many had begun mechanizing their operations with basic machinery and had cotton workers to help with the most labor-intensive tasks. Lastly, a typical Graham County farmer shared farm technology like a combine or ensilage cutter with neighbors through cooperative organizations.[58]

In July 1946 the new Graham County Electric Cooperative (GCEC) acquired the investor-owned Arizona General Utilities system, which relented to legal and financial pressures and sold its properties. The GCEC based its office in Pima and planned to deliver to 95 percent of the county outside the towns, as the latter maintained municipal control over everything within their jurisdiction. The GCEC also acquired the local SSVEC lines, 292 consumers, 128 new members, and eventually extended domestic service to the town of Bylas and to other homes in the eastern section of the San Carlos Apache Reservation. Another group east of Graham County, the Duncan Valley Electric Cooperative, successfully applied for a loan in 1947.[59]

Fig. 5. SSVEC power plant, four miles north of Double Adobe, Arizona, c. 1950. Courtesy of Cochise County Historical Society, Douglas, Arizona.

Even after the loss of service area and the access to federal power sources, adequate amounts of power and money for all the irrigation pumps remained elusive for SSVEC. Members sometimes signed on for electrical service years before they could economically afford to or even before the cooperative could build the service lines. In a field report, one REA field representative predicted that "the growth of these settlements is tremendous and there seems to be an unlimited amount of money available to these farmers." Farmers' investment in all kinds of new pumps and other mechanical equipment foreshadowed service for "big operators and big power users." Issues of power supply, financial solvency, and service continued to plague the cooperative, and its board of directors requested a review from the REA. Following accusations that he failed to adequately respond, Manager Mike Bennett resigned from the board in 1952. Howard Helmers, a veteran of both the REA and Arizona utilities, replaced Bennett and began an intense period of expansion.[60]

The 1960s brought SSVEC new domestic consumers. The wartime and postwar activities at the U.S. Army post Fort Huachuca ensured a large residential population in nearby communities. To accommodate the new growth, the small community of Fry abandoned its uninviting name and incorporated as Sierra Vista. Sierra Vista attracted both military and nonmilitary personnel who came from places where they expected reliable electrical service. Because the base could not accommodate the demand, SSVEC gained an enormous domestic load as well as a membership of primarily suburbanites not native to Arizona. Towns like nearby Patagonia opted to receive cooperative service rather than continue with their often broken and unreliable local system. The cooperative's focus as an exclusively electric utility contributed to its reliability but put it at a disadvantage when towns like Tombstone left the cooperative to allow the state's largest private utility, Arizona Public Service (APS), to manage its gas and water service as well. The tremendous growth in service territory worried southern Arizona's cooperatives.[61]

The cooperatives depended on both water and steam power generated through the APA, but with increasing loads, more consumers, and competition with municipal utilities, they were unsure about future availability and the longevity of their power supply contract. In 1961 they formed the Arizona Electric Power Cooperative Association and became one of three such organizations to receive an REA loan for a generating plant and transmission system.[62] With an energy supply assured, REA power lines crisscrossed southeastern Arizona and connected farms, ranches, towns, and settlements across the region. As a result, the newly electrified region shared many of the profound changes in rural economy, way of life, and community.

"Cochise Would Be Amazed": The Electrified Desert

Expansion and power acquisition allowed the fulfillment of the Agricultural Extension Service's prediction that electrification "should result in great forward progress in agricultural and home life in all the communities affected."[63] By delivering electrical power, the REA cooperatives of Cochise and Graham counties introduced to the region a new technology and type of utility, one owned by its consumers and not a private company. Each profoundly influenced the economy and lifestyles of the consumers in their service areas.

Electricity's economic and demographic impact in Cochise County was visually and environmentally profound. The success of the cooperative, the quality of the soil, and the opportunity to tap the area's groundwater enticed settlers from Texas, California, and elsewhere to the arid Sulphur Springs valley. In 1958, SSVEC's accomplishments served as bragging fodder for the national REA. A *Rural Lines* headline, "Cochise Would Be Amazed," evoked the dominance of the Chiricahua Apache in the region's pre-industrial past.[64]

Electricity essentially changed the region's predominantly ranching economy into an agricultural one. Electrical pumping helped transform the desert valleys of central and southern Arizona into irrigated valleys. Technology helped reconcile the vexing combination of fertile soil and arid conditions that had alternately first attracted, then frustrated, and ultimately discouraged early settlers again and again. Pumping groundwater raised production, diversified crops, and temporarily increased land values. Since that time, the rural electrification program, cooperative, and system would further diversify the economy in non-agricultural industries.

Even the idea of electrification was enough to lure new settlers. As early as August 1940, the *Arizona Range News* reported that the promise of electrification, coupled with the paving of local roadways, had enticed enough newcomers to create a housing shortage. Between 1950 and 1960 the county's rural population increased by 92.4 percent. Many of the new arrivals had left the Texas panhandle, where farmers had so depleted the ground-

Fig. 6. Field of sage near San Simon after installation of electrical pumps. Farmer J. L. Schad is discussing growing, harvesting, and handling methods with Mr. Harvey Tate, Agricultural Extension Service horticulturist, and Dr. Alton Finch of the University of Arizona. Courtesy of Special Collections, University of Arizona Library, AZ 301, County Agricultural Agents Reports, Apache-Yuma, 1942.

water table of the Oglala aquifer that it became too expensive to pump any deeper. Electrical pumping opened vast new farmlands in the Kansas Settlement and the Stewart District as well as the towns of Pearce and Elfrida. Cochise led all Arizona counties in expansion of cultivated land from 1944 to 1950 by percentage. Its acreage of irrigated land grew from 8,260 in 1944 to 25,297 in 1949, and by 1961 the county had opened 60,000 acres to cultivation. In addition to increasing farmland acreage, pumping greatly diversified the crops. With a dependable water supply, the rich soil could grow alfalfa, lettuce, milo (a type of sorghum grain) sugar beets, wheat, barley, chilies, maize, cotton, and even sage.[65] (The environmental consequences of these dramatic changes are discussed in the conclusion.)

Specialists from the REA and the AES conducted studies on irrigation pumping in order to emphasize efficiency and pro-

Fig. 7. Cotton field in Sulphur Springs valley, Cochise County, Arizona, after electrification and pumping for irrigation, c. 1950. Courtesy of Cochise County Historical Society, Douglas, Arizona.

vide assistance to farmers switching from manual to electrical equipment. They collected data and maintained records on the conditions and pumping costs for each crop. The county agent coordinated efforts with REA officials to advise consumers of the benefits and most efficient use of their new electrical pumping equipment. Educational programs and personal visits convinced skeptics that because of the labor saved and additional efficiency, electrical pumping was cheaper than other methods of irrigation.[66]

In southeastern Arizona, the electric cooperative's new systems contributed to the mining economy as well. The Phelps-Dodge Corporation, operating out of Douglas, appealed to Bliss directly, while the Bisbee Chamber of Commerce formed a special committee to ensure the use of copper on the project. The mining success bore another synergy, since the electrical system helped extract the copper used for REA's electrical wire nationwide.[67]

The expansion of cultivated land and the mining industry brought a greater need for unskilled labor. With a growing market and recent damages to crops in California, lettuce and cotton production required the recruitment of Mexican workers under the Bracero program begun during World War II. These new "guest" workers increased the numbers of non-farm residents and reversed a trend by which, according to the census, it was far more common for rural non-farm dwellers to have electrical power than farm dwellers. Even those who owned large farms tended to occupy a "nice home in town" and "maintain their farm buildings as cheaply as possible."[68] By the time the Bracero program ended in 1962, it had spawned four labor camps within the Kansas Settlement, and workers lived in dormitories that had electrical kitchens and laundry facilities. It remained somewhat rare for the houses of workers to be fully equipped with electrical appliances. Since large numbers of Spanish-surnamed men labored as farmhands or domestics, most Arizonans of Mexican descent were classified as non-farm residents and as renters. Although the census numbers do not indicate the level of electrification in Mexican American homes, by the 1950s only 20 percent of those homes had private bathrooms and hot running water, compared to 57.1 percent of Cochise County homes that could claim the same standards.[69]

Likewise, Native American laborers owned fewer urban amenities than the average resident. A social worker visited two Apache and four Navajo cotton camps near Safford. The Apache camps had nothing but a communal water tap and toilet. One of the Navajo camps had new buildings equipped with electricity and gas. Still another included electrified housing units.[70]

For southeastern Arizona, the increase in domestic electrical use, though contributing significantly to the systems total electrical load, was always of secondary interest to local planners. Electricity had proved essential for the region's economic growth, but not in the way the Country Life Movement and federal agencies like the REA and AES had assumed. Still, as in the REA application process itself, gender, ethnicity, and other regional characteristics determined the nature and extent of domestic use among cooperative members, and therefore the new technology inevitably influenced traditional rural domestic practices.

Reaching the Rural Domestic Consumer

"All of our meetings were built around getting electricity," explained SSVEC member Terry Croasdale. Women were members of cooperatives, but they were also active in the Farm Bureau. It is difficult to measure the impact of such activity on electrical use, but educational programs, marketing, and economic incentives exposed potential consumers to plenty of propaganda.[71]

The region's major agricultural newspaper, the *Arizona Producer*, supplemented REA literature and printed advertisements that touted safety, energy conservation, and satisfaction to women who used stoves or other electrical appliances. Advertisements boasted that electricity "has made city homes of farm homes" and implied that electrical use was a determining factor in upward mobility.[72]

The SSVEC encouraged consumerism through four methods that involved more borrowing opportunities from federal programs. First, the cooperative's board of directors accessed federal group loans from the Electric Farm and Home Authority and the REA to provide individuals up to $400 for wiring, plumbing, and appliances. Second, members of the cooperative were also eligible for rural rehabilitation loans under the Farm Security Administration. These loans worked the same as the REA's loans, but with additional opportunities to purchase farming equipment and pumping plants. Third, members could apply for irrigation loans through the Water Facilities Division of the U.S. Department of Agriculture. Finally, the board of directors could arrange group loans to purchase equipment.[73]

Through frequent newsletters, the cooperatives also encouraged load building and hence appliance purchase and use. Articles discussed the purchase of various new, labor-saving electrical appliances within the context of domesticity. A column from SSVEC's quarterly newsletter titled "Watts with the Women" focused on household and electric cooking hints and recipes. SSVEC and GCEC hired women to promote the purchase and use of appliances. Promotions offered to pay people as much as $100 to swap their gas appliances for electric ones. Newsletters announced meetings as well as instructions for electrical use and safety measures. Moreover, the cooperative encouraged consumers to pay attention to their electric bill. Editors frequently printed the average number of kilowatt-hours consumed by small appliances in the newsletter. Ultimately, the newsletter tried to cultivate a sense of investment and ownership in the cooperative, ensuring loyalty and understanding even through troubled times such as frequent power outages.[74]

All of the promotion seemed to have effectively publicized the new technology, if not convince people to embrace all of its amenities. Even people still awaiting electrical service flocked to demonstration meetings at centralized places like McNeal, Douglas, and Willcox that offered lessons on better lighting: how to distribute it, how bright to make it, how to avoid eyestrain. But while they might have been educated about electricity's potential use in the home, most members of the cooperative chose to acquire appliances and electrical equipment selectively. A simple lightbulb was the first priority for many rural residents. Typically, a farmer or rancher installed indoor plumbing next, increasing sanitation and bathing and arguably reducing cleaning times for laundry and cooking.[75]

As a matter of economy, financially conservative rural people only changed over to electrical products when necessary. For example, the family of rancher and SSVEC employee Frank Shelton never bothered to change out their windmill, which had

Fig. 8. Demonstration classes like this one instructed women on the use of electrical appliances, n.d. Courtesy of Sulphur Springs Valley Electric Cooperative, Willcox, Arizona.

pumped water in the house prior to the REA, until maintenance issues made it more feasible to switch to electric pumping in 1951. Some families already owned several gas-powered appliances, so they could be discriminating in which electric ones they chose. Only if they did not already have a gas range would they replace a coal stove with a cleaner, electric range. Climate and culture also contributed to how consumers used and purchased certain appliances over others. With cool summer nights there was little need for fans or other cooling devices that one might expect so far south, and with a mild springtime there was little call for poultry brooders. The REA appraiser who evaluated Graham County speculated that "the large proportion of devout Mormons in the area, emphasizing as they do evils of the coffee habit, will have no coffee percolators."[76]

Radios and refrigerators probably provided the most valuable service to the southeastern Arizona population and had the most profound influence on the range of traditional local rural customs. *Rural Electrification News* consistently reported that nationwide, the radio, for which the battery could now be recharged electrically, was the most popular appliance. It offered constant entertainment, education, and exposure of rural families to new ideas, new places, and, for some immigrants, new languages. Refrigerators not only rid the house of the cumbersome iceboxes but made the process of preserving and storing food safer and healthier, an especially important issue in a desert environment. Ranchers found that rather than waiting until winter for slaughtering cattle or engaging in various methods of meat preservation, deep freezing allowed the activity to continue year-round. Farmers could store the abundance of food they produced each season and save it for later in the year, eliminating the lengthy process of drying and canning. For Mexican American families, this relegated traditional meals previously prepared out of necessity to essentially a nostalgic, cultural status. "What's to it [cooking] now that all this prepared food has come into being? Everything is in the refrigerator and freezer!" remarked Carlota Félix Delgado.[77]

While no longer participating in the operations of the cooperative directly, the AES's county agents, extension specialists, home demonstration agents, and youth programs helped promote the transition to electrical machines to sustain a high and consistent electrical load. The AES continued to share expertise and act as a liaison between cooperative management and its members. Both the national and local agency produced manuals on electrical terminology, adequate energy supplies for appliances, and the care and safety of home electrical systems. They employed the latest scientific advances in nutrition, psychology, sanitation, and health, as well as industrial concepts in organization such as time efficiency and energy conservation, advocating that rural Arizona homemakers could make great strides in improving the daily lives of their families by introducing urban amenities.[78]

One way government programs hoped to integrate rural society into an urban order was by assisting women in making purchase decisions. As an objective of its farm production programs, the Department of Agriculture promoted rural America's gradual transition into consumer culture. The AES's instructional style and programming choices assumed that all rural families arrived at decisions only after careful, rational discussion and examination of all known information and that families had the means, time, and ability to deliberate toward decision. Because mechanized equipment was too expensive to justify for small farms, county agricultural agents were supposed to promote the need to purchase cooperatively. The AES office in Tucson published a pamphlet titled "Guideposts in Buying Household Equipment," which provided basic guidelines for asking questions, comparing features, considering installation needs, dealer, manufacturer, safety, and guarantees. Consumer programs proliferated after World War II. In 1950, 77.7 percent of the state's farm and ranch homes had electricity, reflecting a postwar surge in rural living improvements and new home construction. Developers boasted new, fully electric homes.[79] Between 1960 and 1970 most homes in Cochise and Graham counties were heated with means other than electricity. Television approached the radio as the most popular appliance. Likewise, farm use of food freezers and automatic washing machines surpassed the rest of the county.[80]

The availability of lighting and plumbing allowed schoolhouses to acquire appliances. The curriculum could then supplement adult educational programs by exposing children to the new technology. At a minimum, electrical lighting allowed rural children more hours for studying. Nationwide, science and home economics teachers alike incorporated lessons about electricity and electrical use into their curriculum even if the students did not have it yet in their homes. These efforts sought to curb the tendency of young people to leave the farm for the city and to raise interest in rural living opportunities. Perhaps most importantly, the *Rural Electrification News* reported that filmstrips aimed "to create a desire for more extensive electric service. Such desire is the load builder that ensures the success of electrification projects."[81]

As with today's generation gap concerning the use of technology, children's understanding of and fascination with electrical power elevated the influence of young people in their parents' modernized homes.[82] The 4-H program, a division of the AES similarly cultivated electrical use and care of electrical equipment in schoolchildren. The communities of Elfrida and Whitewater in Cochise County boasted the most popular rural electrification clubs (supervised by County Agent Mark Bliss). Students at Whitewater completed an exhibit of lamps, light cords, toy electric motors, electric doorbell hookups, and other electrical devices. They gave three public demonstrations on constructing electrical devices. One member of the Elfrida club won a $200 scholarship offered by the Westinghouse Company in the National Rural Electrification Contest. Tommy Patterson, a descendant of Elfrida's original homesteader, received county and state awards for projects involving the construction of portable motors and the wiring of houses. Articles from *Rural Electrification News* suggested that the homes of 4-H members often used more power than their neighbors.[83]

The AES-sponsored home demonstration clubs targeted women in hopes of raising the rate of appliance purchase and use in diverse rural communities. Home demonstration agents of different classes, races, ethnicities, educational backgrounds, and locales all worked for the Home Extension Service in conjunction with AES to cooperatively plan comprehensive training projects for rural homemakers. Radio stations broadcast the AES's instructive advice, safety lessons, and ideas for household modernization into both electrified and unelectrified homes.[84]

Several scholars have noted that time studies never fully determined whether the new electrical gadgets resulted in less work for the housewife, since household tasks became relegated to women, who now performed them in isolation. Yet women in the Sulphur Springs valley recall that appliances like electric irons and washing machines made a difference in the nature of their work. Electric irons were considerably lighter than the old irons and could maintain a consistent temperature without scorching clothes (or hands). Electric washing machines shortened what was once a cumbersome, full-day family activity in traditional rural communities. New technologies spurred by electrification either allowed women to join their husbands in farm operations outside the home or freed them to work within the community or in town. Many chose the electric cooperative itself. Women in southeastern Arizona (and nationwide) took on prominent roles in the cooperative. Women founded cooperatives, constituted the majority of office staff, and served on boards of directors.[85]

However, Joan Jensen's study of the AES's activities in New Mexico found that the agency's influence on the use of electrical appliances often depended on how well individual agents crossed ethnic and socioeconomic lines, since the government's educational programs focused primarily on white, native-born middle-class women. Still, agents in Arizona rarely segregated clubs by race or ethnicity, operating under the theory that modernization could assimilate such groups.[86] Studies indicate, however, that ethnic women used technology as a tool to empower themselves.

Chicana women were often employed as domestic servants in the Southwest by the 1940s in order to supplement the poor wages of their husbands who labored at the nearby mines, farms, and ranches. These women knew well that appliances could make housework less burdensome. Chicana historian Vicki Ruiz has chronicled the way Mexican American women not only used their traditional, domestic role to participate in

civic activities but, beginning in the 1920s, responded to consumer culture as a "catalyst for change." The 1954 film *Salt of the
Earth* emphasized the priority this group ascribed to better housing with plumbing and other basic amenities. Striking Chicano
mineworkers in New Mexico demanded domestic technology as
well as equality and work safety.[87]

Yet, the midwestern and southern homesteaders of Cochise
County had been socioeconomically separate from Mexican
American women for years.[88] Likewise, most of the home demonstration agents in southern Arizona hailed from the middle
or upper middle class and held college degrees. They knew only
English and frequently criticized traditional Mexican cultural
practices or at least failed to incorporate them into programs.
Some agents customized each club's program to address, and
sometimes combat, differences in language, literacy, or traditional customs among its members. However, the cost of project materials, geographic isolation, fear of deportation, and a
transitory lifestyle in the case of Mexican migrant workers likely
inhibited club membership. Agents assumed "the immutability
of the family wage, a stable nuclear family, an acceptance of the
sexual division of labor, and mandatory primary school education for children."[89]

According to historian Katherine Jellison, it was the government's view that native-born white women, "unlike members
of other ethnic groups . . . were potentially capable of becoming full-time homemakers on industrialized farms." In contrast,
many immigrants and Mexicans resisted such entrepreneurial
activity in favor of traditional communal living. Likewise, federal
agencies charged with addressing rural needs believed that most
Native Americans rejected ideas of private land ownership and
lacked the money to acquire mechanized equipment.[90]

The San Carlos Apaches tested such theories when postwar
conditions expanded the Graham County Electric Cooperative's
service area to include their reservation. In 1943 the San Carlos

Apache Indian Agency had requested power from SSVEC to supply its day school, mentioning that of the 750 Apaches living in the district, many families desired service (75 in the town of Bylas alone). The Indian agency had worked with the Apaches for years, pushing a home economics curriculum through its own extension service and schools. An REA appraiser credited the teachings of the mission school for raising a desire for power on the reservation, but the World War II relocation programs and military service had exposed Native Americans to urban life.

As wartime work skills and cattle sales increased wealth, more people moved out of traditional dwellings and into government-built housing concentrated around the Native American communities of San Carlos and Bylas, allowing easier access to a central power source. The REA's Graham County electrical survey reported that Native American cottage owners indicated their intention to use electricity in ways almost identical to their neighbors: electric lights, radios, irons, refrigerators, and washing machines. Tribal chairman Clarence Wesley built his house on the reservation's border with the town of Pima so he would be close enough to the electrical line. By the 1950s, GCEC, within whose service jurisdiction San Carlos now fell, began securing permits to construct lines across the reservation in order to serve the trading posts and homes in Bylas and Calva.[91]

Power and Localism

In his book *Rivers of Empire*, Donald Worster emphasizes that the federal government's massive water storage and irrigation projects of the 1930s redistributed power to the economically elite, exacerbated racial and class divisions, and threatened the yeoman farmer's dream of opportunity and independence. However, the experience of southeastern Arizona illustrates that smaller communities took advantage of government programs (although not without struggle) to realize the agrarian dream.

County agents partnered with local leaders and their mostly white rural constituents to find solutions for a struggling ranching and mining economy through community cooperation, organization, and education. The REA also targeted areas with evidence of cooperative traditions and financial responsibility. The latter provision tended to favor land and homeowners who had experience with cooperative organizations and modern tools, who had good histories with financial loans, and who shared similar economic interests and views of life.

In southeastern Arizona, much of the land was homogeneous in its desert valley topography, and by the time of the Great Depression it was privately owned by people of a common cultural and rural heritage. Many were fairly recent settlers intent upon farming, and many were likely familiar with how electrical power could be beneficial in that effort. Government agencies guided the effort, but the Sulphur Springs county agent ultimately placed the responsibility of the region's rural electrification beyond his personal efforts and those of cooperative leaders. The community had to prove a viable system. Responding to a service request inquiry from a Solomonville teacher, Bliss advised that "the securing of electrical lines does and should rest largely with the initiative of the people living in any community."[92]

The process of electrification influenced regional development beyond the fields and in the home. Far fewer people attend the annual meetings today, but many local people still feel tremendous pride in the cooperative's operations and accomplishments. The cooperative and its electrical system cemented relationships between neighboring towns and settlements. When the Bureau of Indian Affairs advocated the inclusion of all of the San Carlos Apache Reservation within an irrigation district's delivery area, Graham County Electric's Native American members protested by insisting that the cooperative provided better service. The SSVEC hosted annual meetings with pit barbecues, bands, and door prizes and attracted almost eight hundred people in the early 1950s. In addition to electing members for the board of directors, members living on remote farms and ranches came to see friends.[93] Only in recent years, as new residents unfamiliar with the cooperative's history and structure move into the community, have consumers begun to think of the cooperative more as a utility than as a local institution.

Furthermore, the cooperative served as a major employer. Before SSVEC even began operations, it fielded job applications from engineers across Arizona.[94] As the project expanded, line construction became one of the area's primary occupations. Linemen were often former cowpunchers who ranched to supplement their income. The cooperative launched a training program in which groundsmen could advance to journeymen linemen and eventually supervise crews. Locals such as Bill Hill and future general manager Howard Bethel returned home from World War II and found work in the developing power systems. The electrical cooperative was a good place to work, learn a trade, and enjoy a satisfying career while remaining in a rural setting.[95]

However, even with access to electricity, traditional rural work ethics and financial pressures steadfastly remained. Out of economic necessity, many rural men and women continued to fill the hours with additional jobs or combined some farming with ranching. They also took advantage of more than one choice for energy. After the REA delivered power to isolated farming communities like the Kansas Settlement and approved the system feasibility of the market, gas utilities followed and offered a less expensive alternative. Still, most residents agree that electricity "made all the difference in the world," and over the years, electrical loads grew consistently.[96]

"Actually, life wasn't all that bad" before electricity, commented Twila Shelton of the Kansas Settlement, "but I know what it was from going without all those appliances to having all this

. . . and it's pretty nice. . . . People today take it for granted . . . you don't miss it 'til the well runs dry." And of course, electrical power lines brought all the conveniences and concerns of urban life into rural Arizona's homes. On the eve of the twenty-first century, Nelson Peck of the GCEC observed: "Today I go home and turn on CNN, where before there was no such thing as the world, there was Pima, Arizona."[97]

The REA did not single-handedly industrialize the region, but it did initiate that industrialization. As SSVEC engineer Gordon Sloan observed, "Like the edge of a knife, electric cooperatives cut through the first barrier." With enough water, farmers diversified their crops and production. Government-sponsored extension programs trained and encouraged community members to use new techniques and machines in agriculture and the home, thereby nurturing a desire for domestic use that ensured a consistent electrical load and a strong system. As farmers grew more prosperous, they could afford additional amenities. Once the load increased, electrical rates fell. The REA's 1937 annual report estimated that of the state's 575 cooperative members, about half of the farms on irrigation projects owned refrigerators and 30 percent had electric ranges, far above the national average. "Electric power," it reported, "is making it possible for Arizona farmers to reclaim and put under cultivation many acres of arid land, by providing an economical method of irrigation. Among the first to take power from the new REA lines were farmers wishing to operate irrigation pumps."[98]

In many respects, the REA's activities in southeastern Arizona echo the success stories that many have told about other areas of the country. The story also illustrates that while the REA program served as a vehicle for achieving rural electrification and as a foil to investor-owned utilities, residents still had to prove they could build a sustainable system, one that would eventually unite a rural region characterized by scattered ranching settlements and rural traditions into a technological region of great agricultural promise and appliance-filled homes. What made the ssvec different was that the community so clearly defined the cooperative's goals. Several Arizona communities desiring electricity had submitted loan requests to the rea prior to World War II, but only ssvec successfully negotiated a loan to build an electrical system for the primary purpose of irrigation pumping. Individual farming and ranching techniques in the region had failed, and many homesteaders had joined cooperative-type organizations in order to accomplish common goals. But what is probably most interesting about this story is that a rural organization based on ideals of cooperation and community helped promote a dream that celebrated the individual yeoman farmer through an urban technology.

The case of southeastern Arizona gives credence to the claim that the rea was one of the most successful New Deal programs for "helping people to help themselves." However, the struggle to convince the rea that pumping would provide enough of an electrical load to sustain a system indicates that the rea's method of evaluation favored, above all else, a safe financial investment. Government engineers determined whether the number of kilowatts consumed could pay for the cost of the project, whether electrical power would fuel the economy, and whether electrical power would raise land values and increase production. The economic appraisal explored every financial aspect of the community. Although the rea and its cooperatives did not blatantly racially discriminate service, its loan-approval policies gave preference to certain groups, particularly landowners and homeowners. Therefore, even when certain groups were a part of the electrical system, their access to and use of electricity remained limited.

The rea had early success in southeastern Arizona, but rural communities faced different issues and challenges in other parts of the state. The rea's evaluation system became more tedious, demanding, and detailed in the years after World War II. Even the REA would not always consider serving sparsely settled areas such as the White Mountains. As the following chapter shows, this more diverse geographical setting, land base, economy, and population presented additional challenges for those desiring electrical power.

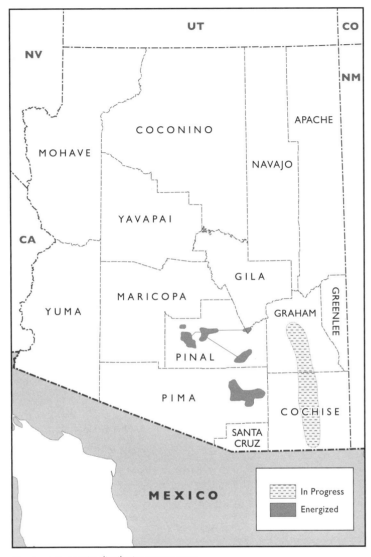

Map 3. REA cooperative distribution system, 1940.
Source: RG 221, National Archives and Records Administration, College Park, Maryland.

Map 4. REA cooperative distribution system, 1952.

Source: RG 221, National Archives and Records Administration, College Park, Maryland.

2

Power through Diversity

The Integration and Industrialization
of the White Mountain Region

In 1946, Lawrence Lee flicked the switch for the Lakeside, Arizona, power plant twice each night at nine o'clock, signaling residents that it was time to light their kerosene lamps. Like so many other local electrical systems in rural America, the Lakeside plant could neither generate enough electricity for around-the-clock service nor enough power to deliver to anyone living beyond the center of town. Less than thirty miles away, in Whiteriver, Superintendent R. D. Holtz of the Fort Apache Indian Agency complained to Commissioner of Indian Affairs William A. Brophy that the existing generating facilities had become too old and expensive to operate. Acquiring an outside electrical power source, he stressed, would be "of tremendous importance" for the agency.[1] Elsewhere on the Fort Apache Indian Reservation, the privately owned lumber mill at McNary produced the region's largest amount of electricity, but the mill owners failed to provide power to all of its workers for domestic use.

Meanwhile, community leaders from the neighboring town of Lakeside met to discuss the regional problem of accessing electrical power, and in 1946 they incorporated the Navopache Electric Cooperative. One year later, the Rural Electrification Administration's federal loan program financed an electrical distribution system that would interconnect all of the communities in Arizona's White Mountains. The cooperative replaced the local Indian agency, private companies, and the investor-owned utilities that had first delivered electrical services to only a limited number of settlements. The new system would technologically and economically redefine the region, while maintaining the historic interdependence of its diverse communities.[2]

The Navopache Electric Cooperative emerged out of the shadow of World War II to deliver electrical power across the southern half of Navajo and Apache counties in central eastern Arizona. Like the Sulphur Springs Valley Electric Cooperative in southeastern Arizona, Navopache became an influential community institution, but it faced different power requirements and different developmental challenges. Navopache overcame physical and cultural barriers amid the hostile political climate of the Cold War to meet the power needs of a rapidly growing population and economy of the White Mountains.

The White Mountain region, located in the southern portions of Navajo and Apache counties, is distinct from other parts of Arizona in topography, resources, and settlement. From its wide, rolling hills and snow-capped peaks to the extinct volcanoes near the town of Concho, the narrow valleys and washed-out plateaus in the shadow of the 11,470-foot-high Mount Baldy have historically provided settlers with potentially arable land. The lush ground cover includes grasses, dropseed, and mesquite in the lower valleys, while thick forests of cedar, juniper, ponderosa pine, spruce, and Douglas fir grow in the areas of higher elevation. Snow blankets the region through May and June. Plentiful streams have always provided an adequate water supply, but they run through narrow box canyons that make it difficult to access water. This limited the region's potential for irrigation and consequently extensive agribusiness.[3] In addition, Navopache's geographically, ethnically, and economically diverse service area encompassed several early Mormon settlements, parts of New

Mexico, the Apache-Sitgreaves National Forests, and the Fort Apache Reservation.

Sharing a Setting

Owing to these environmental conditions, the White Mountains produced a more heterogeneous economy to complement its diverse population than the predominantly farming, mining, and ranching industries that dominated much of rural southern and central Arizona. Many residents preferred occupations based on individual land ownership, such as farming and ranching, but lumbering and fishing also contributed to the region's economy. In addition, several government agencies claimed early jurisdiction over large areas of the White Mountains and its forestland resources. The White Mountain Apaches, Hopis, and Navajos constituted almost half the population. The tribes claimed most of the land base in Navajo County and 66 percent in Apache County. From 1930 to 1950 the Census Bureau considered about 80 percent of Navajo County and all of Apache County rural. Whereas Cochise County counted about six people per square mile, Navajo and Apache counties often numbered fewer than two. Among the sparsely settled inhabitants, however, communities of Mormons, African Americans, Spanish Americans, and Native Americans sought to tap into the region's rich natural resources, and later its electrical power system.[4]

The landscape of the White Mountains enforced isolation, so Native and non-Native communities operated both independently and interdependently. Prior to non-Native settlement in the mid-nineteenth century, several Apache bands, including the White Mountain, Cibecue, Corrizo, and Canyon Creek Apaches, claimed the region as home. These informally organized bands responded to their new environment and interacted with the local Pueblo societies in different ways. Lipan, Mescalero, and Chiricahua Apaches raided Spanish and Pueblo settlements for food, livestock, and slaves, but as anthropologist Henry Dobyns has observed, the ancestors of the White Mountain Apaches relied more on hunting, gathering, and horticulture.[5]

Even as a non-Native presence in the area increased, White Mountain and Cibecue Apaches seldom relied upon raiding for sustenance. They instead raised beans, corn, and squash for generations. Many of the White Mountain and Cibecue Apaches even served as scouts under General George Crook, the officer who pursued the Chiricahua's Geronimo until 1886. The U.S. Army therefore stationed its soldiers high upon a mesa, within the scouts' homeland. Established by the War Department in 1870 at the confluence of the east and north forks of the White River, Camp Apache (later named Fort Apache) was one of Arizona's earliest Native American forts and reservations.[6]

In 1897 Congress demarcated the lands north of the Black River as the Fort Apache Reservation and the area south of the river as the San Carlos Apache Indian Reservation. Together these reservations encompass five thousand square miles of forests, arable land, a half million acres of grazing land, and extensive mineral resources. The former includes much of the White Mountain Apaches' original home range as well as familiar landmarks that evoked Apache origin, identity, and spirit. Unlike many less fortunate Native tribes, the White Mountain and Cibecue Apaches received a land base that offered several options for agricultural and industrial development.

While those at the neighboring San Carlos Apache Reservation bore the burden of integrating a new society made up of several different Apache bands, those living on the Fort Apache Reservation interacted with increasing numbers of non-Natives, including American soldiers stationed at Fort Apache as well as Anglo, Mexican, and Chinese employees of the newly established Indian agency at the nearby town of Whiteriver. From about 1890 to 1910 the fort operated as a self-contained settlement comprising a steam-powered sawmill, farms, a granary, meat plant, dairy, hospital, chapel, lime kiln, bakery, stone quarry, blacksmith shop, and school. Entrepreneurs and missionaries also joined the diverse military setting that foreshadowed the region's intercultural influence, interdependence, cooperation, and communication in later years. For example, these new arrivals introduced new modes of dress, housing styles, and living standards to the Native inhabitants.[7]

The streams and forests of the White Mountains attracted non-Natives to the area throughout the late nineteenth century for nonmilitary reasons as well. These early settlers obtained land in the White Mountains through Congress's land distribution acts such as the Timber Culture Act and the Timber and Stone Act. Modeled on the Homestead Act (1862), the legislation granted or sold public lands parceled out for individual family farms. The settlers brought their own cultural values and ideas regarding agricultural development and community organization. Spanish-speaking shepherds drove their herds from the Rio Grande in New Mexico into Valle Redondo, or Round Valley, eventually homesteading lands near present-day Springerville and St. Johns for farming. Based upon this early settlement, their descendants distinguished themselves from later Mexican immigrants.[8]

The arrival of Mormons in 1877 likewise introduced a new set of cultural traditions to the area. Brigham Young of the Church of Latter-Day Saints (LDS) in Utah sent two hundred settlers to the Little Colorado River valley, a high, remote, frequently dry, and "wind-wracked" area of the Colorado Plateau no one else had settled, or seemed to want to settle. Like their brethren in the Gila River valley to the South, these Mormons founded or joined many farming and ranching communities, including Snowflake, Joseph City, Shumway, Show Low, St. Johns, Heber, Pinedale, Pinetop, and Taylor. A small group established the town of Lakeside as a sheep ranch in 1906. Others moved southeast of these population centers to the Round Valley settlements of Springerville, Eagar, Nutrioso, Alpine, and Greer.

The Mormons' emphasis on community building over money-making drew them toward cooperative social and economic organizations that would become a valuable asset for organizing the delivery of public service utilities in later years. The LDS Church promoted communalism as a way to ease the struggles of the individual farmer or entrepreneur. Through a communal form of organization known as the United Order, Mormons sought to realize their dreams of religious service through utopian societies in which families shared property, labor, and profit.

However, the communities who settled along the lower part of the Little Colorado River struggled to survive. Frequent droughts and floods prevented them from building permanent dams or raising sustained crops. Those further upstream along Silver Creek, a major tributary of the Little Colorado, found more success by reorganizing their settlement away from strict communal values. William Flake and Erasmus Snow, who joined their surnames and founded the town of Snowflake, largely rejected life under the United Order and aimed to support their communities through cooperatives. According to historian Thomas Sheridan, "that transition from communalism to cooperative individualism accelerated as Mormons streamed into other parts of the territory."[9]

Arizona's Native Americans had farmed communally for almost three millennia, but the Mormons aimed to cultivate their own community-based agricultural societies through strategies that would help them to meet their agricultural needs. They began growing subsistence crops along the Black and San Francisco rivers through gravity irrigation, and over time they improved the system by introducing techniques for soil and water conservation. Several LDS communities formed irrigation companies or agricultural districts to promote water storage. Around 1880 the Round Valley Water and Storage Ditch Company constructed Lyman Dam, one of the area's largest water-storage facilities.[10]

Yet irrigation companies faced formidable geographic challenges. The White Mountains remained remote and inaccessible throughout the early twentieth century, even with the availability of water and the introduction of infrastructure. The road from Holbrook to Whiteriver traversed fifty miles of high, barren, rocky mesas. It followed Silver Creek through the towns of Snowflake, Taylor, and Shumway and crossed the nine-thousand-foot White Mountain summits. In fair shape when dry, the area's sole transportation route became almost impassable when wet. This was a major problem in an area where snow often fell through springtime. Over the years, inaccessibility continued to prevent successful water storage for farming or stock-raising. Furthermore, much of the White Mountain region lay within a watershed from which the Salt River Project (a Bureau of Reclamation irrigation and power system serving the Phoenix area) drew its water supply. The White Mountain communities could not legally develop an extensive irrigation or water-storage system after the approval of the Bureau of Reclamation project in 1903 because, according to Arizona water law, Salt River valley residents claimed all the water within the Salt and Verde rivers and their tributaries.[11]

Many migrants had enjoyed at least some industrial technology in Utah before coming to Arizona. However, most could not carry their pot-bellied heaters over the rough terrain of northern Arizona into the White Mountains. Thus the early pioneers, while aware of the alternatives available in urban areas, lit the fireplace for both cooking and heating and used tallow candles made from beef fat for light. The area's pine and juniper forests provided adequate fuel, but many families huddled in bed for additional warmth.[12] After the railroad arrived in the late 1880s, people gradually abandoned candles for kerosene lamps. A few households upgraded to gas lamps they ordered from mail catalogs. Others eventually acquired those pot-bellied heaters, which burned faster and produced greater heat than an ordinary fireplace or woodstove. Some were lucky enough to live in a town where someone ran a small generating unit. By the 1920s, entrepreneurs had begun operating small power plants to provide lighting and energy for their house and sometimes a few neighboring homes, but local enterprises most often served storekeepers, the church, and the local school.

The White Mountains' early electrical systems were local, temporary, portable, and vernacular in construction. With the wires strung across the treetops, electricity added a memorable addition to Lawrence and Esther Lee's wedding celebration in Lakeside. Lee, a self-taught electrician, operated Lakeside's first four-cylinder diesel engine light plant from five o'clock in the morning until nine o' clock in the evening. Primitive wiring or limited budgets allowed many homes to boast at least one lightbulb with a single cord and key switch, but few other appliances. The single bulb, however, was significant. When the plant shut down at night, customers lit gaslights, which failed to illuminate the room nearly as well as the electric bulb.

Not everyone in the area thought electrical power was necessary. Esther Lee recalled that one project to build a hydroelectric plant on Rainbow Lake raised fears that the dam would prevent fish from spawning. Disgruntled fishermen reportedly destroyed it with explosives. But most of the newer residents in the White Mountains, including Indian agency employees, viewed electricity as a tool for transforming the region.[13] The experience of establishing communities through cooperative action would provide valuable training for incorporating electrical power in accordance with their growing needs.

Communal efforts to bring electricity to their settlements involved expanding the services of existing private irrigation companies, but ventures to construct a larger, regional electrical system ran into several barriers. Between 1925 and 1930 the Show Low and Taylor Irrigation Company reorganized into the Show Low–Silver Creek Water Conservation and Power District. Members eventually constructed dams on Show Low Creek and Silver

Creek to serve their six-thousand-acre project. Each dam had a hydroelectric plant that allowed the district to generate its own power, but as with many other rural communities across the country, the need for system feasibility seriously hampered the chances for electrical service. Both power supply and consumer demand proved inadequate to sustain a viable independent system. The relationship between high consumption and low rates could be frustrating to progressive-minded communities, since customers increased their electrical use only when rates decreased.[14]

A Question of Native American Power

Obtaining a large power supply that would require a large service area meant including White Mountain Apache lands at a time when few considered the reservation's inhabitants to be viable electrical consumers. Apaches tended to raise livestock, and only supplemented stock-raising with farming (during a season with exceptional rainfall, the area's rich black soil grew a heavy crop of corn). Furthermore, the agency and its school were located on mesas high above streams, making them impractical recipients of water and, by extension, hydroelectricity.[15]

However, one private utility showed an early interest in developing hydroelectric power potential on the reservation to serve communities off the reservation. In 1910 the Apache Power Company requested a permit from the Indian Irrigation Service at the Fort Apache Reservation to develop hydroelectric power on the Black River, a tributary of the Salt River and part of the water reservoir of the Salt River valley. The proposed plant site on the Black River lay equidistant from Globe, a copper-mining town about forty miles from Fort Apache. Developers believed that Globe would not only provide a large market for electrical power but that electricity would be a boon to its inhabitants. However, while denying any type of covert plan to rob Native Americans of their resources, the Office of Indian Affairs' superintendent of irrigation, Charles Real Olberg, observed that the potential power of the river was of no benefit to the Native Americans, since arable land was scarce. Before the Black River project became a reality, the expansion of the Salt River Project's hydroelectric system effectively killed the proposal.[16]

The Apache Power Company application remains significant because its submission coincided with Arizona statehood, when the development of power sites on reservations set the Office of Indian Affairs (OIA) in opposition to the state's desire to control water development within its borders. The discussions surrounding the proposed project made it clear that few corporate or federal officials considered Native Americans as consumers of electrical power. The Apache Power Company planned to build its generating facility on the border of the White Mountain and San Carlos Apache reservations, but the power generated was not meant for Natives' use. Rather, as the duties of the Fort Apache Indian Agency expanded, the Indian agency became not only the reservation's fastest-growing electrical utility but also the region's. Only when those interested in building a regional electric system included the reservation in their plans would anyone in the White Mountains enjoy central station service.

Hydroelectric development of the White Mountain region began with the OIA.[17] However, the Indian agency utility primarily served the domestic needs of its employees rather than the tribal members. In 1903 the government installed a waterpower dam, canal, and plant to furnish lighting and pump water in the town of Whiteriver (on the northern fork of the White River), exclusively for domestic use. The plant required continuous maintenance. To make matters worse, its riverbank location and poor construction raised the concern that a flood could wash the plant away. Most importantly, the plant's generating capacity could no longer support the agency's size less than a decade later. In 1914 the Indian agency at Whiteriver requested a hydroelectric plant that could provide lighting and water pumps not only for the administration's buildings and the day schools but also to operate shop machinery, an ice plant, and a flour mill. Indian agency superintendent Charles L. Davis claimed that electrical "service for the school and Agency will enter into almost every activity here."[18] A larger power plant would make it possible to extend power use beyond the agency's needs and apply the use of electricity to the government's policies of Native American assimilation.

Consistent with the ideology of Progressive reformers, OIA administrators and engineers had great faith in technology to solve the myriad problems of the industrial age. They considered electricity a vehicle for encouraging both industrial and agricultural advancement on the reservation, as well as assimilation. Although several earlier treaties had offered land parcels and encouraged the agrarian lifestyle on reservations, the Dawes Allotment Act of 1887 had marked a shift toward assimilation in federal Native American policy. The act was not applied to the Fort Apache Reservation specifically, but it divided many other reservations up into 40-, 80-, and 160-acre parcels on the model of the Homestead Act in order to encourage Native Americans to adopt the so-called American values of self-sufficiency and self-reliance through individual land ownership and farming. Primarily stockmen, Apaches irrigated about 1,800 acres of the reservation, but only in small patches insufficient to serve as a primary form of sustenance.[19]

Finding irrigable land within the boundaries of the 2,300-square-mile Fort Apache Reservation was difficult, but OIA administrators advocated permanent settlement for the historically nomadic tribe as the only way in which "the civilization of the Apache can be accomplished." Irrigation would allow this permanence by making it possible to live off the land. "The Indians of this reservation are only slowly taking on civilization and such an enterprise as this would enable them to make considerable progress," agreed one engineer. The local Indian agency,

Fig. 9. Fort Apache Indian Agency facilities at the town of Whiteriver, Fort Apache Indian Reservation, c. 1937. Courtesy of Nohwike' Bagowa, the White Mountain Apache Cultural Center and Museum, White Mountain Apache Tribe, Arizona. Wayne Truman Pratt, photographer.

however, hoped to use electricity not only for irrigation pumping but for domestic needs as well.[20]

In 1922 Congress decommissioned Fort Apache as a military installation. The OIA established the Theodore Roosevelt Boarding School at the site a year later, dramatically raising the domestic power needs of the Indian agency. Starting in the 1870s, the federal government had established boarding schools to supplement agriculture as a tool of assimilation. The schools removed Native American children from their home environment in order to instill the values of industrial American society through academic and vocational training. With the over 250 Apache students already at a boarding school in Whiteriver, the buildings and dormitories on the Theodore Roosevelt campus at Fort Apache accommodated another 250 Native American students, primarily Navajos. The new facilities dramatically raised the OIA's domestic power needs with additional construction. Yet, when the first children arrived at the new Fort Apache facility, many reported severely dilapidated buildings with patched

Fig. 10. Students at Theodore Roosevelt Boarding School at Fort Apache Indian Reservation, with electrical power lines in the background, c. 1937. Courtesy of Nohwike' Bagowa, the White Mountain Apache Cultural Center and Museum, White Mountain Apache Tribe, Arizona. Wayne Truman Pratt, photographer.

roofs and no central heating system. Once the boarding school acquired its own diesel plant to provide electrical power, additional construction followed. Industrial and administrative buildings, teachers' cottages, a laundry house, a blacksmith and carpenter shop, three traders' stores, a post office, a flour mill, ice plant, hospital, and storehouses completed the new, education-centered Fort Apache community.[21]

The boarding school's growing energy demands motivated OIA officials to reconsider bringing hydroelectric power to the reservation. Assistant Commissioner of Indian Affairs E. B. Meritt argued that the Salt River Reclamation Project's claims to the Salt River's tributaries squandered the power possibilities for the reservation. He quantified the loss at almost $20,000, not including the non-monetary loss to the Apaches, who "are be-ing deprived of something to which they are justly entitled."[22] Superintendent Olberg likewise argued that the OIA's moral ob-ligation to provide Native Americans with irrigated lands super-seded the water rights of Salt River valley residents. The OIA ap-pointed engineers to revisit irrigation and power development possibilities on the White and Black rivers in spite of the region's inaccessibility. Engineers determined that electrical pumping was the most economical method, because the agency's location on a high mesa made it too high for gravity irrigation.[23]

These plans for irrigation pumping required only a small in-crease in power generation, but the arrival of Superintendent William Donner ushered in a new era for electrifying the Fort Apache Indian Agency and its facilities almost exclusively for domestic use. In 1929 Donner commenced a road and housing construction program for the reservation, and in 1933 an ambi-tious six-year construction and remodeling plan began. The lat-ter included consolidating the OIA power facilities by replacing the existing plant with a hydroelectric plant and transmission line to the Theodore Roosevelt Boarding School. The new plant would reduce electrical power costs by several thousand dollars a year and expand opportunities for domestic use. It would al-low employees to use the most modern appliances for laundry and cooking and to avoid the annoyance of flickering lights. Additional power lines and transformers would run from Fort Apache to Whiteriver. To support the effort, Donner requested the services of a field matron to teach Apache women the proper management of a modern, industrial-era household.[24]

Despite Donner's efforts, the new system did not extend elec-tricity to Apache residences. Federal policy encouraged Native Americans to adopt a lifestyle similar to other Americans in theory, but both cost and priorities limited household access to electrical power. Furthermore, traditional Apache housing was not conducive to modern American life. Even by the 1930s, most

Apaches still lived in wickiups rather than framed houses that could be wired for lighting and multiple appliances. Wickiups were domed structures most commonly constructed with bent branches and covered with brush, canvas, and blankets. Living in nontraditional housing, such as clapboard cottages clustered close to towns like Whiteriver, increased their chances of living in an electrified home. Those Apaches who chose to live in frame houses demonstrated a profound change in their belief system, which included the tradition of burning a dwelling in which someone had died.[25]

Meanwhile, the non-Native population on the Fort Apache Reservation consumed electrical power liberally. Janet Lynn Wilson, the daughter of an Indian agent, recalled using electrical power and several appliances in her household as a child in the 1930s. Although a grant from the Public Works Administration allotted money to the local Indian agency to repair its hydroelectric plant and electric lines in 1937, Superintendent Donner insisted that meters be acquired the following year. "It is a constant fight to hold down the current with no restrictions" on employee use of electricity, he noted. His supervisor rejected Donner's request, but Donner ordered meters installed on individual buildings at Whiteriver, missions, and stores to try to gauge and control excessive electrical use.[26]

In spite of these efforts at energy conservation, the local Indian agency's power requirements tripled over the next decade, and the Indian Irrigation Service's electrical operations resembled those of a small-town utility. The higher-paid OIA personnel demanded more appliances, and the original electrical power systems struggled to accommodate the demand for refrigerators, washing machines, irons, and other household appliances. In addition, the Indian agency used electricity to pump water to farmland as well as to the lawns and gardens around the Indian agency. The power plants expanded their delivery to reservation schools, hospitals, and local Christian missions.

Fig. 11. Whiteriver Indian Agency office building with nearby electrical distribution line, c. 1943. Tad Nichols Collection, Cline Library, Northern Arizona University. Tad Nichols, photographer.

As the load surpassed the local Indian agency's power capabilities, administrators continued to search for ways to increase power production while reducing power use. Plant operators restricted pumping to nighttime, when domestic use tended to fall, and began charging the missions a minimal rate for services. Yet, Superintendent Donner considered the reservation's Apache population when making these conservation-minded decisions. When someone raised the possibility of cutting off power to the local, independently owned stores, Donner objected on account of the adverse impact it would have on the Native American customers.[27]

The considerable electrical demands on the Fort Apache Reservation also extended beyond government needs. C. W. Crouse, superintendent of the Fort Apache Reservation, first introduced lumbering to the region in 1910. He reported to Commissioner Cato Sells that the local inhabitants on the reservation and at the Fort Apache military fort did not exploit the full potential of the plentiful timber resources. Crouse also surmised that lumber revenues and jobs from a local sawmill could benefit the White Mountain Apaches and supplement their cattle-raising income.[28] As private companies followed, so did power demands and electrification opportunities. The industry provided yet another source for power production and distribution on the reservation.

The Lumber Industry

The forests of the White Mountains, both on and off the reservation, provided such plentiful lumber that residents referred to the area around the non-Native communities of Lakeside and Pinetop as "Sawmill Valley." Tree trunks reportedly measured seven to ten feet in diameter, some so large that today residents like to reminisce about using them as dance floors. By the 1940s the company town of McNary, located on lands leased from the White Mountain Apaches, was the largest population center in the region, the backbone of the regional economy, and the White Mountains' most ethnically diverse town. McNary also housed the area's largest power generator.

A private lumber company exploited the region's timber resources while at the same time supporting a functioning community for its employees. By the 1920s, the lumber industry had so denuded the forests of Louisiana that companies began to look elsewhere for work. In 1923, M. W. Cady and James G. McNary purchased lumber mills in the White Mountains of Arizona. They created the Cady Lumber Company and changed the name of the town of Cooley to McNary. Along with their equipment, the businessmen brought their experienced African American employees to supplement local Apache workers. The company also hired workers from the old homesteading Spanish and Anglo families living nearby. Each ethnic group constituted about a quarter of the workforce. Reorganized as Southwest Forest Industries in 1935, the company grew to become the largest mill in the region, employing more than seven hundred workers.

Because of its remote location, McNary needed to be self-sufficient. Harsh weather made it even more difficult for residents to travel to major population centers. Winter brought so much snowfall that residents could travel only as far as they could walk. The new lumber company constructed two- or three-room wooden houses for all of its employees, a general store, an extensive commissary, shops, a movie theater, a pool hall, a bowling alley, a hospital, and a network of utilities that included telephone and electrical services.

McNary was not the White Mountains' only sawmill to run its own power plant, but it was the largest. The town's electrical system capitalized on the company's operations by efficiently recycling industrial waste for power generation. Sawdust and wood scraps were burned to fuel large turbines that provided electricity for both the mill and the manufacturing plant. The company offered electricity to its workers for a fee, but it shut down the system at midnight because the power plant's primary purpose was to run the sawmill.[29]

McNary's residents received electrical and urban benefits that other rural residents across the country did not. Unfortunately, the distribution of electrical power was not altogether equitable. Low wages and housing segregation echoed the Jim Crow policies of the South. McNary's residents were segregated, both in terms of housing and otherwise. White families lived in homes on the north side of town, an area workers referred to as "On the Hill." There, management and staff resided on a street lined with large, freshly painted, and well-maintained homes. Others lived further down the hill near a section of smaller, less elaborate homes where water often collected in stagnant pools. Located east of the mill and "Under the Hill," "The Quarters" served as home to the African American workers and their families. For those who paid a four-dollar-a-month rental fee, the company delivered electrical services. African American Vera Blake remembers receiving electricity from the company, but only after an extended waiting period. When she and her husband arrived from Texas in 1942, they moved into an abandoned railway car that, not surprisingly, lacked plumbing or electrical power of any kind. After they moved into a vacated house in The Quarters, the couple had to wait several weeks for the company to set up utilities. More often, working families either could scarcely afford electrical appliances beyond lighting fixtures or acquired them very gradually. Yet electrical power still offered opportunities for men like Rafe Sweet, an African American from Lufkin, Texas, who arrived in McNary to work at the powerhouse in 1954.[30]

Homes for Spanish American workers, who lived across the railroad tracks from the African Americans, were not fully electrified either. Virgie Fernandez remembered that her family used woodstoves to heat the water for laundry, dishes, and bathing. Rosemary Padilla recalls that although McNary's high school provided electric sewing machines for all of the students, white students usually got to use them first.

As on the rest of the reservation, most of McNary's Apache residents were without electricity. When Edgar Perry's family moved from Whiteriver to McNary in 1941, they settled in the Apache village on the east edge of town in a two-room house without electricity or plumbing. The family used kerosene lanterns for light, laundered with a washboard and tub, and ironed with the heavy cast-iron iron. Other Apache families still lived in wickiups and used woodstoves and kerosene lamps. Apache children would later remember the difficulties they had studying for school at night because of inadequate lighting.[31]

Because of its location on an Native American reservation, McNary had to wait many years for full electrification. New Deal agencies such as the Farmers Home Administration and the Federal Housing Administration only lent money to landowners, and since the reservation had not been included under the Dawes Allotment Act, the White Mountain Apaches' lands remained in federal trust. After Southwest Forest Industries sold off the McNary sawmill in the mid-1950s and a development company took over the town operations, non-Native residents who adopted McNary as their home expressed great frustration over the town's legal position. Because it was located on federal land, the town was not subject to the jurisdiction of the Arizona Corporation Commission. Residents were not allowed to develop a town government to take over public services, and outside contractors failed to manage the utilities successfully for the lumber company.[32]

Private efforts to build a regional utility system for the White Mountain communities and to bypass the social, economic, and technical limitations of local generating units faced similar land-status barriers. In addition to the Indian agency and the lumbering industry, the U.S. Forest Service also occupied many acres in the Apache National Forest. For years, Holbrook's Lloyd Henning, a local politician, newspaper publisher, businessman, and entrepreneur from Lakeside, struggled to negotiate rights-of-way and maintain a private telephone and electric utility amid the complicated bureaucracy of the corporate and government agencies. Obtaining rights-of-way across Native American reservations proved complicated, as companies had to submit formal documents including articles of incorporation and detailed maps identifying the route. All requests had to go through the secretary of the Department of the Interior. At one point, Indian agency superintendent Charles Davis reported Henning's company to the Arizona Corporation Commission for charging exorbitant rates. Until the matter was settled, Davis refused to grant Henning a right-of-way across the reservation. In 1936 and 1937 Henning wrote a series of angry letters to the superintendents of the Navajo and Apache reservations regarding the Indian agencies' delinquent accounts. Henning eventually abandoned his electrification plans to focus on telephone services.[33]

Henning's experience reveals that competition over service areas on federal lands such as reservations and national forests proved exceedingly complicated. Meanwhile, the White Mountain area's only long-distance transmission line ran from Winslow to Holbrook. According to a former Navopache Electric Cooperative linesman, each of the early local electrical systems in the White Mountains suffered from severe physical, economic, or legal limitations. Many only generated enough voltage to extend electric service a few miles, making it impossible to achieve coverage for the entire region.[34]

By 1940, changing demographic and political conditions offered more promising opportunities. A larger customer base, federal plans to develop the hydroelectric potential of the Colorado River, and the creation of the Rural Electrification Administration would drastically change the nature and scope of electrical service in the White Mountains. The non-Native residents of the White Mountains, like their neighbors to the south in Cochise and Graham counties, viewed the REA as a solution to their electrification problems.[35]

Navopache Electric Cooperative: A Postwar Electric Cooperative

Prior to World War II, individual communities in southern Apache and Navajo counties had made several attempts to secure REA loan money. Just weeks after the program's creation in August 1935, the Lyman Water Company in the town of St. Johns solicited an REA loan. Ever since the Great Depression forced many urban migrants to return home from the industrial cities, places like St. Johns faced increased congestion and competition for land and food. Power development would allow the community to become self-supporting once again. Pumped water promised to expand the amount of arable acreage, but domestic uses for electricity interested the company as well. In the application, James A. Girand, who had tried to develop hydroelectric power in the area for years, stressed the community's predominantly Mormon makeup and claimed that this indicated a tradition of "energy and thrift." Yet before the REA completed a thorough evaluation of the project, Girand also oversaw an application for the farming town of Show Low. Despite the earnest appeals, the REA closed its case files on both projects "due to the lack of interest by the applicant."[36]

It is more likely that miscommunication among the region's potential REA members derailed the proposals. REA funding required that no other utility in the area had the means or the desire to extend lines through a given service area, since the presence of existing systems weakened applications. Another local irrigation district planned to construct a hydroelectric dam. In addition, during the REA's survey process, local businessman F. L. Fish installed a small power plant, apparently expecting the REA to take over its operations. The Fish Lumber and Light Company, which provided energy for only small appliances to forty customers in and near Lakeside with a mile and a half of transmission line, severely undermined the claims of the REA application. Unfortunately, once Fish submitted papers to the Apache County Board of Supervisors and the Arizona Corporation Commission, the modest system qualified as an existing utility in the service area proposed. With similar small power plants at Lakeside and on Silver Creek near the town of Shumway, the region's power production remained inadequate for farming operations, and Fish's enterprise struggled financially.[37]

Not easily dissuaded, six Lakeside community leaders with educational and political backgrounds, five of whom claimed affiliation with the LDS Church, submitted a loan request in May 1937. This one involved a far broader scope than the area's earlier applications. The group hoped to secure an electrical power source and extend power lines to sixty farms between Springerville and St. Johns. After hours of surveying by local residents to assess potential power use, the application and the REA appraiser emphasized the Mormon character of the region's non-Native population, noting their progressive attitude, organizational skill, cooperative experience, cooperative marketing, and record of using modern conveniences. Local AES agricultural and home demonstration agents met with organizers at the local church to raise interest in neighboring communities. The inclusion of small sawmills, cotton camps, dude ranches, and small towns would provide five hundred customers for the system plus eighty more ranches along the distribution lines. The REA still rejected the project as too small and infeasible, but this time administrators saw enough promise to open a file to await more information about expanding the service area.[38]

Lakeside's leaders first incorporated as the White Mountain Electric Cooperative in 1939, one year after a fire destroyed the Fish Lumber and Light plant. After consulting with the county agricultural agent and the applicants, an REA field representative called a general meeting to explain the program to local residents. One hundred ninety customers signed up with the cooperative and requested power line extensions to Alpine, Nutrioso, and even the town of Luna in New Mexico. In addition to those potential consumers, REA suggested that the Lakeside group combine its efforts with the applicants from St. Johns.[39]

Before the applicants could pursue the matter, however, World War II abruptly halted the process. As we saw in the previous chapter, the pivotal role of western states in war production hindered rural power development in the region. The needs of munitions and defense plants limited the available supply. The Truman administration pledged to continue to support the REA, believing it had successfully limited the ability of private industry to control electrical access and use. By 1942 the REA had almost quadrupled the number of American farms receiving electricity. Furthermore, the changes the war brought to Arizona and the White Mountains ultimately satisfied the REA's demands that only a comprehensive, centralized, and dependable system would meet the region's new postwar power demands. The influx of workers and a non-agricultural economy during World War II raised chances of feasibility for REA projects throughout the American West. Increasingly, urban dwellers found refuge in the dramatic mountains and isolated valleys in rural Arizona, only to find themselves cut off from urban conveniences. A tourist industry in Arizona's White Mountains, forests, and lakes was on the rise.[40]

Arizona legislators made inexpensive electrical power generation and distribution one of their top priorities to accommodate the state's demographic changes by taking advantage of federal undertakings, such as the one to harness the water and power of the Colorado River. The REA, the Bureau of Reclamation, and the newly created Arizona Power Authority launched a collaborative investigation to determine the feasibility of building a transmission system through Holbrook to deliver power from the Colorado River through Snowflake or McNary (via Davis Dam on the Nevada-Arizona state line). The project failed to materialize, however, because the report concluded that power development would not be economically feasible.[41]

In May 1943, with the help of county agricultural agents, the REA began conducting a rural electrification survey in Arizona. The state's governor, Sidney Osborn, pledged his support for electric cooperatives after REA administrator William Neal assured him that when materials going to the war effort were released for rural line construction, they would go to Arizona. In 1947 the REA set aside discretionary funds to electrify the state, whose electrical service significantly trailed its population growth.[42]

Organizers at Lakeside were waiting to spend this money. In 1946 they had reincorporated the White Mountain Electric Cooperative and renamed it Navopache Electric Cooperative (by combining the names of Navajo and Apache counties) to clearly reflect the geographic scope. As the new name suggested, this most recent application emphasized greater area coverage to rectify its past feasibility problems. Because of the region's limited economic opportunities, the failure of previous applications had indicated that establishing a regional electric system would be critical to obtaining a loan.[43]

When the REA's auditors assessed the feasibility of a loan to the White Mountains in 1947, the area was virtually devoid of distribution or transmission lines to serve 886 potential members. Only 7.8 percent of homes in the White Mountains received central station service, as opposed to 21.7 percent in the state; less than 1 percent had individual electric plants, compared with 4.2 percent in the state; and 3.2 percent had telephones, versus almost 20 percent statewide. The procedure for the postwar REA appraisal included gathering even more extensive data on income, loaning, and other financial history than before the war. Unfortunately, Apache and Navajo counties remained the poorest in the state, and it was anticipated that barely half of the residents would be able to pay for electrical power for normal household requirements. Stock ranches made up 70 percent of the farms in Navajo County, and while the number of farms increased throughout the 1940s, their average size shrank, a phenomenon that suggested an unstable agricultural economy. Mormon farmers owned an average of eighty acres, only twenty of which were irrigated by the gravity method. Many of them longed for electrical pumps. Native Americans made up 70 percent of farm operators, but their property was valued at a fraction of other farms and dwellings in the state. Tribal members grazed their livestock cooperatively, but Native American farms of three to five acres per family consisted of only gardens and small crops.

In addition to a poor financial situation, low population density also remained a problem. Large federal landholdings like those of the Apache National Forest and the White Mountain Apache reservation, as well as the few railroad and highway systems, dictated sporadic settlement patterns. Most of the area included in the application had too few customers who lived too far apart to make building an electrical system economically feasible.

However, postwar activity promised to improve transportation and economic conditions. The railroad ran through both Holbrook and McNary, and national and state highways crisscrossed other potential cooperative service areas. These new corridors offered potential rights-of-way for power lines. The region's economic future also promised greater diversification. In addition to lumber and sawmills, the area hosted local industries like planing mills, furniture factories, tanneries, canneries, and fruit-dehydrating factories. Local leaders predicted new lumber-related businesses in the areas of sash and door manufacturing and molding. The manganese mine at Heber, the U.S. Forest Service, and the OIA employed several permanent and temporary workers. Incomes were on the rise, and the area's industrial and recreational development required electrical power and promised stable, year-round power demand.[44]

In accordance with its new postwar practices, REA system engineers conducted sample power- and appliance-use surveys to judge the domestic load the area might carry. The sample included several properties that would provide potentially heavy seasonal power loads. The National Forest Service had responded to postwar demands with leases for summer cottages throughout the area. After the war, many Americans had the time and money to travel, and some of them had recently discovered the White Mountains' recreational opportunities. REA organizers anticipated significantly more new homes, cottages, and resorts in places within and around the Apache-Sitgreaves National Forests, such as Lakeside, Alpine, Show Low, Pinetop, and Greer. Persons interviewed by the REA indicated that they would use many more appliances if more reliable and affordable electrical power became available, and the project's appraiser predicted a higher summer load encompassing 10 percent of the region's total use, at least in the domestic arena with irons, radios, and washing machines. Finally, electrical power promised community development through major construction projects. Lakeside and Woodruff planned to build elaborate new churches, while Pinetop hoped to build a headquarters for the American Legion. Several small towns, including the Apache village of Canyon Day, anticipated future water systems and hoped to use electricity for pumping them.[45]

The REA's investigations indicated that many of the White Mountain communities would soon generate a large enough electrical load to make construction of a power system economically feasible. Taking growth—more importantly, anticipated growth—into account, the new Navopache Electric Cooperative aimed to integrate several systems across a substantially larger area than previous applications had suggested. Upon receiving project approval, Navopache set out to build a stable regional electrical power grid through both line construction and system acquisition. The initial Navopache system lit less than two hundred houses. However, in addition to the small power plant in Lakeside, organizers looked to acquire the power systems from St. Johns; the system from Snowflake, Taylor, Heber, and Show Low; the heavily Mexican American communities in Luna and Reserve in New Mexico; and the Fort Apache Reservation.[46]

A System of Integration

An extensive, reliable electrical system like the one Navopache had promised to awaiting consumers required a considerable amount of power generation. The cooperative's leaders in Lakeside naturally looked to the large, Bureau of Indian Affairs–operated, government-owned industrial generators located on the Fort Apache Reservation as valuable components of the region's emerging power system. In addition, gaining the Southwest Lumber Company as a power customer would not only provide a large industrial consumer but, more critically, secure integration of the company's power plant (the largest electrical generator in the area) into the cooperative's system. In short, the commercial and agency generators offered power plants, industrial load, domestic customers, and access to the federal trust lands of the reservation for extending power lines. Integrating the power plants meant integrating Navopache's consumer base. To acquire adequate power generation, the cooperative would have to acknowledge Apaches along with its potential non-Native consumers.

Wartime experiences, including their relocation to urban areas, had drawn many Native Americans (several of whom had boarding school training) even further toward electrification. Soon after the war, White Mountain Apache tribal member Charles Kitcheyan exhibited this level of interest when he sought aid from the tribal council to wire his McNary home.[47] At the same time, REA and BIA correspondence indicated that tribal leaders sought electric lights and basic appliances for their members to "encourage a higher standard of living and education among them." Superintendent R. D. Holtz believed that acquiring electricity would "be a very forward step for the Apache Indians to take and many of the Indians have indicated considerable interest in obtaining electricity for their homes." The cooperative assured the REA of its willingness to deliver electricity at affordable rates not only to the BIA facilities but also to "as many Indian families who have permanent homes who would desire electrical service."[48]

The restriction to "permanent homes," however, meant that those Native Americans who lived in traditional Apache structures would not receive power. Despite the assimilative efforts of the boarding school and mission schools, most of the reservation's 3,417 Apaches, including many in McNary, still lived in wickiups. Max Colbert, the REA appraiser, randomly sampled power use on the reservation. He included two Native homes and one store where owners had purchased power from the local Indian agency. From the data he collected, Colbert predicted that most Native families would use enough electricity to qualify them as minimum power consumers.[49]

On a political level, the White Mountain Apaches had been considering electrification for purposes of tribal use and investment since the Navopache cooperative sought permission to run its lines across the Fort Apache Reservation in 1946. Seeing an opportunity to extend electrical service not just across but throughout the reservation, the tribal council passed a resolution granting permission to survey a line from Lakeside to McNary. The resolution included a twenty-foot-wide, 24,445-foot-long right-of-way to the Navopache Electric Cooperative to cross open grazing land and construct, operate, and maintain a transmission line. The tribe also requested financial compensation for any damages the line might cause to growing timber (another source of economic development for the tribe). Soon afterward, the council permitted Navopache to survey a power line from McNary to several other reservation towns.[50]

Following REA's loan approval, Southwest Lumber (still operating the utility as a "company proposition" for the McNary townsite) agreed to turn its operations over to Navopache and to cooperate in servicing Southwest's other nearby company towns of Standard, Maverick, and Overgaard. Several years later, General Manager Joe Gardner recalled the anxious discussions: "We had to do a lot of negotiating with McNary to receive any power. We studied all types of programs through which we might get electricity, we looked into water power and other sources, but there was no power available."[51]

The path of Navopache's first power line illustrates the eventual success of Gardner's efforts. It ran from McNary through Pinetop and into Lakeside, the organizers' hometown. McNary's residents, including its local American Legion Hall and the African American Fraternal Order, eventually became members of the Navopache cooperative. Southwest maintained a long-term seat on the board of directors.[52]

The acquisition of the McNary power plant was also an essential component to an extensive electrical system and the electrification of the reservation. One of the first routes workers staked ran twenty-five miles through McNary, Whiteriver, and Fort Apache. Fifty Native American residences in these communities qualified as potential power users. The cooperative picked up seven commercial customers in Whiteriver and fifteen small Native American residences along the way to Fort Apache. Continual service to Canyon Day and the village of East Fork added about eighty more residential customers. The wholesale power contract with the Indian agency promised power to the reservation villages for ten years.[53]

At about the same time the cooperative acquired the McNary plant, Navopache overcame governmental red tape and finally absorbed the Indian agency's entire Whiteriver–Fort Apache distribution system. Indian agency customers then joined the cooperative. Agency facilities such as that at Whiteriver could produce more than 400,000 kilowatt-hours annually in addition to the energy developed at the Fort Apache standby plant. In return, an outside power source would be "of tremendous importance" for the agency, since its existing generating facilities had once again become too old and expensive to operate. Besides, the OIA's regional office in Phoenix had been attempting for years to relinquish their utility responsibilities on the reservations.[54]

The cooperative pursued the purchase of other small, private systems as well. When the population increased in Springerville and Eagar, the cooperative launched a successful bidding war with Central Arizona Light and Power Company for the Round Valley Light and Power Company. Acquiring this system and the St. Johns's Northern Arizona Utilities Company finally allowed Navopache to serve the remote towns of Blue, Hannagan Meadows, and Cibecue in eastern Arizona as well as New Mexico communities that had requested service.[55]

Regional Difficulties

Spurred by demand from several communities, Navopache built more distribution lines and acquired several systems over the next twenty years. The region's diverse landscape, cultures, and economies continued to present obstacles to electrification. Many in the formerly small Mormon sawmill communities in the White Mountains predicted a future in leisure and recreational sites, and developers eagerly began the construction of various ranches and resorts in anticipation of central station power. Prospective members verbally granted easements to extend lines across their property, but the U.S. Forest Service was less accommodating. The agency refused to grant rights-of-way or easements across forestlands where a power line might interfere with its own existing infrastructure, scenic views, or watershed. The Forest Service had strung a phone line across treetops along a valley floor, and the power lines had to run a quarter of a mile away in order to avoid interference. This forced the cooperative lines onto the sides of hills or canyon walls, making construction and maintenance difficult and costly. Then, the owners of the Beaverhead Lodge in Hannagan Meadows, located within the Apache National Forest, had pre-wired the lodge and already purchased electrical equipment for their kitchens and cabins. Forest Service officials cited "the high value of the scenic strip" when they refused to grant a right-of-way along a section of the forest known as the Coronado Trail.[56]

In other ways as well, the very landscape that enticed visitors provided Navopache with numerous challenges for system construction. Mountains and canyons in the south and west contrasted with the wide plains further north. Most of the farms lay in narrow valleys and washed-out plateaus. The line superintendent reported serious problems caused by stormy weather and topography that prevented crews from even staking out a possible line route. In contrast to the desert landscape, ice and snow hindered maintenance crews in the White Mountains. With elevations ranging from five thousand to twelve thousand feet, crews had to clear heavily forested areas and erect lines over hard rock. It was several more years before the cooperative could afford to construct extensions to Maverick, Blue, Hannagan Meadows, Young, and the Apache village of Cibecue. Three contractors who had experience building REA power lines in places like Texas and the Midwest severely underestimated the landscape of eastern Arizona and went bankrupt trying to negotiate the topography between Springerville and Reserve, New Mexico. With few roads, deep valleys, and rock-lined cliffs, workers had to literally carve out a right-of-way through the barren landscape. Continuous maintenance issues included heavy snow, mud, icing, flooding, high winds, and interference with phone lines. Wires became fatigued because of winds and moisture damage and required frequent replacement. Moreover, all of the lines had to meet REA safety standards and construction specifications.[57]

Other issues also posed challenges for extending electrical service. A lack of permanent residency prevented some minority workers, whom REA administrators believed were more transient than Anglos, from receiving electricity. In order to justify the loans for rural lines, REA applications had to ensure electrical demand in a proposed area in the future. The company town of Elk Mountain—primarily inhabited by Spanish American workers—contained forty-three shacks for the workers, a small general store, and a sawmill but had no running water or sewer system. The community submitted forty-four membership applications, but the REA noted that most of the town's residents were temporary migrant workers. Due to the nature of their work, such users would likely move on and make collecting any past-due bill difficult for the cooperative.[58] Given these feasibility issues, Navopache's rapid expansion came less from new construction than from the acquisition of nearby, extant, but independent electrical systems and their power supplies.

Still, throughout the 1950s and 1960s, large portions of the area had no rural electric distribution or transmission lines, nor had any private power company been willing to extend services. Claiming to have paid their five-dollar connection fees more than a decade earlier, the two hundred residents at lodges and ranches in the Blue, Hannagan Meadows, Young, and Eagle Creek communities wrote their U.S. congressman, Carl Hayden, pleading for a way to compel Navopache to deliver service. Navopache's general manager, Dewey Farr, also appealed to the senator while he tried to placate his awaiting customers. The women's ranching organization near Blue River, known as the Cowbelles, led the movement to get REA power to their community for just sixteen potential customers. They, along with Apaches in Cibecue and Cedar Creek, hoped to build a large enough customer base to justify the cost of constructing lines over mountainous and wooded terrain.[59] Unfortunately, cooperatives like Navopache faced not just geographical and economic barriers but political ones as well.

Cold War Competition

System acquisition allowed Navopache to claim forty-two hundred members and nine hundred miles of power lines by 1959. The continued construction of Cold War–era defense plants, military bases, research laboratories, and manufacturing plants promised to significantly increase the state's population and power needs. However, national political problems hindered the cooperative's further expansion locally, and many peripheral rural communities would have to wait several more years for electrical power. With the start of the Korean War soon after the cooperative began to grow, federal loan programs refused to lend money for purposes not considered essential to national defense. Since all building materials had to meet REA specifications, the rationing of already scarce metal and wire necessary for construction posed a considerable obstacle to constructing rural lines. Navopache's contractors continued cost-cutting practices by building lines with salvaged materials or using small conductors and stringing them along poles spaced widely apart, but there was little else they could do.[60]

In addition to competing for funding, the new cooperative faced intense suspicion and political firewalls as it continued its quest for area coverage. The Cold War climate had spread resistance to New Deal programs in general, and some private utilities called REA systems nationwide socialistic. SSVEC's general manager, Mike Bennett, lamented, "I don't see why it would make us a socialist [sic] if we owned our cooperative after paying for it over a period of thirty-five years." While private power interests had fought against the REA from its inception, McCarthyism revived the 1920s debate over private and public power. Members technically owned each cooperative, but private enterprise cast cooperatives as government-owned competition and unnecessary tax burdens on American citizens. In Arizona, private utility interests claimed that the Corporation Commission, the state's regulatory body, granted service territories on a county-wide basis. On that point, they continually challenged cooperatives for service territory and accused many of them of misusing their federal loans. Such actions threatened to terminate the REA altogether. The Truman administration vehemently defended REA interests and the "right of each community to decide" the nature of its electric service, but from 1953 to the early 1970s, investor-owned utilities issued aggressive political attacks on cooperatives to discredit the cooperative movement.[61]

Under the name of "America's Independent Electric Light and Power Companies," private utilities advertised in national magazines such as *Redbook, Reader's Digest, Look,* and *Saturday Review* in the late 1950s. Employing the Red Scare rhetoric of the day, the advertisements warned that government involvement in the light and power industry "leads down the road to socialism." They complained further that people who received electricity through federal power sources were exempt from paying taxes in their electric bills and stole business from loyal and honest citizens. One promoter of REA interests, Clyde Ellis, expressed his outrage over the accusations with his own powerful political metaphors: "The perversion of the Christian concept embodied in this advertisement transcends the bounds of all civilized decency. It is a disgrace to America and to American journalism. It can, in the long run, bring nothing but discredit and ultimate destruction upon its sponsors just as the tactics Hitler and Mussolini returned to destroy them and their followers; just as political and economic dictators will always be destroyed in a world where Christian principles and thinking people survive."[62]

Despite such impassioned defense of the REA, the anti-REA arguments were convincing to many urban people who misunderstood the REA program. They mistakenly believed that the government funded rural systems through appropriations rather than through loans that required repayment. This highly charged atmosphere made it harder for cooperatives to receive any appropriations. Congress even threatened to raise interest rates on funds for cooperatives' expansion.[63] REA administrator Norman Clapp tried to counter misinformation with words that emphasized democratic ideas of equality. "It therefore becomes a matter of sound resource development and national welfare," he professed, "that rural areas achieve a practical parity with urban areas on the availability of electric power. It is also a matter of simple fairness that electric service should be available to rural people as abundantly as it is to city people." He added, "The rural territories which power companies passed up in disdain have now become attractive to them."[64] Navopache's general manager, C. Mac Eddy, phrased the situation less diplomatically, accusing the power companies of trying to "skim the cream" from Arizona's rural cooperatives, particularly those who now served big industries in rural areas rich in energy consumption, such as ski resorts.[65]

Private power companies began to compete for consumers in Arizona cooperatives' territory. This problem, known as "spitelining," began to occur more frequently across the country. To encourage customer loyalties, the companies printed editorials which argued that REA-funded cooperatives would charge exorbitant rates because government requirements would necessitate hiring professional personnel and private contractors and purchasing expensive office equipment outside the local area. They warned that anyone whose impatience for private utility service motivated them to sign up for the cooperative would live to regret it. The smarter consumer would wait for the private, experienced, tax-paying utility to serve them under the rules and regulations of the Arizona Corporation Commission.[66]

The public relations campaigns were effective. In St. Johns, REA representatives reported, "These people certainly have turned cold toward REA since our first discussions with them earlier in the month." The owners of the Northern Arizona Utilities Company insisted on several conditions, including free service and additional representation on the board of directors, before they would join the cooperative. Their system encompassed 340 cooperative members who yielded $27,000 in annual revenue. When Central Arizona Light and Power Company merged with the Arizona Edison Company to form the Arizona Public Service (APS), Navopache lost some key service areas to investor-owned utilities, notably Snowflake and the irrigation district in Show Low. The Snowflake–Silver Creek Water Conservation and Power District decided to purchase its power from APS, which underbid REA's standard cost of 2.5 cents per kilowatt-hour. The district then reserved the right to furnish power to all potential consumers between Holbrook and Snowflake. Eventually, APS would serve consumers throughout Navajo County north of and including Snowflake. In 1960, APS purchased the struggling Verde Electric Cooperative even as Navopache tried to absorb the neighboring cooperative into its service area.[67]

Navopache and Arizona's other cooperatives were losing the Cold War. The competitive climate throughout the era placed them on the defensive. Urban constituents believed the REA had already served its purpose and that the agency was no longer appropriate to postwar needs or values. They wrote to their congressional representatives like Senator Hayden, claiming that the government unnecessarily sponsored competition in a free-market society and that tax dollars should no longer support the government department. In response, cooperatives lobbied back, insisting that the rural market was too small to be a threat to commercial power companies and accusing investor-owned companies of "economic dictatorship" through "absolute monopoly." Navopache's general manager, Sanford Gordom, begged Senator Hayden to impress the importance of rural electrification on the congressional Budget Committee by insisting that the REA still had much to accomplish. "The remaining jobs to be done," he insisted, "concern those rural people who were so far out of feasibility even in the early days that up to now have not been served."[68]

By the 1960s, directors of many cooperatives began to realize that they needed to follow the national lead of the National Rural Electric Cooperative Association (NRECA, formed in 1942) and organize a private lobby group on a state level to combat anti-REA rhetoric and promote cooperatives' interests. Among other vehicles, the NRECA produced a publication called *The Rural Electric Minuteman*. On the state level, the Grand Canyon State Electric Cooperative (GCSEC) coordinated the mutual support and expansion of various rural electrical cooperatives in Arizona. The GCSEC began publishing *Arizona Currents* in 1964 as a medium through which to fight off the attacks on public power or even just publicly funded power distribution as socialistic and communistic and "to promote the benefits of being a member of a public power group."[69]

The GCSEC saw its first crisis play out in a very public fight over service territory in southern Arizona between the Trico Electric Cooperative, which extended across the rural areas of Pima, Pinal, and Santa Cruz counties, and the Tucson Electric Power company. This conflict revealed that REA cooperatives could not continue to settle the problem of territorial jurisdiction on a case-by-case basis. Attorney James McNulty repeatedly defended the legal status of cooperatives and their rights to exclusive territories in the courts and in front of the Arizona Corporation Commission. Meanwhile, cooperatives worked with the REA to draft state legislation to protect their service areas even after a municipality may have expanded and annexed the area. The Arizona Corporation Commission ultimately took oversight of Arizona's seven REA cooperatives, including Navopache, in the early 1960s and officially set their service boundaries.[70]

As the political climate of the Red Scare continued to limit Navopache's expansion, the cooperative's many members publicly supported protective REA legislation. A petition from more than 340 constituents bolstered by a tribal resolution from the White Mountain Apaches accompanied a letter from Navopache's general manager, Sanford Gordom, in support of national rural electrification legislation. Introduced to the House of Representatives by Congressman William R. Poage (Democrat) of Texas, the legislation acknowledged that rural electrification in the United States remained incomplete. The bill would allow the creation of a government-sponsored Rural Electric Bank to supplement the traditional financing of electrical cooperatives like Navopache, which needed additional funds to continue extending lines to its territory along upper Eagle Creek and through large parts of the Fort Apache Reservation (a private cooperative bank was later created for this purpose).

Unlike the consistent legislative support from Senator Hayden, who had retired by this time, Arizona senator Paul Fannin (Republican) opposed the rural electrification bill on the basis of economic priorities. In times of inflation, Fannin wrote to constituents, the government needed to conserve large portions of the federal budget for national security matters. Navopache's Gordom pleaded with Fannin, noting that electricity fueled the lumber industry, hospitals, sawmills, and radio stations—all essential components to the ongoing efforts for military operations in Vietnam. Even by the late 1960s, with 98 percent of American farms electrified, the White Mountains' reservations and remote, sparsely populated areas of Blue, Hannagan Meadows, and Eagle Creek north of Clifton still waited for power. Gordom even tried to defuse Cold War suspicions with the rhetoric of the emerging civil rights movement by urging consideration for all rural people. Minority groups like the Apaches, he argued, also received great benefits from electrical cooperatives. Electrical power had allowed the expansion of industrial and educational facilities for Native Americans across the West. "The job is not yet done with the Indian," Gordom pleaded. "It might be pointed out that not too good a case is being made for the American Indian, but in truth, he is the man who deserves the greatest consideration because of his low standard of living, through no fault of his own."[71] The congressional Committee on Agriculture narrowly approved the bill, but it ultimately met defeat in the House of Representatives.

Although Gordom lost the battle, his arguments seemed like a good strategy. The political movement to fight poverty and advance civil rights helped counter Cold War rhetoric and lend support to the REA program by renewing the Progressive Era concerns about the quality of life in rural America seen in the Country Life Movement. Thirty percent of Americans still lived in rural areas that in turn claimed 40 percent of the nation's poor. President Lyndon B. Johnson appointed a National Advisory Commission on Rural Poverty to investigate the issues, and the group published its findings in a 1967 report titled *The People Left Behind*. At the same time, Congress launched investigations into the roots of rural poverty and even held hearings in Tucson to focus on the plight of Native Americans on reservations.[72]

With the REA loan program again under threat in the late 1960s and 1970s, Gordom continued lobbying Republican senator Barry Goldwater for more funding. He consistently distinguished his cooperative for the libertarian-leaning senator by emphasizing the demographics of the Navopache service area and its economic role in fulfilling the spirit of President Johnson's Great Society and the War on Poverty. He cited the depressed areas on the Fort Apache Reservation and in Catron County, New Mexico (in Navopache's service area), and the benefits of electrifying local sawmills that employed "many minority groups."[73]

Unserved non-Native residents invoked similar rhetoric in letters to their congressional representatives. Stella Hughes, chairwoman of the Committee to Get REA on Eagle Creek, claimed with certainty that electrical power would develop farms and ranches and encourage more people to build homes and attract tourism. She also invoked the Progressive Era concerns about the living standards of rural people: "Can you help us?" she wrote politicians and cooperatives across the state. "How about this great propaganda on War on Poverty? Don't you think we come under the heading of a depressed area? Until we have electricity, we cannot progress."[74] The desperation of Hughes's plea attests to the profound changes she saw in her neighboring White Mountain communities after electrification.

Multicultural Marketing in the White Mountains

Once Navopache Electric Cooperative overcame issues of feasibility, geography, cost, and political hostility, the region's prewar power plants and their customers ultimately formed one system and became the primary electrical provider to the White Mountains. The communities within the service area generally supported Navopache's goals, attended cooperative meetings, and shared electricity's impact. Many of the changes echoed the patterns of use in southeastern Arizona, but the electrification process also reflected conditions unique to the White Mountains. This region had historically been home to diverse communities, yet the new power system tied communities together in new ways: physically by power lines, socially through technological

Fig. 12. Meeting of the Navopache Electric Cooperative, n.d. Particularly throughout the 1950s and 1960s, members attended such meetings in large numbers. Courtesy of the Navopache Electric Cooperative, Lakeside, Arizona.

changes, economically through corporate agreements, and politically to combat attacks from private companies and anti-REA legislation. Nevertheless, those who formed and operated the cooperative held different cultural values from many of their members, especially those on the Fort Apache Reservation.

To expand central station service, Navopache needed sustained electrical use, or load. National and local institutions helped the cooperative promote electricity for farms. By the 1950s, Arizona's electrical cooperatives joined those in Texas and New Mexico in organizing meetings with the State Board of Water Engineers, AES's county-based agricultural experiment stations, state colleges, county committees, U.S. Soil Conservation Services, the U.S. Geological Survey, the Farmers Home Administration, and the REA to provide farmers with information about irrigation.[75] However, Navopache had to balance the White Mountains' demographic and economic diversity with the need to promote high domestic use as well.

From the beginning, Navopache pushed heavy domestic use of electrical appliances throughout its service area. General Manager Dewey Farr launched the Arizona Farm Production Power Use Program to encourage communities to hold regular appliance demonstrations. In 1948, Navopache was the first Arizona cooperative to hire an electrification adviser, a former home economist with the Arizona Edison Electric Company in Yuma. In the 1950s, General Manager Joe Gardner promoted educational activities such as movies and demonstrations in diverse communities such as Reserve, New Mexico, in order to increase power use and load. Members there, primarily Mexican Americans, had for the most part continued to live traditionally and therefore consumed minimal power. In response to such efforts, REA officials praised Gardner for his personalized working relationship with both dealers and members.[76]

In the same way that *Currents* educated SSVEC members, the *Navopache Transmitter* encouraged electrical use with regular features about appliances, news, rates, and advice both general and specific to the region. It frequently invoked a cartoon electrical plug called Handy Watts (modeled after the NRECA's Willie Wiredhand) as an educational mascot. Watts offered advice on safety issues such as caring for extension cords, caution against overloading wires, and tips on energy conservation. He might have advised readers, however, to do as he said, rather than as Watts did. "Every day is like a Saturday. Heating your water the electric way," sang the animated plug as he scrubbed himself in a bathtub, an obvious safety hazard.[77]

In spite of Watts's best efforts, all that training still translated into selective appliance purchase and use. An REA-administered survey showed that most residents of Navopache's service area expected to use electricity primarily to light their barns, but their top three appliance choices—iron, radio, and washing machine—echoed national statistics. Many Navopache housewives bucked some nationwide trends and bypassed the expensive re-

© NRECA

Fig. 13. REA cooperative mascot
Willie Wiredhand/Handy Watts.
Courtesy of the National Rural
Electrification Cooperative As-
sociation, Arlington, Virginia.

frigerator, since the chilly temperatures of the White Mountains
made it unnecessary. Some of the most popular items sold at
the McNary General Store were electric irons, skillets, and coffee makers. Longtime resident Vera Blake still boasted about her
electric lemon squeezer in 2000, but as with most communities,
appliance acquisition depended on financial resources.[78]

Home demonstration clubs arguably played a more significant
role in conditioning White Mountain residents for electrical power than they had in southeastern Arizona. Club activity peaked
at a time when residents were seeing the first of Navopache's
power lines erected. Extension agents and home demonstration
agents had to aggressively cultivate a desire for electricity from
each of the different White Mountain communities in order to
expand the electrical system. They prepared potential power consumers with cooperative and industrial values by teaching home

management efficiency in workshops for sewing, housecleaning, organization, and design. By far, the most popular electrical programs focused on the most basic use of electricity: lighting. The Sanders and McNary clubs held two extensive workshops to teach homemakers the value of adequate lighting and how to improve lighting with better bulbs and shades. Subsequent sessions included electric cooking directions involving a range, blender, and food mixer.[79]

However, the program faced the challenge of a culturally diverse clientele. The state's AES worked closely in Native American communities across Arizona but felt particularly successful on the Fort Apache Reservation. The perception prompted one proud agent to boast, "Homemaker Clubs are cutting across religious barriers and are bringing women of all creeds into a common group."[80] These programs' actual success in introducing electricity into the Native communities depended on a variety of factors, not the least of which was the sensitivity of the agent toward cultures other than her own. Under the Donner administration, similar work had begun at Fort Apache as early as the 1930s to encourage modern and industrial values. Initial programs, administered through the OIA, focused on issues of sanitation and food preservation, but a program also worked to replace wickiups with frame houses with kitchens and gardens. Florence D. McKnight, the agency's extension agent in the late 1930s and 1940s, complained about what she viewed as cultural hurdles to her success. In addition to the language barrier, Apaches were "slow to give their friendship." A young Apache woman named Bessie Printup who hailed from the Sherman Indian Boarding School in Riverside, California, helped McKnight adjust to the reservation, although the agent still limited much of her interactions to those who spoke English. Having worked with the Sioux, McKnight faced more resistance to her instruction among the Apaches and struggled for an explanation. "The Apache woman," she speculated, "has no idea what you mean by organizations, clubs, or such and this training will be difficult since she is naturally not inclined to work in groups." However, once McKnight adjusted her work habits by meeting with Apache women individually, she was successful in encouraging them to either acquire their own sewing machine or visit the area office to use one. Some of her students even displayed their machine-made pieces at the Whiteriver Fair along with more traditionally crafted handmade items.[81]

Fort Apache women were not the only challenges for Navajo and Apache County extension workers. Agents complained more frequently about implementing programming in the White Mountains' many Latter-Day Saints communities. While the women of Lakeside and Show Low relied heavily on the REA and public service representatives for electrical training, the White Mountain LDS women responded far less enthusiastically. "Part of this failing," one agent rationalized, "is due to the fact that they are kept very busy outside their homes." Each ward (church community), she explained, required several people to fill its offices, thus monopolizing local leadership. St. Johns alone included eight wards, with two at St. Johns, two at Eagar, and one each at Vernon, Alpine, and Nutrioso, and Chambers. Local community leaders had already found active posts through their church that either duplicated or undermined the work of extension agents and homemaker clubs. The LDS Church sponsored "relief societies" that sewed for needy church members and offered lessons on improving homemaking techniques and money management. Home extension agents argued that relief societies stressed a different type of pedagogy: training women through lecture rather than the "learn by doing" technique of the AES. As a solution, the AES hoped to work with, rather than in competition with, the relief societies.[82]

As they had in Cochise and Graham counties, extension agents targeted children in the White Mountains through popular 4-H clubs. Here, agents also attempted to at least partially cross ethnic and cultural barriers, but legal restrictions limited such efforts. In 1946 the AES held community meetings with parents and children in both Native and non-Native communities to brainstorm about supplemental school instruction that would expose children to electrical appliances and their uses. The AES organized five White Mountain Apache clubs and published two newsletters before being notified that Native children, as wards of the federal government and under BIA jurisdiction, were not eligible to be official state-sponsored 4-H members. The clubs continued in an unofficial manner until 1956, when the state's 4-H leader officially recognized the all-Native clubs. That same year, agents advised forty Apache families on the selection and use of electrical equipment, ten times more than during the previous year.[83]

Access to electricity and its accompanying educational programs allowed Natives and non-Natives alike to use appliances and incorporate them into their rural lifestyles. However, the physical impact on the Native American domicile was profound. Electricity altered household work and transformed the structure of the Apache home. Unlike non-Native homes, traditional Apache housing could rarely be safely adapted for electrical wiring. For many, the nontraditional Native home was defined by the presence of electricity.

Anthropology student Inez Capps observed the White Mountain Apaches in the 1950s and thought that their attitudes toward housing had been slowly changing. She surmised that an acceptance of Christianity had allowed some Apaches to forsake traditional beliefs about death and that they may have no longer felt, for example, that they had to abandon the house if someone died. Without such a belief, building a permanent home made more sense. Perhaps even more influential, boarding school education, military service, and the relocation of thousands of Native Americans to the cities altered younger Apaches' housing expectations.[84] One returning Korean War soldier wrote officials at the

Bureau of Indian Affairs (BIA) to plead for his people: "I do know those Indians could have at least a house to live in: shower, bed, tables, chair, TV, radio, at least live like the rest of the people . . . those people there don't even know what life is."[85]

Unfortunately, many Native Americans could not qualify for new housing under the GI Bill, even though the AES's Home Extension Service oversaw the construction and served as an adviser for furnishing more than one hundred new homes for soldiers returning from World War II and the Korean War. The bill did not overtly discriminate against Native American veterans. However, even if Native Americans technically qualified for new housing, the legislation required applicants to guarantee their loans with a property mortgage, and the federal government held Apache lands in trust. Similarly, non-Natives could tap funding sources like the Farmers Home Administration to fund the construction of irrigation systems or to wire houses as a home improvement. Yet the legal status of tribal members and tribal trust lands disqualified most reservation residents. With the help of the Veterans Administration (a sponsor of the GI Bill), the BIA set up a vocational school to teach the carpentry skills to build solid frame homes of lumber or stucco and wire them for electrical lighting. By 1952 one could find sewing machines, refrigerators, electric irons, and radios in many Apache homes, and children would often bring irons and radios back and forth to boarding school.[86]

In 1956 the Fort Apache Agency's own extension program launched a community development program to promote "better home conditions," improved health, and utilities like water systems. The program included extending Navopache lines from Whiteriver to Cibecue and serving two additional communities along the way.[87] Using profits and credit from successful tribal enterprises such as the White Mountain Recreational Enterprise, ownership of modern, electricity-ready homes became within the financial reach of most tribal members during the 1960s.[88]

The introduction of newer federal housing programs, part of the War on Poverty, also expanded funding opportunities for Native Americans. The White Mountain Apaches embarked on an extensive housing program, taking advantage of new federal housing programs known as "self help" and "mutual help." Unlike previous federal housing programs, these promoted clustered housing and living. Each new housing unit offered electrical wiring and power. A government social worker praised the Apaches' use of money for home improvements such as wiring and electrical hookups.[89]

The transformation from traditional reservation life was not lost on the community. The Fort Apache Reservation's residents acutely felt the economic changes that Navopache's central station service introduced. A cartoon in the *Fort Apache Scout* made light of how modern housing challenged the popular stereotype of the Native American. It pictured two homes sporting antennas in the background, while in the foreground an Apache man scolds a white woman in a car with New York license plates: "Lady, I don't care WHAT you saw on TV, this IS Fort Apache."[90]

The cooperative fostered a relationship with the White Mountain Apaches, because Navopache's electrical system depended upon the reservation's residents for both power production and domestic use. In addition to entering rights-of-way agreements, Navopache advocated for the tribe on other aspects of industrialization such as road maintenance and road building. While the presence of McNary and the Southwest Lumber Company's profitable lumbering activities on the Fort Apache Reservation had introduced Apaches to industrial work and technology, Navopache offered programs to selected trainees. When White Mountain Apache Ted Declay qualified for Navopache's safety and job-training program, he became the cooperative's first Native American groundsman. In this capacity he worked alongside the children and grandchildren of some of the original non-Native White Mountain settlers.[91] Apaches continued to join the cooperative directly as individual members (rather than through the Indian agency) even while tribal officials gained more direct control of other non-electrical utilities such as water and sewage through the White Mountain Utility Authority. Navopache had sought tribal resolutions to support REA-related legislation since at least the 1950s, but the Apache tribe finally achieved a direct voice in cooperative management in May 1975. A BIA representative served on Navopache's board of directors for years, but the cooperative appointed thirty-year-old Apache Raymond Endfield Jr. to the position. As representative of the cooperative's fourth-largest district (out of eight), Endfield was influential in making recommendations and improving member services to then over 66 percent—and over 90 percent by the end of the twentieth century—of the reservation's households. The White Mountain Apaches had fully integrated into the region's power system physically as well as politically.[92]

The reservation's industrial activity increased Apache dependence on central station electrical service. Likely influenced by policies that sought to terminate tribal dependence on federal funds in the mid-1950s, the BIA encouraged the White Mountain Apache Tribal Council to invest further in lumbering. This action gave rise to the Fort Apache Timber Company out of Cibecue, which rivaled and eventually outlasted the Southwest Lumber Company at McNary. In 1961 the Southwest Lumber Company's newspaper, *The Timberline*, reported that the over four thousand White Mountain Apaches led a life that "blended the old with the new." While 60 percent still lived in wickiups, 40 percent had moved into frame homes "that often boast TV antennas."[93] Many consumers grazed cattle within the Apache-Sitgreaves National Forest and on the Fort Apache Reservation, so rather than use electricity for irrigation purposes, as the original private and agency systems attempted to do, the cooperative provided electrical service to individual Apaches for domestic use. By the 1970s, parts of the Fort Apache Reservation resembled non-Native settlements in the White Mountains. Small communities of 200 to 1,400 dotted the landscape; power lines connected them to larger centers of over 3,000, as in Whiteriver.

White Mountain Apache tribal chairman Ronnie Lupe expressed his view of why Apaches absorbed the changes electrification brought, at least to a point, when he testified at the poverty hearings in Tucson in 1967.[94]

> The Indian people are a proud people and a proud race. We like to retain our culture as much as we can, but since the foreigners have arrived, they brought their own culture and they have the dominant culture. We have the greatest challenge here, trying to learn your culture. We are so overrun with a culture that is no longer ours, but something different, that this becomes a challenge; and Indians love challenges. The more education we have, the more we adapt to a culture that never belonged to us. But I think we can still maintain our culture and there must be job opportunities, but I believe it must unfold on the reservation.[94]

The White Mountain Apache Tribal Council continued to grant the Navopache Electric Cooperative, its primary electrical server, each of its requests for a right-of-way and drew power from the resulting lines to serve its new housing communities and recreational accommodations. These included the developing primary area attractions of Hawley Lake for tourists since the 1960s and founding the tribal enterprises of Sunrise Ski Resort (opened in December 1972) and the Hon-Dah Resort Casino (opened December 1993). Each of these endeavors use large amounts of power for operations as well as servicing gas stations, electrified cabins, and other visitor amenities.[95]

Recreational industries and services also transformed the non-Native local economy from farming to tourism. Electrified facilities welcomed travelers eager to escape the urban deserts of Phoenix and Tucson for the mountain scenery and activity.

By 1959, resorts surpassed sawmills and logging as the leading business in the White Mountains. Even today, similar attractions contribute to the growth of the recreational industry in non-Native towns like Pinetop and Lakeside. The town of Lakeside is located on the popular fishing site of Rainbow Lake, where original settlers had reportedly impounded water for irrigation and Lawrence Lee built his power plant. Electricity from the cooperative also pumped water from the adjacent lake to maintain the greens of its golf course, and served a country club, Lakeside's school, and the local church. By the 1960s, three vice-presidents from the state's largest private power company, Arizona Public Service, maintained summer homes in a 180-cottage home development.[96]

The electrification process had brought all of the White Mountains' rural ethnic communities, and the vacationers who began to flock there, into the industrial era. Rural living in White Mountains homes and resorts was closer to that of life in urban areas. In southeastern Arizona, electrification had made farming possible on lands low on surface water, but in the White Mountains, electricity contributed to the growth of an industrial and recreational economy.

Integrating a Region of Power

Prior to World War II, several conditions in the White Mountains resisted the development of reliable and sustainable central station electric service through private, government, or REA-funded efforts. These included the low economic status of southern Navajo and Apache counties, their low population density, few family farms, geographical inaccessibility, and the cultural practices of several of the Native American residents. Postwar changes in economic income, a future promise of low-cost power from the Colorado River, and improvements in communication and transportation diminished these obstacles and opened up new possibilities for the economy and for increasing electrical use through the recreational tourism industry. The resulting changes allowed applicants to propose a more feasible plan whereby a single REA-funded regional system would serve to electrify all of the White Mountains' different communities even in the face of national political opposition.

The communities of the White Mountains historically depended upon one another's resources, but a centralized, regional electrical system would interconnect these communities in a new way and carry the intercultural relationships and influences of the past into a new era. The presence of numerous government agencies, federally owned land, progressive and cooperatively minded Mormon settlers, an abundance of natural resources, and industry all fostered access to modern electrical service and domestic conveniences. The great diversity of the population and economy helped qualify the White Mountain Apaches and their non-Native neighbors in the southern and central zones of eastern Arizona for an REA loan. As the transmission and distribution lines connected the region's isolated communities and independent electrical systems, the Navopache Electric Cooperative met the socioeconomic needs and requirements of a culturally diverse and expanding economic region where independent and private efforts had failed.

The people of the White Mountains would share not only power lines but also a new industrial technology. Both Native and non-Natives supported the expansion of the project, its purpose, and its role in the region. The power sources within the Fort Apache Reservation connected all of the communities of the White Mountain region and redefined domestic "rural living" for each locale in accordance with cultural values and economic goals. Beyond individual homes, the technology expanded industrialization in the historically diverse White Mountain region in the form of tribal enterprises, recreation, and tourism.

The local resources found in the lush green forests, fish-filled lakes, and rushing rivers of the White Mountains had given the

Fort Apache Indian Agency employees and tribal members a distinct advantage over other Native American tribes, and even some advantage over many rural Euro-Americans, in obtaining the luxuries, and the detriments, of industry and its accompanying lifestyle. Electrical power resources on Native lands and the initiative of non-Natives would provide the means to do so. Company towns like McNary leased reservation land, built powerful electrical plants, and served local customers of all ethnic and economic backgrounds. Non-Native White Mountain communities depended upon the tribe's acquiescence to build a feasible regional electrical system, and the tribe benefited from the legal and economic status of these communities to fund it. This would allow the cooperative not only to consolidate locally generated power but to create a stable, regional, electrical system across all the White Mountain communities.

Navopache's activities illustrate those of REA cooperatives across the West in bringing electrification to Native American reservations within their service areas. Although not everyone within the region received power, REA cooperatives "did not systematically exclude reservations when establishing project boundaries."[97] Moreover, crossing reservations and gaining members and electrical loads was often the most economically feasible route to achieving area coverage. Those living too far from clustered housing, however, usually could not afford extensions without help from the tribe. However, fairly remote villages like Cibecue still received power months before other rural communities in Arizona.

The development of the power system that would eventually stretch across the White Mountains, as well as the use of that power, remained consistent with the traditions of its multicultural communities, diverse geographical setting and natural resources, and historical relationships. The Fort Apache Reservation and the area's available resources contributed to early federal funding for irrigation and power services in the region.

Since the turn of the century, the BIA encouraged electrification as a tool consistent with federal policies of assimilation. Yet the White Mountain Apaches, like their non-Native neighbors, remained culturally and economically distinctive communities.

However, large sections of Native American reservations in northeastern Arizona remained far too remote and isolated for even an electrical cooperative to service. As at Fort Apache, the task of providing utility services and delivery to this area fell first to the BIA. By 1960, electrical utility services accelerated the introduction of an industrial economy and living standards to communities whose location, political status, and cultural traditions delayed the process for years. At the same time, the multiple energy resources located on Navajo and Hopi tribal lands would become integral and critical to significant power needs of not just northeastern Arizona but the entire American Southwest.

3

"A Light in Every Hogan"

Power to Indian Country

Navajo Tom Ration reminisced about a community gathering in an assembly room in Crownpoint, New Mexico, one of six locations for Indian agencies on the Navajo Reservation: "A band was playing. It was a very special occasion. We were all told to look at the ceiling. Someone started the generator, and the bulbs slowly lit, one after the other, with a very dim light. Everyone yelled and clapped their hands with excitement. It was the first electricity at Crownpoint, and I saw it."[1] The event Ration described occurred in 1914, but it would take almost half a century before many other Navajos would share his experience.

In 1956 Congress authorized the Bureau of Reclamation to construct one of its largest hydroelectric power plants, located at Glen Canyon Dam on former Native American land in northern Arizona. At the same time, the Arizona Public Service (APS) solicited the Navajo tribe for a franchise to provide electricity to Tuba City. Four years later, in his inaugural address, Navajo tribal chairman Paul Jones urged people to support electrical power as a worthwhile investment. Jones argued that electricity made a "more sanitary, healthful and pleasant place in which to live. The cost of this power is, of course, something that every family user must learn that he is required to pay in order to enjoy these benefits." He pointed out that more homes in rural Puerto Rico had electric power available to them than did the Navajo Reservation. "It is, however, my hope that in due course of time every Navajo hogan, house or home on the reservation will have in it and available for the homeowner's use electricity and the resulting advantages it entails." Lastly, Jones argued that the Navajo Reservation could attract industry if the tribe provided the basic essentials: water facilities, transportation, and power facilities. Such services improve the health and welfare of reservation households, which could enjoy electric appliances like sewing machines, irons, and washing machines to the same degree as off the reservation.[2]

At the time of Jones's speech, more than half a million Native Americans nationwide were isolated physically, historically, and culturally from the majority of the country's citizens. Most of them lived on reservations. More Native Americans resided in Arizona (83,387) than in any other state, and the census classified 90 percent of them as rural. Only Montana, with 21,181 Native Americans, had a higher percentage of rural Natives (94.6 percent). By 1969 the Department of Agriculture concluded that "Indians are the most rural of the U.S. minority ethnic groups, and they are mainly rural non-farm people. They have low incomes, poor health and housing, and are educationally and technically unprepared for a sophisticated, modern economy."[3]

Despite years of federal policies bent on assimilating Native Americans into an industrial lifestyle closer to an "American standard of living," at the end of the twentieth century there were many unelectrified homes on Native American reservations, particularly on the expansive and remote Navajo Reservation, where 37 percent of the residents lacked access to the service.[4] America's emphasis on electrical power distribution may have transformed the economic livelihoods, everyday lives, and living standards of rural Americans throughout the 1930s and 1940s, but its delivery necessitated certain economic conditions and cultural values. To a larger degree than in other rural regions, the electrification of Native American communities could challenge

Native traditions, lands, and lifestyles, epitomize tribal tensions, and exacerbate political factions. Because Native American religion and identity have strong ties to rural traditions, the electrification of the Navajo and neighboring Hopi reservations served as a harbinger for numerous other cultural challenges associated with urban and industrial life.

Earlier chapters revealed that some of Arizona's Native American communities, such as the San Carlos and White Mountain Apaches, became part of a non-Native power grid primarily because much of the grid's power generation came from resources —water and coal—located on those Native American reservations. Native lands throughout the country likewise held many potential sites—oil, natural gas, uranium—for generating electricity, but private developers hoped to deliver that power to expanding communities, towns, and cities located off Native American lands.

Regardless of the rich energy sources and power plants found on their reservations, the majority of Native Americans remained relatively untouched by the industrial and technological advances of the first half of the twentieth century.[5] Yet rural communities such as those on the Navajo and Hopi reservations did suffer from the effects of internal colonialism. Energy development caused ecological changes that not only undermined traditional herding and farming methods but also compromised sacred sites. Tribal members sustained high unemployment, maintained traditional housing in remote areas, received little education about industrial society, and possessed a legal status that hampered the access of reservation residents to federal welfare programs without the approval of the local Indian agency.

However, Native Americans were hardly passive victims in the face of such changes. While full electrification remains a distant goal, the economic opportunities brought about by World War II and the massive development of energy resources on the Navajo and Hopi reservations opened the door for the electrification of northeastern Arizona. Government-sponsored educational programs inspired a group of new Native leaders to bring some of the elements of industrial society not just to the reservation but to tribal members as well. A private company delivered electrical service to the Hopi villages located along the same distribution lines that powered uranium and coal development. Similarly, the approval of large hydroelectric projects and the emergence of civil rights activism and federal housing programs removed many legal obstacles to electrification and household modernization. Rather than rely upon its trust relationship with the federal government for aid, the Navajo Nation sought other solutions for achieving area coverage. By capitalizing on the intense energy development by private companies on Navajo land, a Navajo enterprise purchased, negotiated, and energized its initial system in just a few short years.

Wires would eventually tie the reservations to the greater metropolitan Southwest, but wires would also connect isolated communities across the Hopi and Navajo reservations of northeastern Arizona, although not to one another.[6] The regional distribution system that emerged reflected the political relationships between the Hopi and Navajo communities and between those communities and non-Native society. Its development also embodied the struggle between valuing traditional lifestyles on the one hand and ambitions for moving the tribes into a modern, industrial society on the other.

Early Power Relations in Indian Country

Physical isolation and a complex relationship with the federal government foreshadowed the growth of a complex electrical infrastructure and largely determined the electrification process in northeastern Arizona, including its late arrival. The approximately 17-million-acre, 25,000-square-mile Navajo Reservation occupies most of northeastern Arizona, but it also includes land in northwestern New Mexico, southwestern Colorado, and southeastern Utah. The 1.6-million-acre Hopi Reservation is positioned within its borders atop a series of three high mesas. The location of these communities on the Colorado Plateau makes them relatively inaccessible from main travel routes. The mesas and canyons lie among miles of flat, semi-arid, unfenced plain, so with elevations ranging from 2,760 to 10,388 feet above sea level, temperatures can often be considerably colder than the rest of the state and present less than ideal conditions for agrarian pursuits. Rolling mountains of ponderosa pine, sagebrush plateaus, red rocks, streams, lakes, and barren foothill valleys characterize the landscape. The natural water supply consists only of intermittent streams and inaccessible groundwater. However, water and soil engineers throughout the twentieth century repeatedly determined the land to be irrigable. Even today, most experts consider the land poor for grazing cattle and sheep, but raising livestock long served as the Navajos' chief source of income.[7]

Both oral history and archaeological evidence suggest that the Hopis and other Pueblo Indians are descended from the prehistoric Anasazi culture (commemorated today at ruins like Mesa Verde). The Navajos also maintain a connection to the Anasazi, a word they define as "ancient ones." Anthropological sources indicate that Navajos may have migrated from northern Canada, although scholars have reached no consensus regarding when they arrived in the American Southwest. While estimates range from AD 100 until about 1525, the oral history of the Diné (as the Navajo refer to themselves) agrees that their ancestors traveled through four other worlds before arriving in their homeland, identified by four mountains located within an area known by many Americans as the "Four Corners."[8]

In the seventeenth century, Spanish colonists identified as the Apaches de Nabajó those people who lived to the west of the northern Pueblos, north of the Zunis, and east of the Hopis. Spaniards described the community as a semi-sedentary one that planted corn and traveled to hunt. With natural resources scattered, Navajos likely moved in accordance with the seasons. They frequently traded meat, animal hides, and minerals such as salt and alum to the Pueblo Indians, with whom they shared some agricultural, cultural, and ceremonial concepts. Most Navajos reportedly lived in dispersed settlements and built special structures for harvest storage. Usually circular in layout, these hogans were made of three forked poles, others of a cribbed log type, and still others of stone. Unlike the Pueblos and the Hopis, the clan-based Navajos preferred these temporary and dispersed residences rather than permanent and communal ones. One can still find areas on the Navajo Reservation with less than two dwellings per mile.

In 1774 the area's Native residents successfully expelled the Spanish from the eastern portion of their territory. After Mexico achieved independence in 1821, additional trade routes opened with the United States. Agriculture, animal husbandry, hunting, gathering, and manufacturing woolen cloth formed the base of the Navajos' economy. The dramatic rise of non-Native settlement and the arrival of the U.S. Army in New Mexico Territory after the Mexican-American War (1846–48) further disrupted Navajos' control over their natural resources and greatly accelerated antagonisms with the U.S. government. The government and the traditionally sedentary Hopis frequently engaged in violent confrontations, but no major military campaigns resulted. However, Mexican Americans and Anglo-Americans expanded their settlements into Navajo lands, and the 1858 Bonneville Treaty robbed the Navajos of some of the best land for cultivation, grazing, and minerals.[9]

In 1863 New Mexico's military, which was in charge of shielding non-Native settlers from Native American attacks, launched a campaign to crush the Navajos. The U.S. troops struggled in the region's uneven and rocky landscape, and at the end of 1864 they marched through the tribe's settled areas, destroying most of the crops, homes, waterholes, and especially orchards while capturing many of the livestock. Along the way they killed 301 Natives, wounded 87, captured 703, and robbed the rest of sustenance. Commanded by the dime-novel hero Colonel Christopher "Kit" Carson, the army then forced the weakened Navajos to emigrate almost four hundred miles on foot to a government reservation located in Pecos Valley called Bosque Redondo in eastern New Mexico, or risk starvation. Known as "The Long Walk," this brutal experience, during which many Navajos died, remains one the most traumatic memories in Navajo history.

In January 1867 the federal government transferred control of the Navajos from the army to the Office of Indian Affairs. Later that year, a report condemning the handling of the Navajo situation prompted Congress to set up a commission to negotiate a peace treaty. Whereas the government relocated many tribes to reservations away from their home territory, the 1868 treaty between the Navajo tribe and the United States returned eight thousand Navajos to at least a portion of their homeland. Over several years, executive orders gradually expanded the reservation to include those Navajos who lived outside the original borders. It eventually encircled a 2.5-million-acre reservation that President Chester Arthur established for the Hopis (also known as Moquis). Disputes between Hopis and Navajos over who had claim to this reservation land would only grow more volatile with time and eventually reduce Hopi holdings drastically. Among other issues, the treaty promised that the U.S. government would construct a number of buildings on the reservation, provide housing for the Indian agent on the reservation, and establish educational opportunities. The last provision, which stipulated one school for every thirty pupils aged six to fourteen, would prove critical for introducing industrial, electrical living to young Native Americans.[10]

The 1868 treaty encouraged the Navajos to take up farming by promising 160 acres of land and tools to any family or individual desiring to cultivate. Such clauses continued the policies of the early republic. Since George Washington's administration, an underlying government policy toward Native Americans aimed to make them farmers, the virtuous vocation of Thomas Jefferson's agrarian dream. In support of these assimilation goals, Indian agents contemplated providing Native Americans with electrical power, but only if it aided irrigation efforts that would support farming as a vocation.[11]

However, while some small, irrigated areas were scattered across the Navajo Reservation, real agricultural opportunities never arose over the next century. Residents built their post-treaty economy around resources that were already located on reservation lands, such as forestry and minerals. The federal government also issued sheep and goats to encourage Navajos to raise livestock—an option they found far more economically successful than depending on scarce and unreliable water supplies for the eight to ten thousand cultivated acres in the reservation. By 1940 the sale of wool and mohair provided one of the primary sources of cash income.[12]

During the first few decades of the twentieth century, trading posts and the railroad spurred outside access to and interest in Native arts and crafts like Hopi pottery. Excess wool from sheep provided plenty of material for women to weave distinctive and commercially popular Navajo blankets. In return, some area traders, such as John Lorenzo Hubbell in Ganado, introduced various industrial goods and services to residents.[13]

These activities introduced industrial elements into Navajo and Hopi society. Electricity in some form arrived relatively early at the reservations, even earlier than in non-Native rural areas, because of to the federal emphasis on education and federal treaty obligations. The local Indian agencies' generating stations provided the first electrical power to many of the communities that had schools and major concentrations of residents. Early administrative decisions determined the direction of electrical systems. At the beginning of the twentieth century the federal government began to administer northeastern Arizona through five separate agencies in addition to a Hopi agency: Southern (Fort Defiance), Northern (Shiprock), Western (Tuba City), Western Extension (Leupp), and Eastern (Crownpoint). Like their Apache neighbors, the Navajo Indian agencies used their generators to act as a small, private rural electric utility to the surrounding region. Local Indian agency employees found themselves isolated in remote areas and desirous of some urban amenities; accordingly, each agency consumed large amounts of power. The agencies' diesel plants sometimes extended service to area missions, trading posts, and their own schools. However, the distribution systems did not extend much beyond a mile or so.[14]

Since the 1870s the OIA had followed a federal policy to assimilate Native students through boarding school education far away from their communities. The OIA located the Theodore Roosevelt Boarding School on the Fort Apache Indian Reservation in 1923 to educate Navajo students. The school's curriculum furthered assimilation goals by introducing students to basic Euro-American academic subjects while exposing them to many amenities of industrial life. Part of this industrial training followed Victorian expectations of gender roles, thus primarily Native girls received training in electrical appliances. Guidelines stipulated that the schools' unit kitchens should include an oven range. The home economics programs for Native girls (many of them Navajos) at boarding schools like Fort Apache's Theodore Roosevelt followed the government publication "The Social Heritage of the Indian Girl and Indian Home Life." The goal was to train girls to conduct domestic work "in the homes of others should they desire to do so." The junior high school curriculum focused on the living conditions of the reservation house, while the high school program examined those in the non-Native town or city. Not surprisingly, the average Native American family could not afford electricity even if they had access to power. In addition to speaking English, a Navajo girl who completed boarding school or even day school was expected to move into a house that would allow her to put her education into practice. Rather than a traditional hogan, she was supposed to keep a home with wooden floors, running water, modern kitchen appliances, and even electrical lighting to which she had been accustomed.[15]

In 1928 the federally commissioned Meriam Report severely criticized the government's boarding school policy. The document accused the OIA of lacking any understanding of the problems confronting Navajos and made several recommendations to correct the system, including returning students to their communities. Although the report did not specifically mention electricity, the resulting policy changes would have long-term effects on the reservation's electrification process. For example, a new day school system promised the construction of several modern facilities across the reservation.[16]

The Indian agencies considered electricity essential for the functioning and safety of their schools—probably their largest power users. Some agencies used coal, wood, oil, or gas for heating and lighting, but inspectors repeatedly recommended that electric plants were safer and more energy efficient. Classrooms, dormitories, and kitchens required heat, light, power, water, sewer, and garbage collection to operate. Government officials believed that "these systems must be maintained on an uninterrupted twenty-four hour basis to ensure the health and safety of Indian school children and Bureau personnel."[17]

Beginning in the 1930s, Commissioner of Indian Affairs John Collier had promoted the installation of diesel engines at the new day schools in order to provide more economical electrical services of lighting, small appliances, and pumping. As they had in the boarding schools, administrators stressed electricity as part of the children's educational training for the industrial world. They reported that day schools "must be so designed and operated as to condition children to want better living, to want to go where resources and jobs are sufficient for decent living, and to be able to succeed by virtue of the training, much of this training must be a conditioning to modern living. This cannot be done in barracks or in dismal structures. It cannot be done in schools that are not equal to modern schools anywhere."[18]

In Ganado, John Lorenzo Hubbell offered to deliver power from his trading post to the local day school. However, coordinating the power supply for buildings often taxed the local Indian agency's bureaucracy and maintenance capabilities with constant problems of system capability, reliability, and overloading the system with additional customers. As facilities expanded, so did power supply needs. For years afterward, school was the first place many Native Americans were exposed to electrical power. Most would not have service in their homes until at least the 1970s. Electricity was simply not a part of domestic life.[19]

The day school system emerged during the Roosevelt administration in the 1930s, but other New Deal legislation would introduce electrical power to the reservation. The creation of the REA in 1935 made little impression on the Navajo tribe, since the new agency targeted most of its funding to non-Native cooperatives and associations. But while New Deal programs like the REA altered the relationship of the federal government to its non-Native constituents, the Indian Reorganization Act (IRA), passed on June 18, 1934, sought to redefine the status of Native Americans. The IRA marked a wholesale reevaluation of federal policy toward Native Americans in the United States, ostensibly ending or at least curbing assimilation policies. It urged Native Americans to organize their own tribal governments and constitutions, encouraged economic independence, and promoted the incorporation of traditional tribal history and culture into the school curriculum. Unfortunately, many of the proposed changes challenged diverse Native attitudes, customs, and ways of life. For example, the Hopis' constitution imposed uniformity across the politically diverse mesa villages. The Navajo Tribal

Council, which had originally formed in the 1920s to negotiate oil leases, eventually reorganized to its current form in the 1930s independent of IRA requirements. Although the Navajos rejected the IRA's conditions for adopting a tribal constitution, Commissioner Collier still sought "a goal of a representative, centralized Navajo government together with a more consolidated approach to federal services to the Navajo."[20]

Under Collier's administration, the Navajo Indian Agency reorganized in order to establish a political center on the reservation. Beginning in 1935, the same year the Rural Electrification Act was passed, the OIA consolidated its scattered agencies to serve fifty thousand Navajos living on more than twenty-five thousand square miles of the reservation at the new Navajo "capital" of Window Rock. This administrative reshuffling required the construction of a considerable number of new facilities, including an administration building, council house, power plant building, school building, warehouse, machine shop and garage, dispensary building, single employee quarters building, seventeen cottages, apartment buildings for both Natives and non-Natives, and two Navajo community washhouses. The agency superintendent boasted that "these buildings are of permanent type of construction conveniently arranged and equipped with modern conveniences," including electrical and plumbing equipment for all. The entirely concrete power plant building held diesel-powered electrical generating equipment. Underground concrete boxes and tunnels constructed throughout the new townsite distributed lines for steam, hot water, electrical current, and telephone service.[21]

With its demand for electricity growing greater than its supply, the new centralized Navajo Indian Agency planned to install two more diesel engines and searched for ways to lower the costs of its systems. Some agencies changed from butane to the less expensive natural gas or coal to save on fuel expenses. Future tribal chairman Peterson Zah recalled that a Navajo worker would regularly haul coal from a small mine like Keams Canyon as fuel for Tuba City's boarding school generator. Employees soon began comparing the Navajo Indian Agency and its electrical operations to the successful the New Deal project that brought affordable power and water to the depressed South. Building Superintendent R. J. Tolson commented, "We do not operate exactly as the Tennessee Valley Authority, but under our new construction program, we are in hopes of developing much cheaper utilities."[22]

For years, area churches, stores, and trading posts could receive electrical power from the closest Indian agency if they supplied a meter, equipment, and a service line. The agency usually sold power at ten cents per kilowatt-hour plus federal tax, and inspectors ensured that the customer conformed to the National Electrical Code. When the Tuba City power plant became overloaded, the agency refused any more non-government customers. Such decisions caused some nearby residents to complain. Daisy Albert accused the office of favoritism toward some former agency employees when agents refused to deliver power to her father, Charlie Talawejei. Indeed, Indian agency employees often used the coveted service to promote the agency's interests and goals. One official agreed to furnish light, water, and other utilities to a public boarding school in Shiprock, New Mexico, only if the school admitted Native American children free of charge.[23]

Of all tribal members, schoolchildren probably had the most experience with using electrical power. Prior to World War II, access to electricity was a by-product of federal Native American educational programs and agency activities. Unlike the Apaches, the majority of Navajos and Hopis lived far from urban centers and power lines. Beyond the introduction of trade items, they remained relatively insulated from the changes in industrialized America. According to anthropologist Clyde Kluckhohn, many Navajos of this period acquired industrial and agricultural implements, purchased factory-made equipment, performed traditional cooking in metal vessels (which often replaced pottery except for ceremonial use), and used containers like luggage, trunks, pots, and pans. However, Kluckhohn adds, "For all practical purposes, the applications of electricity, probably the most conspicuous feature of our machine culture, have not impinged on the Navahos at all." Few towns of any size in Arizona or New Mexico had power plants, telephones, or telegraph communication on or off the reservation. The Navajo Indian Agency installed several radio broadcasting transmitters for the Navajo Central Indian Agency to receive reports. Navajo children, who had grown accustomed to the radio and other amenities at the boarding schools, often listened to cowboy music over the broadcasts from urban centers like Gallup. They would carry their preferences for and opinions about industrial life into adulthood and tribal politics.[24]

Postwar Power Development on the Reservations

After World War II, a new generation of Navajo leaders trained at boarding and day schools advocated their reservation's electrification beyond government facilities. As historian Peter Iverson explains, "When the war came, the old values continued, but new ideas and new possibilities also emerged." Native Americans' experiences during the war further heightened interest in bringing industrialization's social and economic benefits to the reservation. OIA officials estimated that thousands of soldiers and war workers had returned to the reservations without a means to financially support themselves. Many veterans expected the same benefits as their non-Native counterparts regarding modern amenities and skills training to work in an industrial economy. Navajos who had relocated to the cities for wartime employment returned to find few comparable jobs on the reservations. The plentiful raw materials that the reservation provided for industrial purposes, such as wool, lumber, and animal hides, were transported and used in manufacturing elsewhere by means of mechanized equipment and largely distributed to non-Native populations. Irrigation problems prevented many people from farming as a livelihood, and even after the height of stock reduction, ranching generated 44 percent of Navajos' income. As historian Richard White observes, "The once self-sufficient Navajos faced starvation or welfare," while the reservation's most important economic asset, manpower, remained severely underutilized.[25]

The hogan remained emblematic of an average Navajo's living status into the late 1940s. No more than 1 percent of Navajos lived in "modern" housing facilities of a frame-type construction. Those few often had the benefit of living on permanently irrigated land or held skilled positions with the U.S. government. Only about 10 percent of the Navajo population could even afford cabins or "improved" hogans, because such people primarily made their living through various combinations of farming, stock raising, and jewelry making. A Bureau of Indian Affairs study in 1947 suggested that nearly 90 percent of the Navajo people were forced by "adverse economic status to occupy squalid, unhealthful mud and log huts" and that "only improved income could hope to improve housing conditions."[26]

Recent scholarship indicates that, rather than permanently moving to the city for work, many Navajos found a way to continue patterns of traditional Native American life by finding alternative means of local support. They negotiated wage work in order to continue living on the reservation. The reservation's economy remained diversified throughout the middle part of the century, so wage and agricultural work supplemented rug and jewelry sales to tourists. As historian Colleen O'Neill observes, "The Navajo case suggests economic development in the American Southwest between the 1930s and 1960s was a fluid process, one that shaped and was shaped by local systems of power and culture specific to that region. . . . They participated in the 're-working of modernity' in their region, strategically weaving an alternative history of capitalist development that was as culturally specific as the patterns of a Navajo rug."[27] The Navajos' gradual response to electrification seems to have followed a similar philosophy for adapting to modern life on their own terms.

Iverson observes that the period following World War II was "an era of changing perspectives on the part of both the federal government and the Navajos. Navajo tribal officials symbolized this transition." As recipients of boarding and mission school training, many of these former students collectively organized an alumni association called the Returned Indian Students Association. They formed election slates advocating a new, younger, and formally educated Navajo leadership. Councilmen like Howard Gorman and Frank Bradley, also alumni of boarding and mission schools, became powerful political leaders and the tribal council's leading advocates for bringing technology to the reservation.[28]

When the Mountain States Telephone and Telegraph Company requested a right-of-way across the reservation in 1939, Frank Bradley insisted that a telephone company representative clarify what procedures he would take to obtain the permit, and he spearheaded a subsequent tribal resolution that required the company to pay a rental fee. Tribal council chairman Jacob Morgan felt that "it would be proper for the Navajo tribe to receive some benefit from this line the same as Indian traders who pay licenses to do business."[29]

The sentiment that the tribe should be involved in bringing industrial development to the reservation was even stronger a decade later when Navajos could no longer sustain themselves agriculturally. In 1947, tribal council chairman Sam Ahkeah hired former assistant U.S. attorney general Norman Littell to served as the tribe's general counsel. For the next twenty years, Littell wielded his legal talents and forceful personality to influence the tribe's many decisions regarding economic growth and self-determination. In order to realize any significant industrial development, the reservation first required an infrastructure: paved roads, telephone lines, and especially electrical power lines.[30]

The Cold War hindered REA cooperatives like Navopache, but the new political climate helped remove many of the hindrances and restrictions to the Navajo Reservation's electrification. In 1950 Congress recognized the dire economic situation on reservations in the Southwest. Using the model of the Marshall Plan, which targeted its funds for rebuilding war-torn Europe a few years before, Congress passed the Navajo-Hopi Long Range Rehabilitation Act, granting $88 million to infuse economic aid. Although most of the funds were slated for roads and trails ($38,237,680), the bill allocated $250,000 to radio and communications systems and more than $700,000 for the development of business enterprises and common service facilities, primarily school and road construction.[31]

Historian Andrew Needham observes that the bill's congressional hearings indicated legislators' hope to continue the assimilation policies of the early century and of the wartime relocation program. Secretary of the Interior Julius Krug argued that the government needed to help Navajos "overcome their difficulties and achieve a standard of living comparable with that of the nation as a whole." Assistant Secretary of the Interior William Warne claimed the development would get both Navajos and Hopis "out into the main swim of the economy and civilization down there in the Southwest." The act echoed the argument of the early-twentieth-century Country Life Movement that access to technology ensured both equality and democracy. However, according to federal officials, Navajos had some catching up to do in terms of industrial living. Even though Navajo leaders had already experienced such instruction as children and young adults through federal educational programs, Navajos would require "extensive instruction in modernity," Needham explains.[32]

New federal policies toward Native Americans compelled the Navajo Tribal Council to repeatedly assert control over what many viewed as the inevitable industrialization of the reservation through communications and utility services, particularly electricity. During the 1950s and 1960s, Congress began to target certain Native American tribes which it felt no longer needed federal support, compelling Navajo leaders to search for greater economic independence and stability. Invoking the rhetoric of the emerging civil rights movement, advocates of "termination" argued that Native Americans deserved the same opportunities and responsibilities as American citizens. In practice, however, the policy simply continued earlier assimilationist goals and a long pattern of dismissing certain Native American treaty rights, land claims, cultural values, and sovereignty. When targeting tribes for termination, the government often ignored their lack of financial readiness to be cut off from federal dependency without enduring severe hardship. While the Navajos were not identified as a termination tribe, Navajo leaders responded to the threat of reduced funding by promoting the doctrine of self-determination.[33] Tribal leaders launched concerted efforts to bring life on the reservation closer to that of non-Native society, but through tribal institutions and in accordance with Navajo beliefs and traditions. However, when the end of World War II generated outside interest in the energy resources on the reservation as well, leaders also sought to protect their claims to natural resources whenever outside corporations desired their use. Navajos would accept energy development on their land, but they negotiated with corporations in exchange for electricity and the benefits that they perceived it would bring to the reservation.

The Bureau of Reclamation spent almost half a century planning a set of dams that would store and control the water of the Colorado River. The Colorado Plateau's deep canyons offered ideal conditions for building large, concrete water-storage dams of sufficient height to produce significant amounts of hydroelectric power. In addition, the vast mineral deposits and fossil fuels on and around reservation lands ensured that the tribe and its resources would become an integral part of regional power development by the end of the 1950s. Navajo and Hopi lands would become critical to energy development and electrical expansion across the Southwest, fueling the region's postwar economic boom. The populations of southwestern cities exploded between 1940 and 1970. Arizona's capital of Phoenix alone ballooned from 40,000 to 650,000 during that period. Such expansion exhausted local resources. In an effort to sustain the profound growth, urban developers turned to an area inhabited primarily by rural Native Americans, the remote Colorado Plateau.[34] Charles Wilkinson has labeled the development of power plants, mining activities, and drilling projects on the Navajo and Hopi reservations as the "Big Buildup," one of "the most prodigious peacetime exercises of industrial might in the history of the world."[35]

The public has yet to realize the environmental consequences of the Big Buildup (see the conclusion), but its economic and cultural influence on the reservations remains profound. An oil strike yielding millions in royalties alone sponsored several tribal works programs. At the same time, the discoveries of uranium and gas throughout the postwar period yielded other economic possibilities for Navajos. Casual observers would likely agree that corporations purchased the minerals from the Navajos at far below market prices, but these new funds still placed the Navajo government in a position to distribute tribal dollars to its members through scholarships, tribal investments, and the development of reservation infrastructure to capitalize on energy production for Navajo use and benefit.

Navajo leaders, however, did not readily solicit or adopt new technology without extensive debate, discussion, and negotiation. Throughout the 1950s the tribal council entertained the introduction of not just electricity but also radio, telephone, natural gas, and television to reservation communities. The issue of sponsoring a radio broadcasting station exposed the cultural and ideological chasm between the older and younger council members—one that was reflected in the tribe as a whole—regarding assimilation, technology, and "progress." The ensuing discussions illustrated the emerging tension between those who rejected the practicality and influence of new technology and those who felt that it was inevitable and positive if controlled for tribal benefit. First, Attorney Littell urged council members to discuss issues of legality and cost. Would the Federal Communication Commission consider the tribe a part of the BIA and therefore not allow a federal entity to own a broadcasting station? If so, could the tribe afford the expenses one would entail? The council members thoughtfully and enthusiastically discussed the pros and cons of providing increased airtime filled with newscasts of local, national, and world news to its tribal members. These members emphasized the advantages that technology had in decreasing the isolation of Navajos from both each other and the industrial world around them. Better communication was vital on a large reservation where transportation was slow and the population was scattered. Rather than relying on word of mouth, council members could impart fuller information about various topics and issues to their constituents. Lastly, the radio offered professional training and employment for Navajos.

In spite of these perceived benefits, other members of the tribal council expressed concern over content and access. Hoskie Cronemeyer, who had supported English-language instruction and argued against the teaching of Navajo customs in schools, worried about the insensitivity of broadcasters, since some on the existing radio programs from nearby towns and cities had already upset listeners with offensive jokes and comments. Morris Natoni wondered if enough people would listen to the station. He also stressed that announcers should have the proper qualifications, such as knowledge of both Navajo and English, in order to serve tribal purposes. Paul Begay observed that if the purpose of the radio station was to increase communication through area coverage, the tribe should consider making receivers available all across the reservation. Supporters dismissed these concerns, asserting that many Navajos, particularly women herding sheep and weaving rugs, already carried radios with them. Tribally run programming would communicate much more useful information to Navajos than outside stations had. Near the end of the discussion, Cronemeyer was convinced that he should support the measure. "We are noting changes," he admitted. "There is progress, we are in a new era. We do not want to stay back in an old-fashioned way."[36]

The distribution of natural gas spurred similar discussions about "progress." Many council members initially viewed natural gas as a commodity the tribe could sell rather than use. Some council members felt such service would privilege the educated and would conflict with other tribal employment interests in coal industry. Others disagreed with this line of thinking. Jimmie Largo commented that where a person once saw wagons, "now we see cars doing the work and doing it better, and even in our homes, notice of progress, notice of a step forward is seen . . . showing that we are on the up and coming and making progress toward things that are better. In that connection, I think it would be to our advantage to think of making another step and taking hold of this natural gas and use it ourselves."[37]

At the end of the 1950s, the introduction of television on the reservation raised many of the same issues. Howard Gorman persuaded the council to appropriate money to survey the western part of the reservation for television service, particularly regarding the schools and hospitals near Ganado, Wide Ruins, Keams Canyon, and Chinle. Chinle had already begun funding television, because the presence of local trading posts allowed them to get television signals. Ganado residents were raising money for equipment, including a power plant, to relay television stations into the area within the year. Gorman viewed television as a vehicle for education. Other Navajos agreed but admitted to having only a vague idea about its content and impact. Others argued that television would be redundant, no different from radio or newspapers in terms of delivering information. James Musket of Fort Defiance doubted anyone would use a television for educational purposes if he or she could watch something else.[38]

Interest in electricity grew naturally out of these discussions. However, tribal leaders took an immediate interest in controlling its transmission and distribution across Native American lands after the APS requested a franchise to provide electrical service to Tuba City, located on the far western edge of the reservation, for a uranium mill ten miles east. The Navajo Tribal Council unanimously approved a resolution empowering the tribe to issue franchises to utilities in the manner of a municipality or county government. Previously, the BIA had granted easements or rights-of-way to allow utility service through the reservation. When Howard Gorman oversaw the Eleventh Annual Navajo Tribal Fair in 1957, its theme, the "Navajo Parade of Progress," emphasized the tribe's industrial advances, and Tuba City welcomed the first delivery of current with a ceremony and a barbecue.[39]

The events sparked lively discussion over what council member Paul Begay saw as the inevitability of electricity on the Navajo Reservation. "As time goes on," remarked Begay, "and communities continue to develop on the reservation, we will have more of these requests coming in from private utility companies which are in business to provide special services for which they will want to have authority to engage in utility activities on the reservation." In response, Chairman Paul Jones echoed the rhetoric of REA literature by targeting women as the largest beneficiaries of APS's power. He added, "It means a modern way of living in that area."[40]

The administration of Navajo tribal chairman Paul Jones (1954–63) emphasized professional and vocational training for an industrial wage economy. Having lived in New York City and

Chicago, Jones had plenty of firsthand experience with urban, industrial settings. Under his administration the tribal council encouraged broader organizational capability, an emphasis on training, and on-the-job instruction involving continuous supervision in the Navajo Vocational Training Program, the Navajo Farm Training Program, and the Arts and Crafts Program as successful tribal enterprises. Additionally, Navajo leaders began to promote this type of education for Navajo children at forty-three new day schools. These new structures would require substantial resources and modern amenities that used electricity.[41]

Throughout his term, Jones advocated a new, "urban" type of living arrangement for Navajos that was less isolating and more conducive to industrialism. With stock raising disappearing as viable way to make a living, Jones promoted a new type of Navajo community that encouraged the formation of villages and co-operation with non-Native neighbors, rather than the dispersed settlement pattern conducive to ranching and stock raising. This would require a change in residential living: clustered housing rather than the traditional scattered housing. The chairman emphasized other community- oriented goals similar to village or urban life. These included stockpiling firewood and developing gas and power lines. Extending land leases would not just attract industry but also help guarantee federal housing loans.[42]

A portion of the Rehabilitation Act offered low-cost, durable housing for Navajo families requiring it. Leaders argued that the new housing would help instill pride and a sense of home ownership. However, the first steps toward modern reservation housing had begun several years earlier at sites of industrial development, such as housing projects for sawmill workers. Five hundred laborers, mostly Native Americans, constructed Wingate Indian Village in the late 1940s. The sawmills not only provided some additional cash and employment during a period of stock reduction, but they exposed the workers to industrial living conditions. Many of these workers reportedly rebuilt their hogans with stone, which BIA administrators described as "of more substantial type of construction than they have been erecting."[43]

The tribal budget for 1960 continued to support the progress made under the Rehabilitation Act by appropriating $5 million to public works. Navajo leaders addressed rising power needs when the town of Shiprock's electrical needs exceeded the power generated from a BIA steam turbine system in 1950. BIA officials planned to build a new school and expand the Indian Health Service hospital. The Bureau of Reclamation committed its power to outside parties, and an anticipated plant by the Utah Construction Company would take too long to meet immediate needs. The agency asked the Continental Divide Electric Cooperative, an REA borrower, from New Mexico to quote rates for service to Shiprock as an alternative to building another agency generation plant. The BIA's relationship with the cooperative went back to 1948 when the agency contracted a transmission line with the cooperative to deliver the Navajo Reservation's first central station service to communities on eastern end of the reservation (the New Mexico side), including five schools, four trading posts, and a tribally owned sawmill along the way.

This process required some customized negotiations. The cooperative encountered numerous problems negotiating rights-of-way across different tribal lands. Its contracts included both the BIA and individual residents as members. REA officials determined that the Shiprock area also promised substantial electrical usage by the Navajo Indian Agency, the area's coal mines, Navajo farmers, and nearby communities. They even discussed forming a separate cooperative to serve the area. However, tribal leaders protested, fearing that such an arrangement would rob the Navajo Nation of a future power customer when it built its own power station (APS already delivered to Tuba City).[44]

As an alternative, the Basin Light and Power Company of Farmington, New Mexico, evaluated the development of utilities in the Shiprock area and offered several suggestions to the Navajo Tribal Council. One plan granted Basin an exclusive reservation franchise in San Juan County, but this likewise took future control of utilities in the Shiprock area away from the tribe. Another option would be to provide electrical power to the tribe at wholesale rates. The power company would bear the initial construction costs and help with rehabilitation. After ten years, the tribe could terminate the agreement and purchase the facilities. The tribe would also take over the BIA system but remain under Basin management and subsequently provide power to all customers on the reservation. However, the exclusion of three high-use customers from power delivery (the new Indian Health Service Hospital, the BIA school, and the Kerr-McGee uranium mine) concerned some council members. Under a third option, the tribe would build the lines itself. The tribal council could claim jurisdiction over the reservation's utilities from the Navajo Indian Agency. Large appropriations from new oil lease money would allow the Navajos to acquire old BIA lines and construct new ones. Although construction costs would be significant, potential growth of the area indicated that in this way the tribe could maintain control over future utility activity. At a meeting in January 1959, after acknowledging several concerns about payment collection, the tribal council unanimously approved the creation of a utility wholly owned and operated by the Navajos.[45]

The Navajo Tribal Utility Authority

The Navajo Tribal Utility Authority (NTUA) began its operations in 1959 with 15,000 potential customers (only 250 actual) and the mission "to acquire, construct, operate, and maintain utility system properties throughout the entire Navajo reservation for the purpose of supplying electric, natural gas, water and sewer service to the inhabitants." The tribal council maintained a seven-member utility committee, few of whom were familiar with the utility business or its technologies. The committee offered the NTUA's managers guidance and kept the council informed of the details of the enterprise's operations. The utility's appropriations stemmed from the Resources Division of the tribe's executive branch (of which NTUA was a department), the tribal council, and the BIA. The board of directors set policy, spending plans, and rates and hired a general manager, a non-Native midwestern engineer with extensive REA experience, named Philip W. "Vance" Vanderhoof. He in turn hired a staff and workers.[46]

In November 1959 the newly created NTUA negotiated with Farmington's electric utility to construct a transmission line between Farmington and Shiprock and to install a substation at Shiprock. With the help of a Washington DC consultant, Martin T. Bennett, and his staff engineer, Leland Gardner, a Navajo, the tribe's lawyers drafted a temporary agreement with Farmington to provide power to Shiprock until the tribe could supply its own. The commissioner of Indian Affairs approved the plans four months later.[47]

Meanwhile, the NTUA took steps to prioritize area coverage over profit. Whereas power companies had requested rights-of-way across the reservation, they had done so in order to provide sufficient load to make their own power systems feasible and profitable. "When this was brought to our attention," wrote Councilman Maurice McCabe in an NTUA status report, "we realized that if we were to grant right-of-ways and permits for the distribution of power to only those areas which had sufficient load to guarantee feasibility of distribution systems, it would be a long time before we would ever get power to the sparsely settled areas." Therefore, NTUA negotiated an option to repurchase the facilities at cost, less depreciation, in all permits for rights-of-way. NTUA's advisory committee also stipulated that any power systems requesting access across the reservation would need to ensure distribution to sparsely settled areas as well as those with higher electrical load.[48] "The Navajo Tribal Utility Authority will extend every effort to bring utilities services to the Navajo people at reasonable and non-subsidized cost," Councilman Frank Bradley commented. "We firmly believe that this enterprise of the Navajo Tribe will be only a self-sustaining one which will be of great ultimate benefit to the Navajo people."[49] Twenty-six miles of transmission line and twenty miles of distribution lines extended across the area by 1960. Further growth, however, would depend on the tribe's success in accessing some of the power that private companies were generating on their lands.

"We Need Power"

In 1960, APS, which already delivered power to towns near the borders of the reservation like Leupp and Tuba City, purchased coal on 24,320 acres of undeveloped tribal land from the Utah Construction Company. The utility hoped to build a new coal-fired, electrical generating plant on Navajo lands near Fruitland, New Mexico. The multimillion-dollar Four Corners Power Plant would run a high-power transmission line hung along eighty-foot-high towers across Native American lands in order to serve rapidly expanding Phoenix. In return for APS's rights-of-way, the land lease of a 1,250-acre site, and the use of coal deposits near Farmington, tribal lawyers negotiated a critical power agreement whereby the Navajos would receive a significant supply of energy from the new plant. Although nearby residents could not take advantage of the high-voltage electric lines, the NTUA would receive power at wholesale rates for a thirty-year period. Tribal council members viewed this arrangement as an economical way for the tribe to both garner substantial royalties and promote further industrial development on the reservation.

Chairman Jones, Maurice J. McCabe, and Martin Bennett considered the APS contract a great opportunity for the future. They would allow power generation to occur on the reservation, because it complemented their plans to distribute electrical power to all areas of the reservation. The financial deals raised a debate about the need to provide utilities and electrical distribution to the entire reservation. To convince the council, McCabe and Bennett used many of the same arguments local REA promoters of the 1930s and 1940s had used regarding investor-owned utility services. Such utilities had besieged the tribe with requests for rights-of-way and franchises in recent years. However, the companies would only build distribution lines to high-density areas, if they intended to serve tribal customers at all. As was typical of many utilities throughout rural areas, the construction of a comprehensive system with complete area coverage required financial feasibility. The reservation's sparsely settled areas would never receive power under such economic stipulations. In response, tribal leaders authorized a study that would examine how to guarantee affordable power not only to populated communities such as Window Rock or Shiprock but to all areas of the reservation. Bennett emphasized urgency: "We need power, cheap power, as cheap as possible and lots of power if we are going to bring industry onto the reservation."[50]

Beyond APS, other possible power sources for the reservation included the utilities Continental Divide Electric Cooperative and Utah Power and Light Company, which were also already delivering power to the outskirts of the reservation. The latter delivered power to the reservation's northern edge at Red Mesa for oil company sales but not to area homes. Power from the Bureau of Reclamation's hydroelectric dam at Glen Canyon and the Four Corners plant was supposed to become available over the next few years. The tribal attorneys warned the Navajos that if any of these interests engaged in retail power sales on the reservation, there would have to be certain "terms and conditions" to ensure NTUA's interests.[51]

Because of this concern for tribal sovereignty, significant challenges lay ahead in avoiding the regulatory activity that Arizona and New Mexico usually required for utilities to operate within their borders. The tribe could allow APS to produce and transport power, but it could not grant APS the right to sell power on the reservation. NTUA could build its tribal system by systematically acquiring existing systems (much like Navopache). Tribal lawyers had included "option to buy" clauses in original rights-of-way agreements with APS and Continental.

This insistence on protecting a future customer base for a reservation-wide, tribally controlled electrical system came at the expense of the neighboring Hopis. Hopis negotiated a deal for electrical power from APS, but when APS requested a right-of-way from the Navajos to deliver to the Hopi villages, the Navajo Tribal Council insisted on reserving the right of a future tribal utility to purchase the line if they later desired. APS rescinded its request, and the issue delayed power delivery to Oraibi for almost a year.[52]

During the discussions about REA funding, Glen Canyon Dam began to supply continuous hydroelectric power through APS facilities. A central component of the Bureau of Reclamation's Colorado River Storage Project (CRSP), Glen Canyon was located outside Page, Arizona, on the northwest portion of the Navajo Reservation. When building commenced in 1956, the massive and controversial structure had promised the tribe a significant opportunity. The Glen Canyon Dam was part of the federal effort to harness hydroelectric power from the upper Colorado River in order to fund CRSP, and in 1939 the Reclamation Act designated certain groups, including the Navajo tribe, as "preference" customers. Unfortunately, controversy surrounded the endeavor. The creation of Glen Canyon's reservoir, Lake Powell, ignited a backlash campaign by environmentalists (immortalized by Edward Abbey in *The Monkey Wrench Gang*) and threatened the sustainability of plants and animals that Navajos considered important resources. Water also inundated hundreds of archeological sites. Furthermore, erosion has threatened Rainbow Bridge.[53]

As the controversies over Glen Canyon raged within and outside the reservation, power from the dam broadened electrical service opportunities for the NTUA to run all of the tribe's utilities. As part of the federal transmission system, one power line extended from Page across the northern part of the reservation to Shiprock, New Mexico. Under an APS agreement, the company would send any additional power to the tribe for distribution purposes. Despite being outnumbered, tribal lawyer Walter Wolf and Navajo Leland Gardner successfully negotiated with Bureau of Reclamation's Floyd Dominy for a delivery point at Kayenta, Arizona, as a condition of selling the right-of-way for that line. The former power supply agreement also stipulated that APS deliver power to the town of Indian Wells, thus allowing NTUA to switch its power supply between the two stations.[54]

At the same time, the tribe and its lawyers debated the possibility of another hydroelectric source through the Central Arizona Project, another Bureau of Reclamation effort to provide water to southern Arizona. Environmentalists, politicians, and the Bureau of Reclamation wrangled for Native American support to build hydroelectric dams at Bridge Canyon and Marble Canyon in the Grand Canyon on the lower Colorado, one located on Navajo lands. Yet unlike the preferential power user status offered to the Hualapai tribe, Navajos received no compensation under the original agreements due to a complex web of legislation, which privileged the state of Arizona's right to power sites along the Colorado River. The Navajo Tribal Council issued resolutions as a formal protest that threw tremendous strength behind the anti-dam forces. In 1966 the tribal council and its attorneys condemned the dams, but not on solely environmental grounds; they did so in favor of developing the reservation's coal deposits as an alternative energy source.[55] The government never constructed the Grand Canyon dams, but events surrounding their proposal illustrate the priorities and tenacious efforts of the tribal leadership to access available power sources.

Amid this negotiation for power, Navajo Tribal Council members continued to express a variety of concerns. Was the tribe ready for this highly complicated endeavor? Would they need to hire utility experts to assist? Hoskie Cronemeyer was concerned that these power deals would have limited financial return. Others worried that electrical power would be limited to frame houses and discourage traditional hogan living. Dick Bayle raised the issue of safety: "In our way of living, at the present time, it is generally the children who are left at home. If they start to turn on the gas or electricity what is the potential danger?" NTUA general manager Philip Vanderhoof promised that such dangers would be addressed through education, similar to fire safety. He listed other advantages, including more comfortable indoor temperatures and better lighting to alleviate eye strain and encourage the rising numbers of day school children to study at home in the evening.[56]

Ultimately, the council accepted the optimists' arguments and approved of power generation by outside interests in exchange for promises of reservation modernization, employment, and revenue. Paul Jones's address at the ground-breaking ceremony for APS's Four Corners Power Plant on March 10, 1961, further articulated the industrial hopes for the plant on the reservation and NTUA:

> This is a great moment for the Navajo Tribe. The construction of a steam electric plant at this site brings to reality the results of many years of exploration and negotiation.
>
> The principal interest of the Navajo Tribe in projects such as this is to provide jobs for Navajos in construction and operation of the plant itself and a better way of life for all our people through the low cost power, which will be produced here. The electric energy will, we hope, attract many industries, thus creating additional employment opportunities throughout the area.
>
> I can visualize ultimately a grid of power lines throughout Navajoland, electric power in Navajo dwellings and, with the

advent of such power, the acquisition of electrical appliances, including refrigeration, by the Navajos as a step toward bettering their standard of living.

In our long range planning, I am hopeful that electric power in the homes will contribute to our educational program through television. An educational television broadcasting station at Window Rock beaming worthwhile programs to my people is not outside the realm of possibility.

Financially, this power plant will be of great benefit to the Navajo tribe. The Tribe will receive a percentage from the mining of coal and a fair wholesale rate on power. At the same time we shall enjoy the beneficial effect of electric energy wherever it is made available. While the presence of a large deposit of coal at this spot has made it possible, the generation of electric power should support the development of other resources throughout the reservation.

At this moment we are witnessing another great stride forward in the progress of the Navajo people, which is coupled with the further development of Phoenix, Tucson, and other cities.

The Navajo Tribe wishes to express its appreciation to the officials of the APS and the Utah Mining and Construction Company whose friendly understanding of our position and requirements has at last borne fruit. I hope, Mr. Lucking [APS general manager] and Mr. Christianson [NTUA secretary], that I shall have the honor of throwing the switch to energize the lines when the first power comes forth from this great generating plant.

We are entering a new era today—an era illuminated by electric power.[57]

A Utility Like No Other

Because of NTUA's desire both to deliver affordable power to all the reservation's rural communities and to control this delivery under tribal supervision, Martin Bennett suggested the tribe look to the REA for funding. The REA's low-interest loans to certain types of organizations aligned with NTUA's electrification goals. Despite General Manager Vanderhoof's concern that the bureaucracy would hamper expansion, the tribal council authorized and submitted a formal REA application for borrowing almost $2 million. In February 1961 the Navajo tribe began the procedure to submit an application.

Meanwhile, several council members continued to stress their constituents' desire for electricity. Howard Gorman, Allen Yazzie, and Paul Williams indicated great pride in what they were doing and felt the REA seemed like the best way to accomplish their ultimate goal. Gorman expressed confidence that "after oil and gas wells have been exhausted, we will still be receiving the income from utilities." They had not only a smart business venture but one that was conducive to the desires and needs of the people. "The Navajo family, whether they are living only in a summer shelter, in a hogan, or in a modern house, our people want to have the benefits of modern living with electricity in their homes," Gorman argued. "There is a great demand and I would like to see natural gas and electricity in every hogan. People who have these facilities seem happier. They seem to have better health where they have these modern facilities."[58]

Leaders pursued electrical power by hiring non-Natives General Manager Vanderhoof and later Mac Eddy, seasoned REA operators from the Midwest. Navajos understood that their utility resembled REA cooperatives in both intent and operation. However, the REA application would present numerous challenges that highlighted the differences between NTUA and other rural electric utilities. First, the tribe would need to qualify as a borrower. This was not the first time the tribe and agency had entertained this possibility, but NTUA's REA application broke new ground on several fronts. It was the first time a Native American tribe had directly submitted an application to the REA; second, if successful, it would be one of the first instances whereby the tribe would have access to improvement funds from a non-BIA federal program.

Many of the legal barriers that had long blocked Navajos and other Native Americans from obtaining such non-BIA-administered federal services had recently been eliminated. At Chairman Jones's request, Congress had allowed the Navajos to extend leases to their lands from twenty-five years to ninety-nine years. This restriction on land ownership had prevented both tribes and individuals from providing property as security for any long-term loan, including those from the Federal Housing Administration. The additional road construction under the Rehabilitation Act also removed important physical barriers. At the same time, exceptional legal status complicated the REA loan, since the REA typically loaned to corporations or associations. In a memo of nearly thirty-pages, REA's legal department argued that although the tribe was not incorporated, it possessed enough corporate attributes to provide acceptable security for a loan.[59]

The tribal council objected to various REA stipulations that could compromise tribal authority. Attorney Norman Littell attempted to reduce the REA's claim on faulty loan payments to only a lien upon the physical assets of the electrical system and not other tribal properties. Furthermore, the BIA refused to approve the NTUA's "Plan of Operation" or NTUA as a tribal enterprise, recommending it apply as a tribal activity instead. As an activity, they explained, NTUA's "Plan of Operation" would not be subject to outside approval. Perhaps even more telling, the BIA had its own interests to think about. The BIA's concerns were not an atypical reaction from a power customer suddenly subject to a change in its utility services. The government would be a large power user for the fledgling enterprise, and BIA officials were concerned about the fact that the utility would fall beyond the scope of state or federal regulations that controlled the rates of other utilities. Keeping NTUA as an activity rather than an enterprise might prove too complicated for the present management structure. The BIA claimed this would become an issue with an REA loan.

On September 7, 1961, the REA issued a proud press release announcing a loan to the Navajo tribe, its first Native American recipient. Native tribes had been individual cooperative members before, but never direct borrowers. The $1,846,000 REA loan aimed "to supply adequate power for homes, boarding schools and tribal commercial and industrial projects, for construction of 275 miles of distribution lines and twenty-five miles of 69kv transmission lines to serve 765 new consumers." The REA staff agreed to Littell's request of an REA lease for all utility lines and facilities, rather than the agency's usual mortgage, in order "to avoid violation of sovereign immunity of the tribe" and tribal trust lands. This arrangement ensured that the courts could not confiscate tribal lands in the case of a foreclosure. Rather than the tribe entering into power generation contracts, the REA would absorb the rights and commitments for power promised to the tribe from the Bureau of Reclamation through Glen Canyon Dam. This stipulation assured NTUA of a continuous flow of power through lines NTUA built with REA funds. In order to circumvent a nondiscrimination clause on government contracts, the REA added a clause granting preference to local employment in order that the tribe could continue to train and employ Navajo workers. The NTUA would acquire and take over the mortgage for the lines and facilities of another REA borrower, the Continental Divide Electric Cooperative, already serving reservation communities. Finally, it required that the NTUA keep separate books on its electrical operations.[60]

Shockingly, in spite all the preparation and lengthy discussion, NTUA rejected the REA loan. General Manager Vanderhoof and his successor, C. Mac Eddy, believed the NTUA needed to completely sever its dependence on government bureaucracy. They also insisted that it would be too difficult to separate the utility's other interests in gas and sewers from money targeted for electricity. The NTUA could grow much faster, they believed, without such constraints.[61] As it turned out, the REA application process ultimately forced the tribe to make decisions about the role and structure of its utility.

At a council meeting in November 1961, Littell and other tribal lawyers pushed the council to clarify the management structure of NTUA. Council members such as Annie Dodge Wauneka, daughter of Chee Dodge, and Howard Gorman expressed frustration and confusion over not just the complicated nature of the issues at hand but also the dominant role the lawyers had taken; the council, they felt, was losing control. The ensuing discussion stretched over two meetings. Attorney Joseph McPherson assured the council that the BIA was very supportive of NTUA and would likely hook its schools and administrative offices up to a tribal electrical system if assured reasonable rates. He offered the Tennessee Valley Authority as an example of a government enterprise that, although operated by the federal government, was not included in the annual congressional appropriations. REA's loan approval at least partially alleviated the concerns of the BIA's area director, Walter Olson, who remarked: "This action by the tribal council which is designed to improve the management of NTUA is commendable. With the supervision this program will receive under this proposed management board, which will include experts in the utility field, and with the Rural Electrification Administration involved in the execution of a loan agreement, this should become an improved business-type organization."[62]

The tribal council was also wary of having a management board made up entirely of non-Navajos, even if they had more than ten years' experience in the utility business. Arguing that Navajos could also maintain oversight, McPherson cited two recent graduates who had received their degrees in electrical and civic engineering through tribal funds. Although McPherson did not identify him by name, future tribal chairman Peter McDonald had recently earned his degree in electrical engineering from the University of Oklahoma and was likely one of these graduates. McDonald had moved to southern California for engineering work before returning to the reservation in 1963 to build his political career.[63]

Some members remained adamant that the tribal council should maintain sole controlling authority as well as profit from this venture and that they should continue to define NTUA as an activity. "If we place it under a Board of Management," Dillon Platero protested, "we aren't going to learn about it or know what is going on. We need to keep our control of this project." The council then issued a new resolution that maintained NTUA's status as a tribal activity under the direction of the tribal council's utility committee.[64]

Electrification, Expansion, and Energy Exploitation

Despite spurning the loans, NTUA managed to complete the project for which it had solicited REA funds. A 160-mile-long transmission line would deliver electricity from the Four Corners plant in Fruitland, through the New Mexico portion of the reservation, to the new $3 million BIA school in Teec Nos Pos in Arizona and to Navajo users along the way. The process would also employ and train Navajos in the electrical field. This dual purpose of building not just electrical infrastructure but also a skilled workforce was consistent with the intent of New Deal's public works programs established a quarter century earlier. Navajo trainees constructed the line under the supervision of the Reynolds Electric and Engineering Company, whose managers boasted that electrical power had raised living standards and increased the Navajos' industrial experience.[65]

Workers finished another important hundred-mile power line in May 1962. This "backbone" for a future system extended south from Chinle through the middle of the reservation to Indian Wells and to customers along the way. *Navajo Times* boasted that "the availability of this electric power makes possible a better standard of living for thousands of Navajo peoples as well as making possible vast industrial expansion." Local electric supply companies bought out full- and half-page congratulatory advertisements. Just as other utilities had to educate people about the dangers of the new electrical structures, editors of *Navajo Times* had to continually warn people about safety. APS even used a somewhat misplaced advertisement featuring a non-Native child in Plains Indian dress warning customers to use electricity efficiently. Amid much pomp and circumstance, Chairman Paul Jones threw the switch to energize the line. Maurice McCabe and Howard Gorman presided over a ceremony where the NTUA presented an electric radio, hot plate, and iron (donated by local electric supply companies) to Mr. and Mrs. Henry Spake to celebrate the lighting of their hogan in Ganado, the first in the system. The Spakes had remodeled their home in preparation of the event. "I have never been in a place where people needed electricity more, or wanted it more badly," General Manager Vanderhoof commented. "We want to put an electrical outlet and two light bulbs in every hogan on the Navajo reservation. This would ensure the user of an outlet for a radio and a small refrigerator, if they could afford to buy them."[66]

Beginning with 426 electrical customers in 1961, primarily residential, NTUA delivered to 2,282 customers by March 1964. The utility served thirty-five communities over three main areas, each boasting a branch office: Shiprock, Chinle/Kayenta, and Window Rock. Shiprock's system operated from APS power via the Four Corners plant. The Bureau of Reclamation provided the Chinle and Kayenta systems with power from Glen Canyon Dam. Lastly, NTUA acquired lines from the Continental Divide Electric Cooperative in New Mexico. Planners anticipated six hundred miles of electrical lines on the reservation.

The tribe took additional steps to secure needed power. In

1963 it signed a contract with the Utah Construction Company, one of the "Big Six" companies that had built Hoover Dam, to set aside a twenty-four-thousand-acre area for strip-mining coal at fifteen cents a ton. The company received sale profits, while the tribe earned royalties. This arrangement would bring electrical power closer to many Navajos, provide Navajo labor, training, and housing improvements, and possibly fund the reservation's own coal power generating plant in the future.

The following year, in 1964, the tribal council supported a resolution for the development of the reservation's vast coal resources by the Peabody Coal Company. Peabody had signed leases with the Navajo and Hopi tribes to strip-mine a site known as Black Mesa. Secretary of the Interior Stewart Udall submitted legislation for another coal-fired plant in 1967. The Peabody negotiations provided a boon to NTUA's Kayenta and Tuba City branches in terms of revenue, increased electrical requirements (load growth), and power supply. By the early 1970s, Kayenta's substation fed power to the mining activities on Black Mesa. Part of the coal mined there (7 million tons a year) would be transported via electric railroad for seventy-eight miles to power the Navajo Generating Station at Page, Arizona, the boomtown created during the construction of Glen Canyon Dam. A portion of the Navajos' share of Colorado River water also powered the station. To electrify Los Angeles, the rest would combine into a coal and water slurry and slide through an eighteen-inch-wide, 274-mile-long pipeline to the Mohave Power Plant on the Colorado River in southern Nevada. Furthermore, NTUA supplied the electrical power for the construction of the Navajo Generating Station. Having purchased natural gas out of El Paso, NTUA in turn provided gas services to the Four Corners Power Plant. These operations continue to provide just under half of NTUA's electrical load. Many homes located close to chapter (or community) houses like Lechee, just south of Page, received electricity and other services.[67]

For years afterward, those within and outside the tribe would regard these deals as trade-offs that compromised tribal ideals. The loss of Rainbow Bridge as a sacred cultural site promoted outrage at the time, but the ecological consequences of Glen Canyon Dam on groundwater supplies and soil quality would not be fully realized until much later. The sulfur dioxide haze produced from the coal-fire plants, which has significantly reduced the region's formerly pristine air quality, can reportedly be seen from outer space. Navajo and Hopi officials have questioned for some time whether the slurry water used to supply energy for southern Californians—pumped from the same aquifers that provide municipal water to tribal members—compromised the quality and supply of water meant for Native domestic and agricultural use. NTUA's and the tribe's quest for industrial development, a stronger economy, and increased employment raised controversial questions about tribal priorities from tribal members.[68]

An Independent Enterprise

Before anyone could critically examine all of these energy developments, growing pains accompanied rapid expansion. The Navajo Tribal Council, the BIA, and tribal lawyers repeatedly questioned and reevaluated the utility's political and legal status. However, like many other cooperative members nationwide, most council members were untrained in public utilities operations, unfamiliar with the new technology, and hesitant to grant enough money to accommodate the utility's rapid expansion. They largely had to rely upon and struggle with NTUA's managers, tribal lawyers, and government officials to understand and maintain control over the complex legal problems associated with the operation of a utility business.

The tribal government tried to assert its control. As early as 1963, when NTUA general manager Vanderhoof threatened to quit, the tribal council attempted to make the utility wholly

Navajo, selecting Frank Bradley to head the utility committee and Edward McCabe Jr. as NTUA general manager. After only five years, 169 of NTUA's 180 employees were Navajos. When McCabe stepped down after just a few months, the council tapped C. Mac Eddy, whom they had retained as an adviser, to be intermediate general manager until he could train a qualified Navajo. Vanderhoof had brought Eddy out from Ohio a few years prior because of his experiences with REA cooperatives in the Midwest.[69]

The lack of communication and efficient administration became glaringly apparent when, in 1965, the REA notified the tribe that it had not yet used the funding granted to it four years earlier. A confused REA administrator, Richard Wood, wrote Frank Bradley, chairman of the utility committee informing him that his agency had never advanced the loan, even though a substantial part of the line proposed to get the loan, the one to Teec Nos Pos, was already constructed and under operation. He asked for an immediate response, warning that the agency would rescind the loan authorization in order to allocate the money to other borrowers. The council instructed Eddy to request an extension of six months for a reorganized NTUA to study the matter and reapply the REA money to other projects.

Eddy responded to the REA by explaining NTUA's rapid growth as well as his optimistic goals for its operation. "I am," he explained, "familiar with the needs of the Navajo people who are in a transition period that requires electricity to improve their standards of living and to create incentive toward a better way of life. The Navajo tribe has been very liberal with their money, however, any pot has a bottom in it and the bottom is not very far off for the Navajo Nation. If the area coverage is to be obtained for the Navajo Nation, it will be accomplished in the same manner as the cooperatives have achieved this goal."[70]

As the NTUA board tried to substitute another project to use the REA funds, Eddy ensured that the entire operation abided by

REA specifications, equipment, materials, and government standards. Ultimately rejecting the idea of a federal loan in favor of autonomy for the utility, Eddy also determined that things became even more complicated if NTUA had to go through the tribal council for every appropriation. To remedy problems of management and to streamline expansion, he urged the tribe to make NTUA an independent municipal-type enterprise, owned but not funded by the tribe. As we saw with the electrical cooperatives discussed earlier in this volume, this tribal effort faced many political, geographical, and cultural impediments. Operating as a tribal enterprise, NTUA broke not just from the federal government but also from the tribal council. This new organization had to be entirely self-supporting and under the auspices of the BIA commissioner and of a management board peopled by experienced, seasoned directors, both Navajo and non-Navajo. It was the only utility wholly owned by a Native American tribe and operated with 96 percent Native labor. Most NTUA employees recall the change as one of the scariest in their careers. "That was a turning point," reflected Kayenta branch manager and later NTUA general manager Malcolm P. "Mickey" Dalton. "We were on our own, divorced from the tribal budgetary process. Supervisors were given the reins; we had hiring and firing authority. We had to produce, and the whole complexion changed. Self-determination in action."[71]

The tribe gave the new enterprise all the existing facilities and about $3 million start-up money. NTUA would generate its own revenue and fold it back into operations. The new "plan of operation" called for the expansion of utility systems to all of the areas of the reservation that engineers determined were economically feasible. The document also professed that the new NTUA would carry out the purposes and intent of the 1950 Rehabilitation Act and would provide the tribe a return on its investment by charging low rates and employing Navajo workers.[72]

On March 14, 1966, the advisory committee of the Navajo

Tribal Council appointed an independent management board for NTUA. It consisted of four non-Navajos with at least ten years' experience in both public and private utilities, and three Navajos who could learn the utility business from them. The BIA worried about controlling NTUA funding as well, but Eddy predicted a profit by 1966. The new management board streamlined operations so effectively that most of the deficit the utility had accumulated prior to reorganization was gone by the end of 1967.[73] An ironic historical coincidence illustrates the significant changes over a century. The first chairman of the NTUA Management Board, H. L. Carson, went by the nickname "Kit." Sharing the name of the scout who led the Long Walk to Bosque Redondo, Kit Carson (the father of television legend Johnny Carson) had thirty-five years' experience in rural utilities in Nebraska and Iowa, and he and his wife wintered in Phoenix. Other notable board members over the years included councilwoman and health care advocate Annie Wauneka; Navajo Lee Gardner, an engineer and a manager for Pacific Gas and Electric; and long-time politically influential supporters and councilmen Howard Gorman and Frank Bradley.

By 1969 the NTUA system boasted 7,303 customers (4,581 residential), 312 miles of transmission line, 1,130 miles of distribution lines, and 27 substations. The system delivered a substantial amount of power to new BIA schools. Analysts predicted a substantial increase in available power sources once mining operations began at Black Mesa. Eddy described NTUA's strategy for power acquisitions: "We just kept grabbin' and grabbin'."[74]

With NTUA's success, the renewal of non-Navajo Mac Eddy's contract became somewhat controversial and embroiled in inter-council and tribal politics about who should run the tribal utility. Through the support of people like Annie Wauneka, Eddy served as general manager for another two years until Tribal Chairman Peter McDonald asked him to head its new Development Office. (Eddy went on to serve two years with the Navajo

Forest Products Industries and then became general manager of the Navopache Electric Cooperative in the White Mountains.) He hand-picked his Navajo successor, Kayenta branch manager Malcolm P. "Mickey" Dalton. Dalton, educated in the Ganado Mission School like Howard Gorman, began working with NTUA as a contractor and learned the utility technology and the business on the job as a lineman and line foreman. Although Edward McCabe Jr. had briefly served as the utility's first Navajo general manager, his successor Mac Eddy selected Malcolm Dalton as NTUA's first Navajo general manager. Dalton held the post for the next twenty-seven years. The following year, Lee Gardner became the first Navajo chairman of the board of any Navajo tribal enterprise.[75]

As NTUA continued expansion in the 1960s and early 1970s, political, economic, and cultural factors inhibited the utility's mission of providing area coverage and installing "a light in every hogan." Despite immense progress over the years, much of the territory on the reservation still lacked access to electricity. People peppered council representatives with questions: Could they still get power if they were located far away from a power line, and, if so, who would pay for the cost of construction? In 1962 only half of the three hundred eligible homes in Shiprock, those within a six-mile radius, received power. Many people moved into new housing communities built by the Navajo Housing Authority and found they had no electricity due to last-minute changes in plans. Furthermore, land status questions involving the Hopis, federal legislation, cost, and energy shortages slowed system growth. Cultural barriers also inhibited power line extensions (electrical use will be discussed later), but the primary obstacle was usually affordability.[76]

The Navajos' land dispute with the Hopis compounded the obstacles to the reservation's electrical coverage. The Navajos had already denied a right-of-way for APS to several Hopi villages. Two years after granting an extension, REA canceled NTUA's loan when it realized that the utility hoped to apply the funds to extend power lines into land disputed by the Navajos and Hopis where federal construction had been forbidden in order to force the parties into negotiation and settlement.[77] NTUA could neither build into the Hopi Reservation nor on what it claimed was Navajo land around it.

Tensions between the tribes had escalated when the prominent Peabody Coal Company signed leases with both tribal councils in the early and mid-1960s to strip-mine the coal fields at Black Mesa, located directly within land contested by the Navajos and Hopis. Concern over the destruction of land and the environmental effects of strip mining and coal firing became entangled with APS and NTUA power delivery efforts, further biasing traditional Hopis against electrical power in general. The *Healing v. Jones* court case, which lasted from 1958 to 1962, established a "joint-use" area between the Navajo and Hopi tribes. "Joint use" meant that the tribes shared an area designated as part of the 1882 Hopi Reservation regarding ownership and other legal rights. Many accused the decision of being politically motivated, since so many Hopis opposed mining in the disputed territory. Perhaps in defiance or even denial, NTUA system maps throughout this time period do not depict the joint-use area as part of the Hopi Reservation. Hopi protests and refusal to grant rights-of-way prevented NTUA from serving the area for several years. The BIA strictly followed a policy that forbade government construction or development until the court partitioned the land between the tribes. Almost a decade after delivering power to the Hopi village of Moenkopi due to its proximity to Tuba City, APS delivered electricity to Old Oraibi, the oldest continuously inhabited village in the country, as well as New Oraibi, through the towns of Holbrook and Keams Canyon in 1967. Like the Navajo Indian Agency, the Hopi Indian Agency had built power lines to villages some years before, but Keams Canyon Indian Agency's steam plant had limited power to even energize its nearby schools and mission. APS purchased and rebuilt the system, incorporating it into a new power grid. The reservation's BIA superintendent added that electricity was central to improving the Hopi economy by allowing better tourist accommodations. Hopi tribal chairman Willard S. Sakiestewa Sr. looked forward to televisions and "modern electrical appliances" in Hopis' homes.[78]

Intent on building a regional system, NTUA made repeated attempts to purchase the APS systems serving the Tuba City area and the Hopi Reservation. NTUA ran into several legal barriers when it tried to run lines to either Hopis or Navajo tribal members in places like White Cone and Pinon located in the disputed joint-use area. Some Navajo BIA employees at Pinon still relied upon the Navajo Indian Agency office and school to provide utility services through a severely taxed "patchwork electrical distribution system." Yet others remained without electricity even after they moved into mobile homes to be closer to the school generator. In 1974 Congress partitioned the land, allowing NTUA to begin extensions, but cost still exempted several potential customers. Three years later, NTUA finally reported that it had extended distribution lines into the Cottonwood-Pinon section of the joint-use area.[79]

The environmental and cultural mitigation laws of the late 1960s and 1970s also delayed securing rights-of-way and slowed construction, particularly following the federal and tribal legislation such as the National Historic Preservation Act, the National Environmental Protection Act, and the Endangered Species Act, which required environmental and cultural impact assessments to ensure that construction would not disturb any archeological sites or natural habitats.[80] Such findings would often determine the route and length of power lines, adding considerably to expenses. National Park Service lands, or areas where the Bureau of Reclamation's high-voltage lines already ran, forced NTUA to construct their lines down hills, across rugged terrain, and into canyons.

In addition to conflicts with federal lands, internal procedures on the reservation caused problems for achieving full area, or reservation, coverage. NTUA had to obtain permission from local communities in order to extend lines. Chapter houses, which had administered the reservation at the local level since 1927, would host the meetings to inform residents of the procedure for getting electricity and its benefits. It was common for NTUA and chapter houses to all approve line construction, but lack of funding (often raised through fees they charged to individual communities) greatly stalled service. Federal procedures also stipulated that NTUA had to secure homesite leases from each residence into which it fed a line. Other people would move closer to the power line to cut down on expenses, but then they might get into a land dispute with a neighbor. Land claim issues were particularly sensitive in the joint-use area. More typically, people refused to grant a right-of-way because they did not want anyone or anything, including an arm of the tribal government, imposing restrictions on their grazing lands. Those living in the checkerboard areas could not benefit from the tribal system, but they could become eligible members of non-Native electrical cooperatives.[81]

In at least one case, the local population aided the utility in extending services over extreme and uneven terrain. In 1979, workers enlisted helicopters to set the power poles for a line to Navajo Mountain, which reaches 10,380 feet in elevation. As REA cooperatives had realized in the past, NTUA supervisors quickly understood that training local people to erect their own systems was both cost-effective and practical, since only they could tolerate the elevation to complete the work.[82]

Lastly, the energy crisis of the 1970s placed the NTUA in severe constraints. Battles with the nearby town of Farmington over the construction of the Navajo Power Plant (near Navajo Dam in New Mexico) limited needed power for pumping to farms within the Navajo Indian Irrigation Project.[83] As the tribe began efforts to take more control over the development of energy on the reservation, NTUA found itself running low on funding. The utility again applied to the REA and this time accepted the government loan. Once more, the issues of mortgage leases and tribal sovereignty arose. In one of his final acts as a member of President Jimmy Carter's administration, the REA administrator approved the loan in January 1980. In doing so, REA accepted a pledge of revenue for security, the right to confiscate equipment and appoint a temporary manager, but they could not market the utility as a whole. Throughout the 1980s and 1990s, NTUA received over $8 million from the REA, subject to all the stipulations of an REA borrower. By the end of the twentieth century, NTUA struggled with attempts to accommodate its system's growth. In 1965 the Navajo Tribal Council leased property for electrical generation to the Western Energy Supply and Transmission Associates (WEST), a conglomeration of private western utilities including the Salt River Project and APS. WEST's ambitious plans hoped to sustain the non-Native population growth of the American Southwest by generating three times as much power as the Tennessee Valley Authority. The tribe formed the Diné Power Company to promote energy development on the reservation in part to support the largely distributive function of NTUA.[84]

For more than twenty years, the NTUA was the only utility wholly owned and operated by a Native American tribe. In spite of its unique position, the organization participated in organizations and activities on par with REA cooperatives across the state like the Grand Canyon State Electric Cooperative. However, because the tribe owns NTUA, not its members, the not-for-profit enterprise is not an REA cooperative on the model of Sulphur Springs Valley Electric Cooperative, Graham County Electric Cooperative, or Navopache Electric Cooperative.

Although the electrical program in northeastern Arizona commenced almost thirty years after the passage of the Rural Electrification Act, its growth was rapid and influential. A complex power system stretched across a region dominated by Navajo and Hopi inhabitants, altered traditional Native living patterns, and reflected changes and tensions in tribal leadership in the twentieth century. While many Navajos and Hopis had been geographically, culturally, and ideologically isolated from the industrial world, experiences at boarding schools and during World War II nurtured a desire for electricity across an entire generation. Resource development and poverty programs of the 1960s opened opportunities to access it. When this generation secured leadership, electrical power served as a primary component of a larger economic and political vision of self-sufficiency and determination. Having been introduced to, or forced into, an industrial lifestyle through federal administration and education, the Navajo Nation debated, organized, and eventually took control over their own technological development in order to achieve reservation-wide electrical service. In many senses, the Navajos held a unique position among Native American communities, including the neighboring Hopis, in having both economic and political opportunities to form and benefit from operating their own electrical distribution system. These decisions were part of a concerted effort to provide the technological resources that would entice industrial investment to the reservation to stimulate a traditional economy no longer able to sustain itself agriculturally. The NTUA would contribute to tribal goals of independence and self-reliance while it vowed to put "a light in every hogan" on the reservation.[85]

"A Paragon of Paradoxes": Using Power on the Reservation

Rather than become the farmers the federal government intended in the 1868 treaty, Navajos and Hopis entered an industrial world as both electrical suppliers and consumers. By 1960 most individuals on either reservation did not operate commercial farmland outside the Navajo Indian Irrigation Project. In 1968

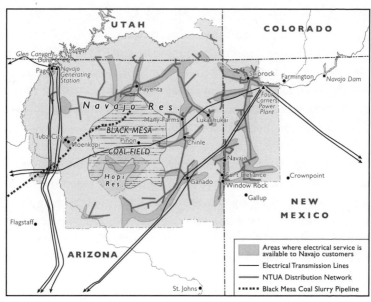

Map 5. Distribution network of the NTUA, 1975.
Source: Compiled from James M. Goodman and Mary E. Goodman, *The Navajo Atlas: Environments, Resources, People, and History of Diné Bikeyah* (Norman: University of Oklahoma Press, 1982).

the *Navajo Times* commemorated the treaty's 100th anniversary with a special edition called "A Century of Progress." In an attempt to replace painful memories of the past with hope toward the future, the Peabody Coal Company purchased an advertisement congratulating the tribe for "A Long Walk to Progress." While the events are hardly comparable, the idea of a long, arduous journey toward electrification certainly reflects the story told thus far. Electricity was familiar to many Navajos and neighboring Hopis years before the technology became available to them, but most did not see the electrification process as inevitable. This is an important consideration for examining electrification, because system feasibility required that electrical delivery and electrical use went hand in hand. Significant numbers of Navajos become electrical consumers and utility customers only after Navajo leaders with backgrounds of federal or missionary education took power, and only when the rise in industrial wage made electrical service affordable.[86]

Previous chapters have addressed similar issues regarding the use and impact of electrification. Therefore the following discussion evaluates what the Navajo Reservation's potential power consumers thought about electricity, how they intended to use or not to use it, and how it ultimately affected their culture and way of life. Electricity alleviated traditional chores of rural life, such as collecting wood and hauling water, but the changes the technology introduced had an arguably more profound impact on the reservation than any of the other regions we have discussed. All of its industrial implications brought along a set of assumptions and values that challenged traditional Native American values and ways of life. Both the Navajo and Hopi societies struggled to negotiate a way to live traditionally within the expanding modern, industrial setting.

As in other rural areas, education and economic need created the community's desire for electrical power, but several sources encouraged domestic use. In addition to exposure through boarding schools, military service, and off-reservation living, many Native Americans first "stepped into electricity through the battery era." Historian Martin Link tells the story of one of the first electrified hogans in Canyon de Chelly, one illuminated by the headlights of an old pickup truck.[87]

Then, as early as the mid-1960s, advertisements in the *Navajo Times* promoted sewing machines, vacuum cleaners, and television sets. Advertisements from appliance stores in nearby Gallup and articles reporting the arrival of electricity in Navajo country reveal much activity and enthusiasm. The ads continually linked electrical power with the idea of progress and modernism. The editors often surveyed tribal members with questions about modernization and sponsored appliance giveaways. Stores from Gallup and Farmington pushed refrigerators, washers, dryers, lamps, fans, and electric ranges. If one could afford them, appliances made sense on the still rural reservation where even in Window Rock the nearest laundromat was forty miles away in Gallup. NTUA also sold some unique appliances tailored to its customers, such as the "Navajo Electric Blanket," which resembled the traditional product with traditional rug designs. Yet not everyone fully supported or understood NTUA's mission. Managers reported considerable vandalism of the lines before they could even be energized. These acts included shooting at power poles and cutting wires.[88]

Several contractors for electrical wiring, including NTUA, also advertised in the *Navajo Times*. Like electric cooperatives, the tribal utility devoted a specific department for training Navajos to wire residential and commercial facilities across the reservation. They only carried out such contracts, however, when engineers determined the sites economically feasible for extensions. NTUA encouraged consumers to use at least two lightbulbs and one outlet for a radio or small refrigerator, warning that a washing machine would require water services in addition to electricity.[89]

NTUA worked to alleviate fears about the safety of electrical current, especially among the elderly. Its managers instructed their district administrators to guide both employees and the general public in the appropriate use of electrical power. Existing service organizations such as the Indian Extension Service, a division of the BIA but modeled on AES, underscored these efforts. While such educational programs resembled those in other rural areas, they addressed the values of northeastern Arizona's residents. No doubt born out of the grand tradition of REA cooperatives' Handy Watts and Willie Wiredhand, a distinctly Navajo interpretation of the congenial, safety-conscious spark plug emerged: a lightbulb called Kee Kilowatt. NTUA employee Laverne Bartos designed Kee and illustrated a comic-book-style pamphlet to instruct illiterate customers about the utility's procedures, purpose, and safety issues (see figs. 14 and 15). The pamphlet advocated the benefits of electricity and appliances by depicting Navajos of all ages enjoying indoor lamps, irons, washing machines, refrigerators, and televisions. As a conclusion, the last frame portrays a young boy napping by a mesquite tree with the caption "Happiness = No more chopping wood for the cookstove," indicating that electrical power increased leisure time. Similar instructive cartoons appeared in *Navajo Times* explaining utility operations and encouraging customers to conserve energy in order to keep their bills affordable. Local chapter houses also took some responsibility for educating consumers about electrical service and benefits. NTUA repairmen addressed the service needs associated with a number of growing appliances in isolated areas that were without commercial dealers.[90]

Similarly, once APS delivered its initial lines into Hopi villages, the company held educational meetings to explain electrical use, power safety, and wiring procedures. Some Hopi families had already purchased power from traders' small diesel power plants. One village gave first priority to a religious institution, much as the Mormon towns of Safford and Thatcher did in Graham County by wiring its sacred kiva. Yet as was the case with the Navajos, cost would inhibit many of them from achieving fully electrified homes.[91]

In addition to programs for power users, NTUA prepared many Navajos for professional positions such as welders, electricians, and administrative workers. Although the workers learned technical skills rather easily, many had minimal schooling and could not fill out the paperwork their jobs required. They enrolled in NTUA-sponsored adult education classes for literacy, writing, and vocational training. Some even asked to bring their wives or other family members with them. More qualified Navajos enrolled in correspondence courses to learn how to operate power and sewer plants. Other educational institutions designed courses according to NTUA's requirements, which stipulated the application of Navajo learning traditions. The NTUA board encouraged

(*top*) Fig. 14. Excerpt from NTUA publication featuring NTUA mascot Kee Kilowatt. Laverne Bartos, "The NTUA Story" (Window Rock AZ: Navajo Tribal Utility Authority, 1968). Copy in Department of the Interior Library, Washington DC. Courtesy of Navajo Tribal Utility Authority, Fort Defiance, Arizona.

(*bottom*) Fig. 15. Excerpt from NTUA publication instructing customers about use and procedures. Laverne Bartos, "The NTUA Story" (Window Rock AZ: Navajo Tribal Utility Authority, 1968). Copy in Department of the Interior Library, Washington DC. Courtesy of Navajo Tribal Utility Authority, Fort Defiance, Arizona.

contractors like Reynolds Electric and Engineering Company to make maximum use of the indigenous workforce. Reynolds's training classroom involved reviews of electrical industry materials, codes, terms, and the operations of AC (alternating current) motors and circuits. Six out of the first twelve students successfully completed the course the first year Reynolds offered it. By 1970, Intermountain High School's curriculum included electricity, and the utility employed almost 250 people, mainly Navajos. Still others would receive on-the-job training, such as former custodian Ted Tenakhongva, a Hopi and Navajo lineman, and future NTUA general manager Mickey Dalton. By 1971, NTUA had its own complete educational program that boasted high school equivalency courses, apprenticeship programs, and a training center that focused on specific skills. All of these employees had to not only learn new work skills but also adapt to the industrial way of daily life that involved modern conveniences.[92]

From the beginning, women were an integral part of NTUA office staff and management, if not technical jobs. However, Navajo women became involved in activities through homemaking clubs that resembled the programs in other regions. The early activities of the local Indian Extension Service in many ways complemented the home economics educational curriculum taught in the boarding and day schools. The instruction introduced new standards of cleanliness that complemented the work of Councilwoman Annie Wauneka, who lobbied for health issues on the reservation. As an NTUA board member, she supported NTUA's goals of electrical, water, and especially sewer services. Therefore, moving into modern frame homes of wood or stone was one of the most important first steps in encouraging modern homemaking. Such houses had become more common on the reservation, particularly in regions close to the railroads. Yet Navajos constructed traditional homes for religious purposes as well. Since the 1960s, many people therefore maintain a ceremonial hogan in addition to their frame houses.[93]

The Indian Extension Service was more successful with Hopis than with Navajos. Shungopavi, Polacca, Oraibi, Toreva, Mishongnavi, and Chipsulavi reported club memberships with over one hundred women. A tradition of communal living may have made the Extension Service's club structure more natural for Hopis than for tribes like the Navajos and Apaches, who traditionally lived more scattered and isolated from one another. Since the 1930s, Hopi girls and women had been able to visit nearby Indian Extension Service offices and make use of electric ranges and sewing machines. Hopi requests for improved sewing supplies and better fabrics reflected some of this influence, and the women showed off their new machine-inspired creations at the tribal, Navajo County, and Arizona State fairs. The Keams Canyon Indian Agency hired home economist Hopi Juanita Kavena in 1953. AES agent reports repeatedly praised the work of the agents on the reservation, expressing hopes that one day the Native American programs could be absorbed into the AES's home demonstration programs in the rest of the state. At times Hopi women even joined non-Native Navajo County women at planning and leadership training meetings. "There is a great need for work among Indians," commented one extension agent. "These Hopi women are further advanced than many groups and welcome extension work." Even if they did not participate in many of the home demonstration programs, Navajo women were responsive to radio programs sponsored by the Extension Service and the Office of Navajo Economic Opportunity. Such programs offered advice about health, commodity foods, and modern influences. They would suggest recipes for preparing traditional foods in the electric oven, allowing women to plan for meals in a different season than traditional methods would have allowed. Like non-Natives, Native American women likely had strong decision-making powers regarding the purchasing of household appliances upon the arrival of electricity. NTUA's Consumer Services Department even hired its own home economist in the mid-1970s to offer demonstrations about the use and safety of major appliances.[94]

APS and NTUA not only had to instruct new users about how electricity worked but also had "to work around tradition, mythology, and everything else" when it came to serving their Native American consumers. Residents in small, isolated towns like Pinon, where generators powered the boarding school and trading posts, had little desire to host the types of urban influences seen on larger reservation towns like Chinle and Window Rock. Electricity presented significant challenges to traditional Native American life, so it was not surprising that children supported the changes more readily than tribal elders. With little understanding of the technology—for example, the concept of grounding wires—some found the occasional short circuit particularly alarming and remained suspicious about issues of safety and cost. Former tribal chairman Peterson Zah recalls his grandfather warning him to be wary of electrical circuits, knowing that Zah would encounter them at boarding school.[95]

At the same time, elder Deesheeny Nez Tracy indicated a willingness to adapt to electrical living and expressed gratitude to the "treaty makers" for educating Navajo children about the industrial lifestyle.

> Among other things, Navajos learned to improve their living conditions and now can maintain nice, clean houses. Many have modern facilities, like electricity and gas to cook and to heat their homes. . . . These all make life easier. Most of us don't have to haul or chop firewood now. I moved into my new home a little over two years ago, and all I have to do is press a button or turn a knob, and I get all the conveniences of a nice, comfortable home. At first it seemed strange and uncomfortable to me, but I got accustomed to it.[96]

The influence and expectations of the younger generations gained significance throughout the postwar period. The tribe's desire to keep young, educated tribal members from leaving the reservation spurred housing programs and developments that would include all the required utilities. During a discussion at a Navajo Tribal Council meeting about improving the condition of Wingate Village, Frank Willeto invoked the children as a reason to adopt new living standards: "When we take children back to the old homeland, our children miss the finer modernization, such as an electrical system and so forth. These things they miss, and pretty soon they would like to come back. So with this in mind Gentlemen, it is a desire of my people to have some way to consider our living standards in this village."[97]

Navajo and Hopi children, likely influenced by their boarding school and urban experiences during relocation, largely preferred to live in "modern" frame homes with all of their conveniences. As with the Apaches, non-Native rural communities elsewhere in Arizona had some influence over the desire for new technology among the Hopi youth through AES-sponsored 4-H clubs. In 1956 the *Arizona Farmer Ranchman*, a newspaper aimed at the state's rural communities, reported the growth of 4-H clubs in the villages of Hotevilla, Oraibi, Toreva, Polacca, Chimopavy, and Keams Canyon. The 4-H community clubs divided into smaller project clubs specializing in various areas such as gardening and clothing, and the village of Hotevilla even boasted an electrification club. This particular club worked with boys on electrical projects and experiments despite the fact that at that time many only used electricity in their school and not yet in their homes. "But," the newspaper qualified, "the boys in the club are looking forward to the day when the community will have a power line or a light plant there."[98]

The Hopi traditionalist movement was probably one of the most dramatic manifestations of how attitudes toward electricity differed along generational lines, not to mention Native American resistance to technology. This loose coalition of Hopi activists identified a wide range of issues emphasizing dedication to Hopi culture, religion, and daily life. Most of the activists did not categorically oppose all industrial changes. They added public utilities to their platform in 1966 as the vehicle through which the BIA and its "puppet" tribal council aimed to destroy traditional Hopi life and create an inevitable financial debt and dependence on a foreign culture. Similar to their position on coal mining, they complained that digging holes for power poles disturbed village markers and desecrated lands. This had indeed occurred on some Navajo lands. APS had taken a leading role in excavating some ancient Native American ruins that workers discovered while constructing its transmission line from Farmington to Phoenix. Furthermore, the issue of easements and rights-of-way made village leaders worry that the power company could take more of their land away if people failed to pay their bills. Others reportedly feared that the static which emanated from power lines would disturb the natural energy forces in sacred areas and visually disrupt the tranquil landscape.[99]

Participants in the traditionalist movement physically thwarted utility construction on two occasions in 1966 and 1968. While there is little record of the 1966 incident, the standoff two years later garnered a little more media attention. On May 8, 1968, the BIA, tribal government, and APS began efforts to build paved roads, power lines, telephone lines, and sewers into Hotevilla in response to a request from over one hundred Hopi petitioners. Elder religious leaders protested. "We do not need those things," explained one. "We have lived here a long time—many old people here are still healthy. We don't need water pipes or electric lights, or sewers or paved road. We have our good spring water. We have our oil lamps . . . These things are no good for the Hopi. It only means taxes that we can't pay. . . . We were instructed by the Spirit how to live. We can take care of ourselves. These public works are all coming in here—it must be stopped!"[100] When one demonstrator blocked the tractors, a scuffle ensued. Some women stood in pre-dug holes to prevent further desecration from the insertion of the poles. They even fought back with a comparable technological weapon when they brought their grievances to the popular national television program *The Steve Allen Show* to generate considerable public sympathies. Public works stopped the day after the program aired, and traditionalists pulled out several of the poles that had already been set and left them lying across the highway. To discourage further removal, the agency superintendent warned would-be saboteurs that the poles were now electrified. Eventually, one-third of the Hopi villages refused power line service. Such tensions created factions that spilt communities like the Moenkopi Pueblos, where homes with electricity were interspersed among those without it. APS had to run individual lines directly to the homes of those who did not affiliate themselves with the sponsoring tribal council.[101]

Not everyone objected to the introduction of power lines. Younger Hopis found a voice in the community action program newspaper *Hopi Action News*. One of the most successful of the War on Poverty programs, the community action program provided seed money to disadvantaged communities nationwide to improve their standard of living. Editorials in the *Hopi Action News* indicated the improvements that were necessary for community survival due to the lure of cities. The newspaper also sponsored an essay contest in which young writers emphasized the generational differences in values and perspectives with regard to electrical power. In November 1966, eighth grader Fannie Kewan cited electricity, a sewage system, and better, government-built homes as ways of improving her community. "When we have electricity," she explained, "our village might be a clean village." Classmate Sarah Jane Sumatzkuku echoed these concerns. In July 1968, student Cheryl Tenakhongva asked, "Must there be a 'civil war' in Hotevilla? Must the younger generation wait for the older generation to die out before they modernize their homes?" The younger generation has grown accustomed to such features at boarding school, she explained, and older people needed to realize they are living in the "atomic age" and not deny such comforts as electricity, water, and sewage to the tribe's younger members.[102] Elders could dismiss such young people as "hippies," but the reality was that Hopi communities reflected a mix of the old and the new.[103]

Even those in the traditionalist movement opposed electricity because it threatened dependence on a foreign culture, not because they feared or misunderstood the new technology. Their manipulation of public opinion through a television program provides some evidence of this. One anthropologist observed that in Moenkopi, villagers made decisions about which appliance to purchase based on whether an item's function was separate from traditional life and, for some, whether it carried an association of luxury. Electricity and other utilities significantly increased villagers' investment in their household, and as a result they spent more money and tied the village closer to the cash economy.[104] A *Hopi Action News* cartoon in September 1966 mocked the ignorance of some, depicting a man on a ladder placing an antenna atop a teepee. He turns to a neighbor and asks, "Whatta ya mean, I gotta have electricity first?"[105] Years later, a nonprofit agency organized by tribal members called the Hopi Foundation installed solar panels on those unelectrified homes, bypassing power lines entirely.[106]

Electricity and modernization created a good deal of conflict among Navajos as well. For some, power lines represented progress; for others, they symbolized the destruction of traditions and rituals. However, for many older Navajos, electricity and electrical appliances served as agents of unwanted change. Elders preferred to live traditionally and naturally rejected electricity. Some still dressed in traditional clothing. Likewise, many women continued to make fry bread over an open fire outside and bathe in sweathouses. Lighting was unnecessary when the sun governed the stock-raiser's schedule.[107] When offered a Euro-American-style house with a propane gas stove, sink, heater, and other appliances, one woman insisted on remaining in her hogan. When her children tried to convince her that the house would make her life easier, she provided the following explanation:

> I can't live in this house; I'm not used to it. I'm going to go out, chop my wood, get my little chips in, start my fire, and cook the old ways. It keeps me alert. It keeps me going. It keeps me . . . looking forward to something [rather] than just sitting here and turn the knob and watch that thing come on. I prefer heating my water on a stove, wooden stove, wood-burning stove. I'd rather get up early in the morning and build my fire the way I'm supposed to. I can't just get up and turn the fire on; it's a short life . . . I'd rather do it the hard way and live longer.[108]

Throughout the 1960s and 1970s, non-Native educators continued to promote new technology as a way to assimilate Native American children. Teachers from Kaibeto Elementary wrote to Senator Barry Goldwater about their desire to prepare children to become "better equipped to enter the white man's world." While their building had received power in 1965, the teachers felt the school needed television to acquaint students with the larger world as well as to deliver programs like *Sesame Street* and *The Electric Company* in order to reinforce English and other skills not emphasized outside the classroom. A non-Native Window Rock High School teacher and a Navajo opened Window Rock's first television sales and service stores in Window Rock in 1963 (there was another in Fort Defiance).[109]

Television became so popular that the tribal council discussed making television reception a reservation-wide service in 1964. The community of Tohatchi asked that the tribe purchase a television signal so that certain communities would not have to bear the cost of maintenance for a signal that people as far as Window Rock and Ganado also enjoyed. Some tribal council members expressed concern that television would encourage laziness, but others countered that television would not only be educational but would be for children in other ways as well: it would keep them at home with their families, "keep them out of trouble" at night, and therefore alleviate "juvenile problems" in favor of family time and recreation. Where even adult Navajos might go to Gallup to watch television, they could instead stay home if the service was offered. Howard Gorman weighed in using the argument that the tribe needed television to keep the children permanently home: "What right have we to deprive our people, our children, especially, where the TVs are already available to them? We cannot stop progress anyway. Sooner or later we are going to have to go all out to cover the whole reservation perhaps." John Brown concurred by emphasizing television as one of the most popular electrical appliances:

> Now there are some people, young people that have gone to schools and people that have worked around towns, worked in cities and they are used to these modern facilities as recreation goes . . . such as TV and shows and all the modern equipment that a person needs such as radios, it has to do with electricity. When they come back to the reservation they feel like if at all possible they would like to have the same conveniences that they have enjoyed where they lived in these border towns . . . the NTUA motto is "Progress for Power." The Navajo people want progress with power. There is a lot of electricity going to these remote areas and for this reason a lot of them are requesting facilities.[110]

In spite of such discussions at the council level, elders like Deesheeny Nez Tracy, who expressed appreciation for some aspects of modern technology, held conflicting feelings about the consequences of electrical appliances. He indicated that modern conveniences allowed more leisure time, and therefore made people lazy. "Our children sit in front of the TV and consume gallons of pop into all hours of the night," he complained. "We seldom hear about a person running at dawn yelling at the top of his voice, or the screams that come from taking an ice-cold plunge or rolling in the snow. We hear only the screaming of the radios and stereo players. Who is to blame? The white man made the inventions."[111]

Even a sampling of anthropological studies reveals evidence that radio and television have contributed to divisions across the generations. The radio threatened to replace storytelling, not only by co-opting the integral role of oral tradition in song and legend preservation, but competition with the device discouraged elders from divulging key cultural traditions, thus causing intergenerational resentment. Radio also challenged traditional patterns of communication, since people no longer sought all their community news from friends and relatives. At the same time, the technology served the goals of the tribal government. The radio's wide audience and rapid delivery of information provided the large reservation with a means to build a sense of community, support traditional language and cultural maintenance, and promote social changes through special programming. Another study conducted in the early 1980s compared the impact of television on families of Euro-American, Spanish American, and Navajo descent. Television was a dominant activity for all three groups, including on the reservation, where only one channel signal was received. It reduced the diversity of activities of a traditional Navajo family who might otherwise engage in family storytelling, discussion, basket weaving, butchering, grooming horses, and playing with children. Unlike its role in other groups, however, television made little difference in Navajo use of household space, remaining by and large "multipurpose, and non-sex specific."[112]

Other appliances seemed to offer less controversial benefits but drastically altered traditional activities and eating habits. As in other rural areas, the refrigerator made a profound cultural impact on Navajos and Hopis. Due to their high cost, many homes began with small units. Ice cream and cold sodas served as an incentive for some, but refrigeration also allowed people to store food and medication and to keep fresh milk for infants. Moreover, it significantly altered people's diets. Gathering fresh fruits and vegetables, processing meat, and hunting were no longer necessary. In many ways, refrigeration improved health, but it also removed fresh meat from the daily meal. Most people bought frozen meat from packing companies, and some complained that the aged meat caused upset stomachs.[113]

Perhaps as profound as the change in diet, the availability of electrical power and other utilities led to a new type of housing for Navajos. The War on Poverty had shed a national spotlight upon the living conditions on Native American reservations through several congressional reports and hearings. As the REA and NTUA expanded their delivery areas, other opportunities for federal assistance in modernizing Native American homes became available as well. Paul Jones predicted clustered housing in Navajo village communities almost simultaneously with the introduction of industry on the reservation, and subsequently electrical power. Congress was reconsidering many federal public housing programs to allow Native American borrowers, and NTUA would be able to service these developments. Studies predicted heavy load growth due to extensive school construction and the industrial development of oil and gas fields. Public housing authority programs highlighted a general trend toward community living, and the mutual and self-help projects tailored to Native American communities made possible the fulfillment of Jones's inaugural hopes. New roads opened the reservation to more tourism, including motels and trailer parks. In some places, former residents returned to their homes to find that electricity had spurred community and small business development. Tribal council members and NTUA promoters like Howard Gorman and Frank Bradley ensured substantial appropriations

Fig. 16. Traditional Navajo hogan, the typical housing prior to electrification. Life Among the Navajo Collection, Cline Library, Northern Arizona University. Veronica Evaneshko, photographer.

to the utility each year. Throughout the 1970s, NTUA coordinated its efforts with housing projects across the reservation, including trailer parks. Eventually, even some of the most traditional Navajos allowed small amounts of electricity, such as a lightbulb or radio, into their homes.[114]

The availability of electricity did not always translate into electrification in terms of access and use. The modern houses built for Navajos were not a practical construction on the reservation, especially if heated with butane gas. In the late 1970s, contractors had built a series of modern, electric-ready home in White Cone, but when Louis and Myra Begay relocated there they could not afford NTUA rates to have power delivered. The relocation commission eventually arranged for a hookup, but it was not enough to keep the Begays in the ramshackle building. The couple eventually abandoned the house and went to live with relatives in a hogan.[115] Another Navajo woman complained bitterly

Fig. 17. Town of Navajo, and example of clustered housing with transmission lines. Life Among the Navajo Collection, Cline Library, Northern Arizona University. Veronica Evaneshko, photographer.

to the Indian agency, her tribal councilwoman, and even her congressional representatives that the school refused to deliver power to her trailer. "Without electricity I not only am without lights," she declared, "but I cannot heat my trailer in the winter except by means of the gas range in the kitchen. As you know, this is both a health hazard and a potential fire danger."[116]

Issues of affordability further hindered many would-be users. Until all Navajos could be guaranteed steady employment, electrical use on the reservation would inevitably remain low. Extensions from power lines to residences, as well as the wiring of those homes for basic appliances, required the skill of experienced operators who would abide by electrical codes. Wiring services and connections fees totaled over $125. As a nonprofit, self-sustaining enterprise, NTUA could not often, and cannot today, afford the full costs of power line extensions to less than six individual homes. The individual or the community must provide the balance. As a matter of priority, some Navajos found that it was neither practical nor desirable to raise the money for electrical power. Paying electric bills would simply add another obligation to their lives, a hard fact that concerned many members of the tribal council. Moreover, electrical use required even a greater expense than simply the bill, because users would also need to purchase appliances.[117]

NTUA historically boasted the lowest rates in the Southwest, but it is critical to note that electric bills claimed a larger percentage of the average Navajo income than of a typical non-Native user. Throughout the 1970s, many consumers did not understand the relationship between NTUA and the tribal government. NTUA power recipients often complained about the electrical rates and services to Dinébeiina Nahiilna Be Agaditahe, commonly referred to as DNA Legal Services.[118] For those who could make payments, Navajos followed the pattern of non-Natives who may have received electricity in the 1930s, acquiring electrical equipment gradually in accordance with their budgets and priorities. First, Navajos usually installed a security light at the eastern hogan entrance. Next, new customers prioritized lighting for studying and the preservation of perishable foods over, for example, an iron (usually the second electrical purchase for non-Natives). Each hogan typically had two bulbs, a couple of outlets, a refrigerator, a radio, and perhaps an electric stove. By the 1970s, electrical appliances were fairly common on the reservation for the 20–40 percent of residents who had NTUA service. About 38 percent of the households owned television sets, 36 percent refrigerators, 21 percent stereos, 17 percent washing machines, 14 percent vacuum cleaners, and 5 percent dryers. These statistics trailed the rest of rural Arizona as a whole, where 85.2 percent owned televisions, probably close to 100 percent refrigerators, 55.8 percent washing machines, and 25.8 percent dryers. However, they are close to the average percentages for Americans ten to fifteen years after they received electricity.[119]

Fig. 18. A Hopi village and tv antenna. Courtesy of National Archives and Records Administration, College Park, Maryland. Photograph by the Environmental Protection Agency, May 1972.

By the end of the twentieth century, those Native Americans of northeastern Arizona who had access to it and could afford it tended to use electricity to some extent. More Navajos entered the wage economy. Now able to afford electrical power, many began moving away from traditional living and into structures more conducive to electrification and more complex wiring. This was part of a long-term change in settlement patterns where, beginning in the 1950s, particularly younger Navajos moved from dispersed family camps to urban centers like Shiprock, Ganado, Crownpoint, and Chinle. These towns offered employment opportunity, public schools, and public utilities. Between 1964 and 1976 the Navajo Housing Authority funded more than a thousand homes of Euro-American style (with some assistance from NTUA). One study reported 76 percent of all of the dwellings on the reservation as having gabled roofs and more than one room. By the 1990s they increasingly lived in lumber (47 percent), mobile (20 percent), and stucco homes (17 percent). Only about 5 percent of the customers reported living in the traditional hogan, but many of them built electrified hogans of modern construction. When NTUA surveyed a sampling of 2,000 (out of almost 30,000 residential customers), 94.3 percent of their Navajo consumers reported owning refrigerators, and almost 90 percent owned televisions and stoves. One could find VCRS, clocks, lamps, and stereos in such homes as well. It is noteworthy that Navajos adopted few of the "time-saving" appliances like vacuums, washing machines, and dryers, whether because of finances, need, or simply rejecting the rhetoric of advertisers or reformers. Except in Hotevilla and Old Oraibi, most Hopi homes had electric power lines running to them. Many of these also boasted televisions and VCRS.[120]

Reconciling modernity with tradition seemed to be the dominant sentiment. NTUA won the grand prize for the best parade float at the 1963 tribal fair by depicting an electrified frame home alongside a traditional hogan. APS made attempts to diminish the obtrusiveness of the lines in its service area. It replaced the standard transformers with much smaller ones, and considered color and size in the line's design.

Photographs and cartoons commented on the symbolism of power lines and what they introduced to the formerly isolated reservation. Amid a scene of intersecting roads and power lines, one cartoonist had a character comment, "What did that white man say? If you can't beat them . . . just join them!" Another depicted two men rushing to leave (or enter) an electrified sweathouse in order to catch the Liston-Clay fight, a popular national sporting event on the television or radio in which the Navajos could now share. One *Navajo Times* article began, "Hogans and houses; sheep herds and electricity; ochre dyes and lipsticks; earthen jugs and TV antennas; emergence myth and typewriter, red man and white man; 'Yahteh' and 'howdy'; traditional and modern, old ways and new trails . . . This is Window Rock—an absolute paragon of paradoxes."[121]

In some instances, electricity could enhance traditional prac-

"What did that White Man say? If you can't beat them.....just join them!"

" BETTER HURRY! LISTON-CLAY FIGHT IS ABOUT TO START...."

(*top*) Fig. 19. "What did that White Man say? If you can't beat them . . . just join them!" Courtesy of *Navajo Times*, April 25, 1963.
(*bottom*) Fig. 20. "Better hurry! Liston-Clay fight is about to start. . . ." Courtesy of *Navajo Times*, November 21, 1963.

Fig. 21. A Navajo family between Chinle and Many Farms with electrical tower in background. Courtesy of Navajo Nation Museum, Window Rock, Arizona, PRC (Public Relations Collection).

tices as well. Rather than smoky fires, lightbulbs illuminated nighttime dance ceremonies, and microphones improved communication at those and other community events. Navajo rug weavers could practice their craft around the clock. As they increased productivity, weavers gained status as the rising commercial popularity of their product enabled them to afford appliances for their households. Inevitably, however, electricity altered weaving as an art form. Appraiser Andrew Nagen, for instance, classifies designs along "pre-electric" and "post-electric" categories.[122]

Capitalism and modernity challenged Navajos, but like many other Native American groups, they accepted it on their own terms and retained the traditional cultural integrity of their households, communities, and governments. Even as early as 1942, Clyde Kluckhohn observed that "the really astonishing thing, as one experiences the totality of Navaho life today, is the degree to which these Indians have taken over aspects of technology without sensible alteration to the distinctive flavor of their own way of life."[123] A 1969 report through the Department of Agriculture suggested that Native Americans had to negotiate between integration and separatism. The report's author, Helen Johnson, observed, "The way to achieve an intermediate position between the familiar culture and the dominant but alien one is not at all clear."[124] In reality, many tribes preferred to walk the line between tradition and progress. Harry Walters, curator of the museum at Navajo Community College, noted, "You often hear: 'All the old ways are gone.' In some ways, this is true. Yet we are still Navajos. The language may be a little different, ceremonies a little different. We may use a pick-up instead of a horse to carry the ceremonial wand on the first day of Enemy way. Nevertheless we are still a unique people." Navajo teacher Rex Lee Jim added, "Our adaptability is a tradition."[125]

Victims or Consumers?

The NTUA, the relationship between the Hopis and APS, and the cooperative efforts of the White Mountain Apaches are just a few examples of Native American access to and use of electrical power. They offer some context for how Native Americans, often cited only as the most unfortunate victims of outside energy development in the West, also exercised tremendous agency in bringing modern services and conveniences to their communities. Despite BIA and corporate efforts to lure them from the reservation to enticing off-reservation labor villages, most Navajos decided to remain and use tribal institutions to introduce the benefits of modern life such as electrical power to their homes.[126] While the Apache tribes joined the regional system of the local REA cooperative, and a private utility served the Hopis, the Navajo Nation utilized federal programs and tribal resources to fund a fiscally independent electrical system serving the tribe's specific needs, rather than receive services as third-party customers. NTUA continues to serve as a model to many Native communities, while the Apache and Hopi examples provide the context for the other options the Navajo Nation's leaders could have chosen.

Electrification was a primary factor in changing people's lives across the country, in rural Arizona, and particularly for Native Americans, but it was not solely responsible for the transformation of Native life in the twentieth century. NTUA attorney Walter Wolf observed: "Reservation life has changed not solely because of the availability of utilities, but because of a lot of factors coming to play at one time . . . the emphasis on hospitalization, and schools, and infrastructure of that nature was made possible because the utilities necessary to operate those facilities became available."[127] On the Navajo Reservation, the self-operated utility of the NTUA contributed to what scholar Peter Iverson has observed as a developing sense of Navajo nationalism amid the growth and change of the United States as a whole. Due to the development of tribal enterprises and other types of self-supporting economic programs after World War II, tribal councils were able to take advantage of BIA and non-BIA government programs in areas such as housing and economic growth in order to receive electrical power. Industrialization encouraged wage work, allowing more people to join the consumer market that purchased home appliances. Electrical power provided the means to industrialize and move toward a living style closer to off the reservation. Extensive modern influences can be observed from the reservation's houses to its new, nontraditional medical facilities.[128]

Former tribal chairman Peterson Zah observed that electricity had a greater impact upon Native American communities than others due to issues of culture, land status, and the level of promotion by tribal leaders. Zah summarized: "The Navajo had to really be innovative and aggressive in terms of bringing electricity to the reservation at a pace that is conducive to people change [sic]. If the Howard Gormans and the Frank Bradleys brought it on too fast, people might have rejected it some degree, but they did it in a way that was in concert with the attitudes of people and the acculturation process that we were going through because of our education." NTUA engineer Leonard Earl similarly expressed his pride in being a part of progress. "NTUA has grown right along with the Navajo people," he observed. Wilford Sorrell reflected upon NTUA's fortieth anniversary: "It's very unique what it's done for the Navajo Reservation. It's not something you can measure."[129]

Electricity did not solve the problems of poverty, substandard housing, health care, and unemployment on Native American reservations. New technologies and massive public works came at a high price. Energy development damaged sacred lands and traditional forms of sustenance, strained Native-white relations, and caused internal factionalism. However, these examples do illustrate that while change, collaboration, opportunity, and modern technology may alter many aspects of a traditional community's lifestyle, sometimes in profound and tragic ways, they do not necessarily lead to its cultural destruction. Navajo leaders in particular equated electricity with their efforts toward "progress," using electricity to gain greater control over the pace and nature of what they perceived, due to the massive energy development by the government and private industry, as an inevitable industrial future. It served as one of several tools Native Americans used to persist and to achieve the independence and experience necessary for the more politically motivated self-determination movements in the years that followed.

Yet Native Americans today remain in the highest percentage of Americans living without electricity. And the largest reservation, the Navajo, leads this statistic at 37 percent. In many ways, federal policy toward Native Americans dictated the rate at which they adapted to modern social and economic conditions. Physical, cultural, and ideological factors as well as cost served as additional hindrances. Legal status could affect electrical distribution when, unlike the White Mountain Apaches, the Navajos lacked proximity to industry. Electricity had only been available through the Indian agencies for employees, local missions, BIA schools, and trading posts for years before it was available to average Native American families. As government wards living in remote communities, Native Americans such as the Navajos and Hopis did not receive electrical power for years and sometimes decades after other areas of Arizona, even though the energy sources lay within and adjacent to their lands.

Furthermore, the Navajo Nation falls short of achieving a wholly self-sufficient, autonomous system within northeastern Arizona's rural region. As in the case of the Apaches, Native lands provided the energy source, but non-Natives were needed to convert that energy into electrical power. Sometimes NTUA even looked for power sources off the reservation. In 1993 the thirty-year power agreement with APS expired and the private utility refused to renew the power agreement on the same conditions. With a better bid, Tucson Electric Power won NTUA's primary power contract.[130]

Emphasizing these realities, however, overshadows significant Native American efforts to achieve and control modern technology and utilities for themselves while overcoming significant barriers of cultural preferences, geographical space, economic limitations, and politics. In *Breaking the Iron Bonds*, Marjane Ambler blames the poverty of Native American reservations on energy policies and reviews the legal history of Native Americans' pursuit to gain control over their energy resources. However, Native Americans sought to use these resources as consumers as well.[131] The story told here further illustrates that electrical development on the reservations should be studied not only within the context of non-Native exploitation but also in terms of Native empowerment. While much of the energy produced on Native lands targets non-Native communities, the development, existence, and impact of a tribal electrical system symbolizes the large degree to which Native Americans can and have maintained control over their resources, culture, and future throughout the twentieth and into the twenty-first century.

Conclusion

The Limits of Local Power

This uplifting of people's lives is the thing over the years that I look back on and feel best about. What I did was a meaningful job. A good example, besides the memories of how it affected my family's life, is going to some of the hogans on the reservations and see[ing] televisions in them, to see a house made of dried meat and stocks and hear a radio going inside. Now I'm not always 100 percent sure that we always create the best when we bring in these life bending changes. But I like electricity's convenience, and I don't know anyone who doesn't. What I am saying is that electric service is not necessary to life, but it's a hell of a nice thing to have. And we as Americans love it. —**Harold Roberts**, Tucson, Arizona, 1977

Harold Roberts worked outside of the service areas discussed here, but his words summarize the pride and sentiments of many rural Americans who initiated the process of rural electrification in their communities.[1] Many others may not have shared Mr. Roberts's rosy view, and certainly one can argue that this wholly positive and progressive attitude toward technological change is infused with cultural biases often influenced by the paternalistic and economic interests, whether they are of middle-class reformers or government officials. But such an attitude is pervasive in the oral histories of rural cooperatives and is shared by leaders in each of the communities reviewed in this study. That view has remained prevalent. Today our leaders hire contractors to wire places as far away and as culturally complex as Iraq and Afghanistan as a means for exporting Western and democratic values in power distribution. Critics will and should question the accuracy and simplistic nature of this strategy based upon a standard of living one outside culture has defined for another.

This study emphasized the efforts of those who consistently and persistently accepted the idea that electricity was a positive or necessary change for achieving economic and social equality. Their views dominate the available source material (both written and oral), oversimplify basic principles of distributive justice, and mask the many tensions people felt over the technology and its impact. These same sources reveal that Americans from culturally and ethnically diverse backgrounds bought into the "technology equals democracy" equation. They actively enlisted electricity to connect to power, both literally and figuratively: to economically build and socially preserve their rural communities through irrigation, tourism, and education. Government policies and programs encouraged each to regard high energy use and wide distribution as an integral component for participating in America's "blessed way of life." Electrical infrastructure defined new regional economies and lifestyles, but not only in ways the technologically elite—the urban, middle-class reformer—predicted or the government determined. Communities, local factors, and individuals also influenced the electrification process.

Community Power in the Rural West

The Arizona State Planning Board observed in 1934 that "the demand for power or electric energy is best measured by the industrial development of the State or community. In other words, if industrial, mining, or agricultural development is to take place, there must be a simultaneous development of some source of power. Electric energy is perhaps the most desirable power."[2] The construction of large hydroelectric dams across the West ended the region's dependence on eastern manufacturing and expanded economic development possibilities beyond agriculture and mining.[3] But these projects benefited only populated areas. Rural places that provided inadequate power in the West became obstacles to industrial development. For better or worse, once these places plugged into a regional power system, electrical technologies altered, enhanced, and sometimes transformed diverse communities socially, politically, and economically.

In some of these areas, the lasting effect of electrification remains to be determined, but it seems clear that communities considered electricity a tool for meeting specific development goals and accessed electricity in ways that met those goals. In arid southeastern Arizona, community leaders built an electrical system to fulfill their vision of an agrarian society. However, they were only able to do so near the end of the Great Depression, when the American economy was shifting to a wartime economy. Such goals were locally driven and often counter to those of government agencies like the REA, which tended to focus on electrifying the household. The residents of the White Mountains sought REA funds to connect and consolidate existing regional power sources largely for industrial and domestic use, but they did so after World War II, amid the tensions of Cold War McCarthyism and renewed questions about public and private power. With a diverse population of African American, Spanish American, Mormon, and Native American communities, this region introduces additional ethnic and geographic factors involved in electrification that provide a comparison to the reservation communities that dominate northeastern Arizona. There, national demands for energy resources, changes in tribal leadership, civil-rights-era activism, and War on Poverty programs contributed to regional and local system building and also to profound cultural changes. Whether electricity was delivered by private utilities, tribal utilities, or REA cooperatives, rural Arizonans ultimately initiated, defined, organized, and controlled this process at the local level.

The electrification of rural Arizona involved many issues and conflicts familiar to historians of the region: federal versus local interests, aridity, interethnic and socioeconomic conflict, industrialization versus preservation of natural resources, agricultural use versus ranching needs, tribal rights versus regional development, private enterprise versus public ownership, and rural versus urban identity. How and when rural Arizonans eventually received and used electrical power complicates models of technological determinism and tales of urban conquest. These stories illustrate that rural Arizonans of diverse ethnic, cultural, and religious backgrounds were far from passive in gaining access to and guiding the impact of the new technology in their homes and communities. Their enlistment of government funds and the influence of federal educational and marketing programs certainly challenged the American West's message of "rugged individualism."[4]

Since the federal government had an interest in 71 percent of the state's lands (whether owning them outright or in trust for Native peoples), it was an influential force in the lives of all rural Arizonans. In some cases, as with the REA, this involvement proved critical in providing a mechanism through which to bring electrical power into isolated areas over long distances. In others, federal interests conflicted. As anthropologist Thomas Sheridan notes, "The federal government was therefore patron, partner, overseer, and antagonist in most rural people's lives."[5] Through the local agencies of the Office of Indian Affairs and its schools, the government continued its role in introducing electrical and communication technology to rural areas. Therefore, Native American reservations were among the first rural areas in the American West to receive electrical power. The OIA usually restricted service to government buildings and supporting personnel, but the Fort Apache Indian Agency and the Navajo Indian Agency often acted as the first utilities for the remote reservation areas.

Designed to encourage local organization and operation, the REA remains one of the New Deal's most successful and influential programs. The Rural Electrification Act had its roots in the country's transformation from an agrarian to an industrial economy during the Progressive Era, and emerged amid the exigencies of the Great Depression. The REA continued to provide the means through which rural communities could build power systems for years afterward. Even the Navajo Tribal Utility Authority, which formed a tribal enterprise rather than a cooperative, based its policies on REA standards. The REA remained a primary funding source for most rural electric systems. Today, many of Arizona's rural electric utilities, Native and non-Native, support one another's interests through organizations such as the Grand Canyon State Electric Cooperative. Eight REA-financed electrical distribution cooperatives had formed throughout Arizona by 1948.[6] As a result, while less than 26.5 percent of Arizona's rural homes received electricity from a centralized system in 1932, 77.3 percent enjoyed these services by 1950.[7] Aided by federal loans, these REA cooperatives provided electrical and telephone service to parts of Arizona that, unlike other parts of the country, included remote ranches and Native American reservations.

Largely through the efforts of local farmers, ranchers, county agricultural agents, and the REA, life in rural Arizona increasingly began to resemble that of cities. Each infrastructure evolved to meet its own local needs, uses, demographics, political structures, and natural resources. Specific characteristics of population density, demography, geography, reliability, and affordability directed how and when rural Arizonans gained access to electricity. Arizona provided its own set of opportunities and challenges for rural electrification: denser and more homogeneous populations, more tree cover, less-extreme temperatures, and fewer topographical variations. Prior to the 1930s, many of the state's rural residents received electrical power from local generators or windmills, yet in the open desert the wind did not always blow and generators frequently broke. Its rough and varied terrain, low population density, national forests, Native American reservations, and rapid postwar growth also contributed to make area coverage a particularly slow process.

Only the physical connection of communities through a common regional power grid allowed more stable and dependable power systems. The REA's requirements of area coverage dissuaded private companies from practicing consumer discrimination. Area coverage necessitated system feasibility, high electrical loads, and therefore high electrical use. As historian David Nye observed, organizing an electrical distribution system under REA required "intensive local planning" and cooperation between neighboring communities across county borders and ethno-cultural differences.[8]

Electrification ultimately allowed many Arizona farmers to diversify beyond cotton, which had become their primary export during World War I and the 1920s. Electrical pumping helped former rangelands produce crops, increasing land values in both rural and urban areas. Dairy production, raising poultry, and fruit and vegetable growing emerged as new options for agribusiness. Electrical pumps promised efficient and reliable pumping vital to local economies that were desperate for a reliable water supply but unable to access power from a storage dam.[9]

Rural electrification also aided the growth of Arizona's lumber and tourism industries, contributing to local economic autonomy. These developments ensured that fewer people left the rural areas for better economic opportunities, and instead enticed urban dwellers to visit for vacation. Electricity allowed the people of the White Mountains to provide recreational and lodging options for millions of urbanites accustomed to modern conveniences. The rural electrification program was a direct and indirect stimulus for job creation. It provided rural people with an alternative to often difficult working conditions in occupations where their efforts ultimately benefited outside corporations and urban areas more than their own rural communities.

The Consequences of Electrification

Local factors also limited electrification's promises. The process did not wholly benefit all rural residents. First, remote areas on the reservations still lack power, and even in areas where residents were some of the first recipients of rural electrification, the process is incomplete. In 1991 the Sulphur Springs Valley Electric Cooperative finally delivered power to the southeastern border community of San Bernardino, where residents living far from well-traveled roadways had continued to operate individual diesel generators. The settlement was located outside the cooperative's service area and too distant from main roads to be considered feasible for power line construction. When the cooperative finally built out to the community, one resident could finally use some of the appliances she had received as wedding presents forty-one years before.[10]

Second, the environmental consequences of electrification are perhaps the most serious argument against any wholly progressive attitudes toward the process. Agricultural expansion in southeastern Arizona had serious ecological ramifications. In 1965, Sulphur Springs Valley Electric Cooperative (excluding the Graham County service area) served 8,600 consumers through 1,970 miles of distribution lines and 250 miles of transmission lines. Irrigation encompassed about 30 percent of the total load for the year.[11] The increased pumping severely depleted the natural water supply. "We farmed more land than we had water for," observed William Gaskell.[12] Between 1947 and 1957 the water table dropped twelve feet in Cochise County's Kansas Settlement. It then fell an additional forty-six feet in the farming community by 1962. In 1952 the Arizona legislature released a study on the state's groundwater and possible conservation laws to govern its use. Despite such efforts, the water table at the Kansas Settlement fell an additional ten feet by 1964. Where once water lay 26 feet below the surface, pumps in the 1990s needed to reach 160 feet. Continued agriculture would require deeper wells, and as energy prices increased during the crisis of the 1970s, pumping costs forced many smaller-scale farmers to take acreage out of production. As the water table continued to drop and the federal government scaled back farm subsidies, farm acreage fell dramatically, and the old ranching families saw the region returning to its cattle-grazing roots.[13] At the dawn of the twenty-first century, some farms found success in growing corn with new sprinkler technology, and the Sulphur Springs valley touted itself as Arizona's emerging wine country.[14]

With these examples of incomplete coverage and environmental consequences in mind, the struggle for access and the controversial impact of rural electrification in the West seemed the most dramatic on Native American communities. Electrical utilities and systems emerged soon after the placement of Arizona's Native Americans onto reservations in the mid- to late nineteenth century, but a century later few Americans were as poor and as rural as Native Americans living on reservations. Geographical segregation and legal status restricted access to electricity in much the same way that urban segregation into barrios and ghettos allowed and allows for different, and usually less, opportunities for their residents.[15] Apache, Hopi, and Navajo tribes in Arizona faced the same issues as other rural people, but their access to electricity varied in accordance with the community's level of segregation, location, land status, political organization, economic position, and cultural preservation. Experiences with electrification varied according to a combination of these factors. The Apaches joined an emerging REA cooperative, the Hopis signed on to a private company for service, and the Navajos formed their own utility.

Across Arizona, technology and urbanization threatened to undermine the unique and traditional identities associated with rural life. The government's historic use of both education and technology as tools of assimilation in Native American communities reveals the most dramatic changes and tensions associated with electrification. The goal of area coverage highlighted and strained the already profound tensions within many Native American communities between those who wanted to embrace modern American life and those who feared the loss of Native identity and culture, and all those in between. Through federal education efforts, the younger generation in both Native and non-Native communities exhibited greater comfort with new technology.

Compounding the internal struggles, Natives, non-Natives, scholars, environmentalists, and scientists have documented the adverse cultural, economic, and ecological effects of energy development on Native American lands and lives through strip mining and hydroelectric dams like Glen Canyon. Glen Canyon and its reservoir, Lake Powell, destroyed or obscured Rainbow Bridge and other sacred sites. Debates over whether to drain Lake Powell continue today. Navajo people, lands, and culture all paid a high price for leasing many of the very energy resources that would electrify the Navajo Tribal Utility Authority's first lines. The conclusions from studies about reservation industrialization strongly imply that for Native Americans, rural electrification was also a mixed blessing.[16]

Electrical power provided Apaches, Hopis, and Navajos with the means to meet future industrial goals, but these communities did not always integrate easily into the industrial economy. Despite rhetoric that encouraged assimilation, the generating companies and government systems provided few opportunities for doing so. Energy development and electrical services failed to provide a fully successful solution to economic problems. Layoffs and accusations of discrimination were frequent despite

the employment opportunities for Navajos that energy development seemingly offered (e.g., at the Navajo Generating Station
at Page). Furthermore, the utilization of natural resources on
the Native American reservations often had disastrous ecological consequences, including pollution, groundwater depletion,
and soil contamination, as well as health problems. Local communities had to surrender grazing lands for company camps.
Many Navajos contend that no one adequately informed them
about the environmental consequences of energy development
and energy operations when they entered various agreements or
contracts such as the strip mining at Black Mesa. They blamed
the tribal council, the BIA, and companies like Peabody Coal.[17]

Negotiating Native American Power

This presentation of case studies does not intend to diminish the
very real environmental changes and gross cultural violations
electricity and energy technologies have inflicted on rural ecolo-
gies and lifeways. Rather, it joins several recent scholarly works
of "new" Native American history in emphasizing other truths
that often get lost in the controversies: the agency, dynamism,
fluidity, flexibility, and even modernization of rural America, including its reservation communities.

Over the years, writers such as activist Jerry Mander have
made vehement and persuasive arguments that technology de-
stroys not only Native American lands but also Native culture
and tradition.[18] However, even Native American activists like
Vine Deloria Jr. have suggested that there is much to be gained
for sustaining tribal life by combining the insights of both traditional and modern technology.[19] "Tradition does not stay stable," explains Keith James (Onondaga/Minsi Lenape); "rather,
it evolves, and Indian life has always been a dynamic exchange.
It involves adaptation, but it always has a core or thread through
it that links it together with what is fundamentally sound and
true."[20] Rejecting the traditional-versus-modern dichotomy,

which implies there are only two choices for Native American lifestyle, today's scholars persuasively argue that while modern technological change and capitalism have economically transformed tribal communities, they have done so without sacrificing those communities' cohesion or cultural identity.[21] Rather, many tribes have used electricity and other tools of conquest and dispossession to "reshape their cultures and societies to keep them alive."[22]

Tribal leaders took and continue to take action to distribute the electricity being generated on their lands to their lands. Like other rural residents, they introduced technological change in order to sustain their economies within an industrial nation. Even among some of the most traditional Navajos and Hopis, evidence from lengthy debates indicates that it was not specifically the technology they rejected but rather the dependence on a system (in this case a power grid) outside their community and the consequences of that dependence. As seen throughout rural Arizona's communities, generations born in the decades after World War II often urged the pursuit of technology. Today, the American Indian Science and Engineering Society, the Tribal Resource Institute in Business, Engineering, and Science, and alliances such as the Council of Energy Resource Tribes (CERT) further attest to the proactive attitude many Native Americans have toward advanced technology.

Getting on the Grid

So while electrical power lines, like all technology, carry political influence and cultural power, that fact should not obscure or dismiss the very real local efforts that helped to distribute electricity and guide its use. Rural electrification was by and large achieved locally in spite of private corporations or investor-owned utilities, and even in spite of the federal government's bureaucratic hurdles. Over barriers of profit, economy, ownership, topography, land, and legal status, rural Arizonans used electrical power to plug in and gain entry into an increasingly industrial society.

Yet as historian Lizabeth Cohen argues, the availability of goods and services has not translated into social and economic equality. The idea of mass consumption promised to offer civil, economic, and political equality in New Deal and post–World War II America, but residential segregation and "dependence on unregulated private markets wove inequalities deep." Profits and markets achieved priority over "loftier" goals of equality.[23] Similarly, without government regulation or oversight, rural or otherwise marginalized communities struggled for access to affordable and viable electrical power. Yet the systems they built reflected local economic, social, and political needs and choices, not those of distant city dwellers. The introduction of electricity did not cause the destruction of the rural West and its communities through urbanization, but the lack of access to, or the lack of local control of, technology threatened the persistence of such communities.

The communities examined here were far from the only ones in Arizona, the American West, the country, or the world who worked to access electrical power. However, they exemplify the various avenues through which different groups of rural westerners in different settings accessed, used, and adapted to new technologies. They can serve as models for how other rural communities might respond to and accept the introduction of new technologies today, if given the opportunity. Together, they also expand discussions about rural economic development in the American West, the impact of technology on economy and lifestyle, and finally, who regulates access to public and private power, both electrical and political. When large private and investor-owned companies controlled power production, electrical technology, transmission, and distribution without regulation, they argued that it was not "economically feasible" for many ethnic and rural communities to access "the grid." Federal policies and programs created the desire and the tools for communities to gain equal and democratic access to the technology. In the end, however, rural electrification was a locally directed process subject to local issues, concerns, and parameters. To understand contemporary crises with the power grid, policy makers may want to review Americans' historical relationship with electrical power production, distribution, and regulation.

Distributing Power: An Epilogue

"Electrical power, it turns out, is not like ordinary commodities," observed columnist Robert Kuttner in an August 2003 *New York Times* editorial about the regional blackout.[24] The collapse of the northeastern power grid, California's deregulation fiasco, the unethical practices of those who led lobbying efforts to deregulate the electrical industry, and the unreliable electrical systems in cities such as New York following the attacks on September 11 and New Orleans after Hurricane Katrina have forced Americans to confront electricity's importance in their twenty-first-century lives. Searching for explanations, the public blamed inept utility management, insufficient energy sources, and transmission and distribution problems. Then, only a few identified deregulation as the culprit. The economic climate at the end of George W. Bush's presidency in 2008 further called into question the wisdom of deregulation. During the presidential campaign that year, most experts instead called for at least some responsible government regulation in industries upon which American lives and lifestyles depend.

Due to the economic ties among the states, California's energy problems and high, deregulated prices spilled into neighboring western states, affecting the most economically vulnerable communities. Arizona Public Service likewise charged higher prices to the Tohono O'odham Tribal Utility Authority and Citizens Utilities, which serve Santa Cruz and Mohave counties, where over a fourth of the population lives below the poverty line.[25]

Arizona began its deregulation process in 1999, but the Arizona Corporation Commission reevaluated the state's plans after California's troubles. Separating power generation from power distribution without oversight, deregulation theoretically increases the competition for customers in the same service area. It relies on the idea that the market will ensure fair rates for power generation. Promoters argue that technological, political, and economic forces have made the "regulatory compact" of the twentieth century obsolete and even burdensome. Meanwhile, electrical cooperatives have formed state, regional, and national alliances to strengthen bargaining power and combat their vulnerability to large energy corporations. In some instances they have negotiated lower-cost power from distant sources, but transporting that power to rural areas of consumption requires even more energy. Once again, this type of activity threatens to physically and technologically leave rural communities behind in a new post-industrial era.

A similar distribution pattern is emerging with twenty-first-century technologies. Since the mid-1980s, wireless, cable, and computer technology allowed rural populations as distant as rural Africa, India, and China to bypass the wired world of power lines for access to urban information and services. However, not surprisingly, many companies favor profitable markets over need. During his visit to the Navajo Reservation in the year 2000, the first for sitting president, Bill Clinton again advanced the idea that equal access to technology fuels and supports a democratic society. He observed that as a group, Native Americans in the West joined a considerable number of poor and rural Americans separated from the opportunities available to the majority by a "digital divide." He cited computer and Internet access as a "key civil rights issue of the twenty-first century" and pledged to bring attention and corporate funding to the issue (the Navajo Tribal Utility Authority began soliciting consumer opinions about offering the Internet in 1999). An article from the *Arizona Republic* in the summer of 2000 reported that experts prescribed technology, specifically telecommunications service, as the remedy to poor economic conditions. Rural communities could use Internet access to help preserve Native American languages, increase long-distance communication, and support entrepreneurship.[26]

Access to the Internet is the most recent manifestation of using technology to maintain traditional values, ensure community cohesion, and allow self-sufficiency. Today, several Navajo communities are "connected," but many others still await a dial tone and electrical power.[27] In 2007, Arizona governor Janet Napolitano launched the Tribal Rural Electrification Program to serve as many as ten thousand Native American households not connected to a power grid. Building upon the work of groups like NTUA, she hoped the solar energy–based program would serve as an example to other rural communities.[28] Rural electrification alternatives such as these skip the feasibility limitations involved in power line construction, maintain community independence, avoid land exchanges, and provide healthier alternatives to polluting coal plants. Still, solutions are not simple, and such debates need to consider local concerns, culture, and economies as well as state and national politics. In 2007 the Navajo Tribal Council and the Diné Power Authority decided to build an environmentally controversial power plant that could conceivably electrify twenty thousand more homes on the reservation for the first time. A grassroots organization, Diné CARE (Citizens Against Ruining our Environment), vehemently opposed its construction.[29]

Renewable energies and wireless technology may eliminate some construction and cost hurdles of the past for rural access. However, if the country shifts toward energy sources like solar and wind power, which often generate power far from the nation's population centers, an infrastructure for electrical transmission and delivery will need to follow. Someone will need to decide where the infrastructure goes and how to fund its construction. Yet many states have joined a growing political trend that encourages the abandonment of government oversight and localized system-building through deregulation.[30] Arizona's representational demographics and topography offer a microcosm for the rural electrification process in the American West. But even that microcosm reveals the complexity of that process across the tremendous economic, geographic, and cultural diversity of rural America.

History shows us that we should carefully consider the consequences before championing the idea that the marketplace alone should control access to electricity through either power generation or distribution. Returning the process of electrical generation to wholly private interests, where only profit and market fluctuation dictate the expansion of electrical systems and the rates charged to consumers, where only private companies design markets without oversight, and where "visionaries" like Enron's Ken Lay and Jeff Skilling see opportunity for market exploitation, may mean that America's "blessed way of life," however different communities define it, might well be one that not every American can share.

Notes

Abbreviations

ACASU Arizona Collection, Archives and Special Collections, Hayden Library, Arizona State University, Tempe

AHF Arizona Historical Foundation, Hayden Library, Arizona State Library, Tempe

ASA Arizona State Archives, Arizona State Library, Archives and Public Records, Phoenix

GCSEC Grand Canyon State Electric Cooperative, Phoenix, Arizona

NARA-CP National Archives and Records Administration, College Park, Maryland

NARA-LN National Archives and Records Administration, Pacific Region, Laguna Niguel, California

NARA-W National Archives Building, Washington DC

NTUA-HQ Navajo Tribal Utility Authority Corporate Headquarters, Ft. Defiance, Arizona

RG record group

SCUA Special Collections, Main Library, University of Arizona, Tucson

SSVEC Sulphur Springs Valley Electric Cooperative, Willcox, Arizona

Introduction

1. Presidential spokesman Ari Fleisher said: "The President believes that [high energy consumption] is an American way of life, and that it should be the goal of policymakers to protect that American way of life. The American way of life is a blessed one." "Perspectives," *Newsweek*, May 21, 2001, 17.

2. Former California governor Gray Davis used the phrase "flagship of

the American economy." Lowell Bergman, "Blackout," *Frontline*, Public Broadcasting Systems, aired June 5, 2001. Roosevelt quoted in Nye, *Electrifying America*, 304.

3. See Tobey, *Technology as Freedom*, for ways Americans marketed electrical use during the Great Depression.

4. Distributive justice is a philosophical, economic, and/or sociological theory regarding the fair and equitable allocation of resources in a society. Capeheart and Milovanivic, *Social Justice*, 29; for an argument supporting the integration of democracy, equality, and economic justice see Zucker, *Democratic Distributive Justice*.

5. See Nye, *American Technological Sublime*, 143–98, for a discussion of how America defined itself through technology, especially electricity.

6. See Myers, "Rejecting the Regulatory Compact," for a historical look at electrical regulation in California; see Williams, *Energy and the Making of Modern California*, for a historical account of the development of energy sources in California.

7. Kurt Eichenwald, "Verdict on an Era," *New York Times*, May 26, 2006; "Two Enron Chiefs Are Convicted in Fraud and Conspiracy Trial," *New York Times*, May 26, 2006; Alex Berenson, "The Other Legacy of Enron," *New York Times*, May 28, 2006; Allan Sloan, "Laying Enron to Rest," *Newsweek*, June 5, 2006, 25.

8. Berenson, "The Other Legacy of Enron."

9. Daniel Yergin and Lawrence Markovich, "The System Did Not Fail. Yet the System Failed," *New York Times*, August 17, 2003; Robert Kuttner, "An Industry Trapped by Theory," *New York Times*, August 16, 2003; David Firestone and Richard Peréz-Pena, "Failure Reveals Creaky System, Experts Believe," *New York Times*, August 15, 2003; Richardson, "Role and Performance of Public Power"; see Hirsh, *Power Loss*, for an extensive discussion of deregulation in the electrical industry.

10. Energy Information Administration, "Energy Consumption and Renewable Energy Development on Indian Lands" (Washington DC: U.S. Department of Energy, March 2000).

11. Castaneda, "Energy in the West"; Myers, "Rejecting the Regulatory Compact." William Robbins examines industrialism and capitalism in general in *Colony and Empire*.

12. Lowitt, *The New Deal and the West*, 227–28; Nye, "Electrifying the West, 1880–1940."

13. U.S. House Committee on Agriculture, Subcommittee on Forestry, Re-

source Conservation, and Research, "Electric Industry Deregulation in Rural Areas," Hearing, 105th Congress, 2nd sess., March 25, 1998, pp. 10–13; U.S. House Committee on Agriculture, Subcommittee on General Farm Commodities, Resource Conservation, and Credit, "Effects of Electric Deregulation on Rural Areas and an Examination of Legislative Proposals," Hearing, 106th Congress, 1st sess., May 26, 1999.

14. Westrum, *Technologies and Society*, 26.

15. Myers, "Rejecting the Regulatory Compact," 38.

16. Brigham, *Empowering the West*; Rose, *Cities of Light and Heat*.

17. Lowitt, *The New Deal and the West*, 33; Brown, *Electricity for Rural America*; Childs, *The Farmer Takes a Hand*; Coyle, *Electric Power on the Farm*; Ellis, *A Giant Step*; Cannon, "Power Relations"; Myers, "Electricity in Orange County"; Kline, *Consumers in the Country*.

18. Frederick Jackson Turner, "The Significance of the American Frontier," in *1893 Annual Report of American Historical Association* (Washington DC: Government Printing Office and American Historical Association, 1894), 199–227, reprinted in Etulain, *Frontier Experience*, 17–43.

19. Marx, *The Machine in the Garden*, 229–42.

20. For discussions about the urban West see Abbott, *Metropolitan Frontier*, xv; Pomeroy, *The Pacific Slope*; Cronon, *Nature's Metropolis*.

21. Hurt, *Rural West since World War II*, 4–5.

22. Nelson, "Rural Life and Social Change," 38–40.

23. Hathaway, Beegle, and Bryant, *People of Rural America*, 5.

24. Barron, *Mixed Harvest*.

25. M. R. Smith and Marx, *Does Technology Drive History?*; Worster, *Rivers of Empire*; Hughes, *Networks of Power*.

26. Nye, *Electrifying America*; Marvin, *When Old Technologies Were New*.

27. In addition to the publications of the Country Life Movement, see President's National Advisory Commission on Rural Poverty, *The People Left Behind*.

28. Kline, *Consumers in the Country*, 6, 10, 19, 131.

29. Rose, *Cities of Light and Heat*; Brigham, *Empowering the West*; Tobey, *Technology as Freedom*; Cowan, *More Work for Mother*; Jellison, *Entitled to Power*; Cohen, *Consumers' Republic*.

30. West, "Walter Prescott Webb," 170, 171.

31. Melosi, *The Sanitary City*; Keating, *Invisible Networks*.

32. Von Hoffman, *Local Attachments*; Matsumoto, *Farming the Home Place*.

33. Brigham, "Lighting the Reservation." For a more direct comparison of

Arizona Native Americans' experiences with electrical power see Glaser, "'An Absolute Paragon of Paradoxes.'"

34. Lewis, "Native Americans: The Original Rural Westerners," 12–13, 27.

35. Iverson, *For Our Navajo People,"* 2.

36. Jensen, *Promise to the Land*; Martin, *Songs My Mother Sang to Me*; Deutsch, *No Separate Refuge*; Pascoe, "Western Woman at the Cultural Crossroads."

37. Ross, "Every Home a Laboratory," 6–7, 17.

38. Nye, *Electrifying America*, 299; "Rural Electrification Progress on the Salt River Project, Arizona," *New Reclamation Era* 20 (October 1929): 151.

39. Polk, "Economic Electric Power Survey," 1.

40. See Sheridan, *Arizona*, 300–316; Economic Research Office, "Rural People in the American Economy," Agricultural Economic Report no. 101 (U.S. Department of Agriculture, 1966).

41. Ross, "Every Home a Laboratory," 23–24.

42. Nelson, "Rural Life and Social Change," 39.

43. See Tobey, *Technology as Freedom*; and Lipsitz, *The Possessive Investment in Whiteness*, 6–8.

44. Groth and Bressi, *Understanding Ordinary Landscapes*, 1.

45. Deutsch, *No Separate Refuge*, 9–10.

46. Needham, *Power Lines*.

47. Hurt, *Rural West since World War II*, 5.

1. Empowering Agrarian Dreams

1. Rosalia Salazar Whelen and Esperanza Montoya Padilla in Martin, *Songs My Mother Sang to Me*, 152–56, 100–117; Frank and Twila Shelton, interview; Weech, interview; Lillie Harrington, "Rural America's Dark Days and Nights," in Sulphur Springs Valley Electric Cooperative, *The Power of Cooperation*, 1.

2. Emily Hoag, "The Advantages of Farm Life," 1923, pp. 133–34, in Manuscript File, 1917–35, Records of the Division of Farm Management and Costs and Its Predecessors, RG 83, NARA-CP.

3. A. Mark Bliss to Carmody, December 14, 1937, SSVEC.

4. After 1930, the Census Bureau categorization makes it difficult to determine the demography of the area. However, in 1950 a special census counted Spanish-surnamed people. U.S. Bureau of the Census, *Fifteenth Census of the United States*, vol. 1, *Population, 1930* (Washington

DC: Government Printing Office, 1933), 157; U.S. Bureau of the Census, *Census of the United States, Population, 1950*, Special Reports, Persons of Spanish Surname, vol. 4, pt. 3, Chap. C (Washington DC: Government Printing Office, 1953), 43; Records of the General Land Office, Bureau of Land Management at www.glorecords.blm.gov.

5. For an in-depth discussion of the demographic diversity in the region see Benton, "What About Women in the White Man's Camp?"; Benton-Cohen, "Common Purposes, Worlds Apart"; Martin, *Songs My Mother Sang to Me*, xi–xvi.

6. Salazar Whelan in Martin, *Songs My Mother Sang to Me*, 145–69; Philip Greisinger, "Land Ownership in Cochise County Arizona," April 1942, 4–5, Manuscript File, 1913–1946, Records Related to Studies, Projects, and Surveys, RG 83, NARA-CP.

7. Benton-Cohen, "Common Purposes, Worlds Apart," 440–41.

8. Schultz, *Southwestern Town*, 45–55; Salazar Whelan in Martin, *Songs My Mother Sang to Me*, 145–69.

9. Field Appraiser's Report, "Arizona 17 Graham," 12, 14, Project Case Files of the Economic Analysis Section 1937–48, Applications and Loan Division, Divisional Records, RG 221, NARA-CP.

10. Benton-Cohen, "Common Purposes, Worlds Apart," 431–32; Greisinger, "Land Ownership in Cochise County Arizona," 6–9; Schultz, *Southwestern Town*, 55–66; Underground Water Commission, "The Underground Water Resources of Arizona" (20th Legislature of the State of Arizona, January 1, 1953), 13, ACASU; "Willcox and Sulphur Springs Valley: Cochise County Arizona" (Willcox AZ: Willcox Chamber of Commerce, 1925, 1938), SCUA.

11. Melcher, "Tending Children, Chickens, and Cattle"; Weech, interview; Benton-Cohen, "Common Purposes, Worlds Apart," 445–51.

12. Schultz, *Southwestern Town*, 57–58, 61; Eleanor Claridge, "Klondyke and the Aravaipa Canyon" (1989), 55, ACASU; "Agricultural Statistics," Economic Analysis, "Arizona 10 Graham," Project Case Files (Entry 3), RG 221, NARA-CP.

13. Ross, "Every Home a Laboratory," 32.

14. Uth, *The Spirit of Cooperation*; Bethel, interview.

15. G. E. Thompson and G. F. Gray, "Dry-Farming in the Sulphur Springs Valley," Agricultural Experiment Station, Bulletin no. 103 (Tucson: University of Arizona, April 15, 1925), 338–56; Schultz, *Southwestern Town*, 90; Benton-Cohen, "Common Purposes, Worlds Apart," 431–33.

16. Schultz, *Southwestern Town*, 92; Bethel, interview; Frank and Twila Shelton, interview; Polk, "Economic Electric Power Survey," 356.

17. *Arizona Range News*, May 24, July 5, 12, 19, August 9, 1899.

18. Esperanza Montoya Padilla in Martin, *Songs My Mother Sang to Me*, 100–117; Sloan, interview; Claridge, "Klondyke and the Aravaipa Canyon"; Melcher, "Tending Children, Chickens, and Cattle," 45.

19. Arizona State Planning Board, "Report of the Power Survey Committee of Arizona Section, American Society of Civil Engineers" (Phoenix, November 20, 1934), Arizona State Library, Phoenix.

20. Ross, "Every Home a Laboratory," 22.

21. Cherrel Batty Weech, "History of Electricity in Pima and the Gila River Valley" (Eastern Arizona Museum and Historical Society, Pima, n.d.); Polk, "Economic Electric Power Survey," 368; Federal Writer's Project, "Safford," RG 91, ASA; Polk, "Economic Electric Power Survey," 368; Ernest Brewer, "Cochise County and Cities," c. 1936, RG 91, ASA; "Memorandum," box 8, Applewhite Collection, MS 17, Arizona Historical Society, Tempe.

22. Polk, "Economic Electric Power Survey," 368; Hoag, "The Advantages of Farm Life," appendix; "Agricultural Statistics," Economic Analysis, "Arizona 10 Graham," Project Case Files (Entry 3), RG 221, NARA-CP; Arizona State Planning Board, "Report of the Power Survey Committee"; U.S. Federal Power Commission, *Arizona Power Survey*, 150, copy in Hayden Library, Arizona State University.

23. Ross, "Every Home a Laboratory," 22–23; see also C. A. Lee, "Wired Help for the Farm."

24. Lowitt, *The New Deal and the West*, 65; Schultz, *Southwestern Town*, 52–53, 61, 78–79, 89; Greisinger, "Land Ownership in Cochise County," 7–8, 19.

25. Rudolph and Ridley, *Power Struggle*, 53; George Norris to Morris Cooke, October 24, 1935, and Cooke to Norris, November 14, 1935, reprinted in *Rural Electrification News*, November 1935, 4, 7.

26. U.S. Federal Power Commission, *Arizona Power Survey*, 56.

27. For more information on the Arizona loan see Glaser, "'An Absolute Paragon of Paradoxes'"; Morris Cooke to Isabella Greenway, August 14, 1935, and J. E. Rankin to Isabella Greenway, June 30, 1936, Isabella Greenway Papers, Arizona Historical Society, Tucson; Rural Electrification Administration, *Annual Report, 1937*.

28. Greisinger, "Land Ownership in Cochise County," 3; Assistant Counsel

G. Simpson to W. L. Ramsey, April 2, 1937, Arizona 00, roll 3, Microfilm Copies of Project Case Files (Entry 3), Records of the Administrator's Office, RG 221, NARA-CP.

29. Harry C. Lamberton to Arizona Corporation Commission, C. S. Beck to John Carmody, June 21, 1937, Arizona 00, Project Case Files (Entry 3), RG 221, NARA-CP; C. H. Southworth, Chief Engineer, San Carlos Irrigation District, "Electrical Districts to Provide Medium for Rural Electrification: A Suggested Plan to Initiate and Administer Approved projects for the Distribution of Electrical Energy," 1935, Greenway Papers; Polk, "Economic Electric Power Survey," 17.

30. Correspondence, "Arizona 10 Graham," Project Case Files (Entry 3), RG 221, NARA-CP.

31. Bliss to John R. Murdock, May 21, 1938, SSVEC.

32. George de Long to Fisher, May 8, 1937, "Arizona 11 Cochise," Project Case Files (Entry 3), RG 221, NARA-CP; Bliss, Cochise County, Reports of County Agents of the University of Arizona Agricultural Extension Service, 1937, 57, AZ 301, SCUA.

33. "Local REA Project Given Temporary Recognition," *Arizona Range News*, September 23, 1938; Bliss to Falkenwald, November 28, 1938, SSVEC; "Local REA Project Given Temporary Recognition," *Arizona Range News*, September 23, 1938; Bliss to Moody, September 27, 1938, Meeting of Incorporators, October 18, 1938, SSVEC.

34. Bliss to J. Cunningham, August 9, 1937, Bliss to R. W. Morrison, August 10, 1937, SSVEC; Bliss, Cochise County, Reports of the County Agents of the Agricultural Extension Service, 1937, 57, AZ 301, SCUA.

35. Cooke quoted in Jellison, *Entitled to Power*, 99.

36. Barbara Rudd, "Woman's Work Is More Like Play on the REA Electrified Farm," *Rural Electrification News*, November 1936, 10–11.

37. Benton-Cohen, "Common Purposes, Worlds Apart," 435; Weech, interview; Peck, interview.

38. Rural Electrification Administration, *Annual Report, 1937*, 134–35, and *Annual Report, 1939*, 168–69.

39. Bliss to Carmody, March 16, 1938, April 20, 1938, SSVEC.

40. Irving, interview, p. 14.

41. Albert Molenaar to C. C. Falkenwald, November 9, 1940, "Arizona 14B Cochise," Correspondence re More Effective Use of Electrical Energy by Members of Cooperatives, 1938–40 (Entry 86), Power and Utilization Division, Divisional Records, RG 221, NARA-CP; Bliss to Carmody,

March 16, 1938, Bliss to Carmody, March 31, 1938, C. O. Falkenwald to Bliss, March 31, 1938, Bliss to Harry McCullum, April 20, 1938, Bliss to Falkenwald, May 23, 1938, and Albert Molenaar to C. C. Falkenwald, November 9, 1940, SSVEC.

42. R. R. Harbour to Nat M. Dysart, May 21, 1938, Bliss to Carmody, March 16, 1938, April 20, 1938, Bliss to Carmody, August 8, 1938, and Bliss to Allen Stickler, April 21, 1939, SSVEC.

43. Bliss to Falkenwald, October 18, 1938, Bliss to O. Harris, April 5, 1939, Bliss to C. J. Moody, December 16, 1939, Bliss to C. J. Moody, December 16, 1939, and Moody to Bliss, December 21, 1939, SSVEC; "Valley Electrification Program Allotted $488,000.00 by National Administration," *Arizona Range News*, May 19, 1939.

44. Progress Report, "Arizona 14 Cochise," January 8, 1940, Progress Bulletins, 1937–40, Information Services and Personnel Divisions, RG 221, NARA-CP; "The Lines Go Up!" in Sulphur Springs Valley Electric Cooperative, *The Power of Cooperation*, 4.

45. Sloan, interview; Weech, interview; Progress Reports, "Arizona 14 Cochise," September 11, 1939, October 13, 1939, Progress Bulletins (Entry 94), 1937–40, Information Services and Personnel Divisions, RG 221, NARA-CP; Terry Croasdale Rowden, interview with Mrs. E. C. Hill, *Arizona Currents*, November/December 1985, 4–5; Progress Report, "Arizona 14 Cochise," January 8, 1940.

46. Frank and Twila Shelton, interview; Sloan, interview.

47. Karen Weston, "Celebrating Sixty-five Years of Providing Power to Southeast Arizona," *Currents: Sulphur Springs Valley Electric Co-op*, September 2005, 25; Terry Rowden, "A Legacy of Light or When the Lights Came On," 1995 (both at SSVEC).

48. "Electric Co-op Offers Prizes for Best Decorated Homes," *Arizona Range News*, December 13, 1940; "Call for Bids on Bowie-San Simon Line," *Arizona Range News*, February 21, 1941.

49. Terry Rowden, *Arizona Currents*, July 1986, n.p. (copy at SSVEC).

50. Mabel Brown, "With a Flip of the Switch . . . ," in Sulphur Springs Valley Electric Cooperative, *The Power of Cooperation*.

51. Mark Bliss, Report of County Agent, Cochise County, 1941, 1942, AZ 301, SCUA.

52. "History of Rural Electrification" (Washington DC: Youth Programs Office, National Rural Electric Cooperative Association), 7; Henry Slattery "To the Editors," *Rural Electrification News*, June 1942, 2; "REA Defense

Committee Advises Co-ops on Protective Measures," *Rural Electrifica-tion News*, March 1942, 8; "Blacking Out the Farm," *Rural Electrification News*, July 1942, 10, 15; Frank and Twila Shelton, interview.

53. Schultz, *Southwestern Town*, 99; Polk, "Economic Electric Power Sur-vey," 61; Arizona State Planning Board, "Report of the Power Survey Committee"; U.S. Federal Power Commission, *Arizona Power Survey*, 150; Mike Bennett to Governor Sidney P. Osborn, December 1, 1941, Osborn to J. Leroy Lancaster, December 17, 1941, and James H. Cun-ningham to Sidney Osborn, August 15, 1941, RG 75, ASA; Minutes, "Ari-zona 14 Cochise," March 13, 1945, RG 221, NARA-CP.

54. G. J. Long to Boyd Fisher, May 8, 1937, "Arizona 3 Apache," Project Case Files (Entry 3), RG 221, NARA-CP; U.S. Federal Power Commission, *Arizona Power Survey*, 1, 71–75; May, "The Arizona Power Authority," 55–56.

55. Correspondence, 1949 "Arizona: Miscellaneous Legal," Correspon-dence regarding REA Borrowers, 1948–51, Papers of Claude R. Wick-ard, 1945–53, Office Files of REA Administrators and Acting Adminis-trators, Records of the Administrator's Office, RG 221, NARA-CP; Henry Richter to R. J. Beamish, "Arizona 14 Cochise," Entry 8, Project Case Files, 1939–1945, Records of the Administrator's Office, RG 221, NARA-CP; Minutes, December 14, 1943; June 22, 1947, "Arizona 14 Cochise," Minutes of Meetings of Borrower Cooperatives, 1943–51, Cooperatives' Operations and Management Divisions, Divisional Records, RG 221, NARA-CP; Third Annual Report, Arizona Power Authority, RG 75, ASA.

56. Field Appraiser's Report, 3–4, 13, 19, "Arizona 17 Graham," Project Case Files of the Economic Analysis Section, 1937–48, Applications and Loans Division, Divisional Records, RG 221, NARA-CP.

57. Mike Bennett to Governor Sidney P. Osborn, December 1, 1941, Os-born to J. Leroy Lancaster, December 17, 1941, and James H. Cunning-ham to Sidney Osborn, August 15, 1941, RG 75, ASA; Minutes, July 10, 1945, March 13, 1945, October 8, 1946, "Arizona 14 Cochise," Minutes of Meetings of Borrower Cooperatives, 1943–51, Cooperatives' Opera-tions and Management Divisions, Divisional Records, RG 221, NARA-CP.

58. Field Appraiser's Report, "Arizona 17 Graham," Project Case Files of the Economic Analysis Section, 1937–48, Applications and Loans Division, Divisional Records, RG 221, NARA-CP; Field Activities Report, March 19, 1949, "Arizona 17 Graham," Field Activities Reports 1946–51, Applica-tions and Loans Division, Divisional Records, RG 221, NARA-CP.

59. Clyde Wickard to Harold Patten, John Mudock, Carl Hayden, Ernest McFarland, March 1951, "Arizona 17 Graham," Correspondence re REA Borrowers 1946–51, Field Activities Reports, 1950–51, Applications and Loans Division, Divisional Records, RG 221, NARA-CP; Cherrel Batty Weech, "History of Graham County Electric Co-op, Inc." (Eastern Arizona Museum and Historical Society, Pima, n.d.); Peck, interview.
60. Minutes, Annual Meeting, Sulphur Springs Valley Electric Cooperative, Inc., February 8, 1949, Minutes of Meetings of Borrower Cooperatives, 1943–51, Cooperatives' Operations and Management Divisions, RG 221, NARA-CP; "Travel 10 Field Reports, 1948–49," "Arizona 14 Cochise," Field Activities Reports 1946–51, Applications and Loans Division, Divisional Records, RG 221, NARA-CP; Field Activities Report, May–June 1953, February 14, 1952, "Arizona 14 Cochise," Applications and Loans Division, Divisional Records, RG 221, NARA-CP; E. M. McAleb, Minutes, Regular Monthly Meeting of the Board of Directors, December 9, 1952, SSVEC.
61. Hubert Wales to Alvin J. Wetmore, March 21, 1953, GCSEC.
62. McNulty, interview; "Co-op to Erect Power Plant," Arizona Electric Power Cooperative Scrapbook, Arizona Electric Power Cooperative Corporate Headquarters, Benson AZ; Clapp, "Re-Energizing Rural Electrification," 4.
63. Bliss, County Agent Report, Cochise County, 1944–45, AZ 301, SCUA.
64. U.S. Bureau of the Census, *Number of Inhabitants, 1960* (Washington DC: Government Printing Office, 1962), 4–8; Schultz, *Southwestern Town*, 93; Opie Rundle Burgess, "Sulphur Springs Valley," *Arizona Highways*, April 1958, 12–13; "Cochise Would Be Amazed," *Rural Lines*, July 1959, 15–17.
65. Sloan, interview; "Shortage of Houses," *Arizona Range News*, August 16, 1940; Rural Electrification Administration, *Annual Report, 1938*, 188–89; Burgess, "Sulphur Springs Valley," 10–12.
66. A. Mark Bliss, Cochise County, County Agent Report, 1941, 19, 23, 28, AZ 301, SCUA.
67. G. R. Michaels to Bliss, June 27, 1939, and P. Y. Beckue to Bliss, September 11, 1939, SSVEC; Rural Electrification Administration, *Annual Report, 1938*, 188–89.
68. Schultz, *Southwestern Town*, 93; "Cochise Would Be Amazed," 15–17; Field Appraiser's Report, "Arizona 17 Graham," 7, Project Case Files of the Economic Analysis Section 1937–48, Applications and Loan Division, Divisional Records, RG 221, NARA-CP.

69. Frank and Twila Shelton, interview; U.S. Bureau of the Census, *Census of the Population: 1950, Special Reports: Persons of Spanish Surname*, vol. 4, pt. 3, chap. C (Washington DC: Government Printing Office, 1953), 3C, 59; U.S. Bureau of the Census, *Sixteenth Census of the United States: 1940, Housing, Volume 2, General Characteristics, Part 2, Alabama–Indiana* (Washington DC: Government Printing Office, 1943), 102.

70. Report of Florence Miller, Area Social Worker, Records of the Phoenix Area Office, Educational Branch, Central Classified Files 806, RG 75, NARA-LN.

71. Terry Croasdale, "Memories Shared of SSVEC Beginnings," *Arizona Currents*, November/December 1985 (copy at SSVEC); Weech, "History of Electricity in Pima and the Gila Valley"; Schackel, "Ranch and Farm Women," 107.

72. Ross, "Every Home a Laboratory," 136; *Arizona Producer*, July 22, 1939, 9.

73. "Valley Electrification Program Allotted $488,000.00"; "Local REA Project Given Temporary Recognition," *Arizona Range News*, September 23, 1938; Pre-incorporation meeting SSVEC minutes, November 21, 1938, January 3, 1939, Minutes of Meetings of Borrower Cooperatives, 1943–51, Cooperatives' Operations and Management Divisions, RG 221, NARA-CP.

74. *Co-op Quarterly: Sulphur Springs Valley Electrical Cooperative*, January 1968, SSVEC.

75. Ross, "Every Home a Laboratory," 25; *Co-op Quarterly: Sulphur Springs Valley Electric Cooperative* 2, no. 6, SSVEC; Mae Baldridge, Cochise County, Home Demonstration Reports, 1951, AZ 302, SCUA; U.S. Federal Power Commission, *Arizona Power Survey*, 54.

76. Frank and Twila Shelton, interview; Field Appraisal Report, "Arizona 17 Graham," 3, Project Case Files of the Economic Analysis Section, 1937–48, Applications and Loans Division, Divisional Records, RG 221, NARA-CP.

77. "Electricity and Rural Health," *Rural Electrification News*, August/September 1947, 4–5; Clyde Wickard, "Electricity and Rural Health," *Rural Electrification News*, April 1947, 2; Francis J. Sette, "Running Water and Rural Health," *Rural Electrification News*, May 1941, 7–11; Frank and Twila Shelton, interview; Socorro Félix Delgado in Martin, *Songs My Mother Sang to Me*, 59.

78. Mae Baldridge, Cochise County, Home Demonstration Reports, 1951, AZ 302, SCUA.

79. "Guideposts in Buying Household Equipment," Circular 207, College of Agriculture, University of Arizona Agricultural Extension Service, December 1952; Ross, "Every Home a Laboratory," 15, 150, 185–87; Cohen, *Consumers' Republic*.

80. U.S. Bureau of the Census, *Census of Population and Housing, Detailed Housing Characteristics, 1970, Arizona* (Washington DC: Government Printing Office, 1972), table 63.

81. "Electrified School an REA By-product," *Rural Electrification News*, April 1937, 16–17; "Another Filmstrip, 'The New Rural School' Is Now Available," *Rural Electrification News*, May 1937, 32; Harry Slattery, "Education in the REA Program," *Rural Electrification News*, April 1941, 13; Frank and Twila Shelton, interview.

82. Wright, *Electricity in the Home*; Grace Ryan, Report of Home Demonstration Agent, 1954, 35–36, AZ 302, SCUA.

83. Bliss, 4-H Club Report, Report of County Agent, Cochise County, 1941, 21, AZ 301, SCUA; "Electricity Plays Part in 4-H Program," *Rural Electrification News*, September 1937, 26; Gertrude L. Warren, "Why 4-H Clubs Welcome REA," *Rural Electrification News*, July 1939, 16–17; "Rural Electric 4-H Clubs," *Rural Electrification News*, September 1940, 11–13.

84. Ross, "Every Home a Laboratory," 1, 27.

85. Kline, *Consumers in the Country*; Cowan, *More Work for Mother*; Jellison, *Entitled to Power*; Bethel, interview; "$1,000,000 Business Women: Their Communities Endorse These Women Board Members," *Rural Electrification News*, October 1946, 4–5, 22.

86. Ross, "Every Home a Laboratory," 3, 52–53; see Jensen, "Crossing Ethnic Barriers," 220–30, for AES activity in New Mexico.

87. Ruiz, *From Out of the Shadows*, 65–71; Herbert Biberman, *Salt of the Earth* (Independent Productions/International Union Of Mine, Mill and Smelter Workers, 1954).

88. Benton, "What About Women in the White Man's Camp?"

89. Ross, "Every Home a Laboratory," 43 (quote), 72, 100.

90. Jellison, *Entitled to Power*, 9–10.

91. Weech, interview; Peck, interview; Stanford Research Institute, *The San Carlos Apache Reservation: A Resources Development Study* (Phoenix: Stanford Research Institute, Mountain States Division, 1954), 10; Addenda to Appraisal of Arizona 17 Graham, Project Case Files of the Economic Analysis Section, 1937–48, Ernest Stefan to Richard Richter, "Traveler's Report," "Arizona 17 Graham," April 22, 1948, Field Activi-

ties Reports 1946–51, Applications and Loans Division, Divisional Records, RG 221, NARA-CP.

92. Bliss to W. G. Hastings, April 26, 1940, SSVEC.

93. Peck, interview; Annual Reports, SSVEC; "Last Year at the REA Annual Meeting," *Arizona Range News*, February 1, 1952.

94. Benson to Bliss, October 7, 1937, SSVEC.

95. Bethel, interview; Van Romney, DVEC [Duncan Valley Electric Cooperative], to Farr, President, GCEC, July 10, 1952, and Arthur King to Martin Gentry, October 26, 1938, SSVEC.

96. Sloan, interview; Frank and Twila Shelton, interview; Bethel, interview; Schackel, "Ranch and Farm Women," 107.

97. Frank and Twila Shelton, interview; Peck, interview.

98. Sloan, interview; Rural Electrification Administration, *Annual Report, 1937*, 134–35.

2. Power through Diversity

1. Lee, interview; R. D. Holtz to Commissioner of Indian Affairs, December 31, 1946, and Tribal Relations/Acts of Tribal Councils July 1946–December 1947, file 3-064, box 123, Central Classified Files 064, Fort Apache, RG 75, NARA-LN.

2. "Arizona 13 Navajo," Records of Economic Analysis, Applications and Loans Division, RG 221, NARA-CP; Clark Fullerton, "Joe Gardner Traces Navopache Electric's Development," *Hilites: Electric Service for Rural Living*, April 1981, 1, 4.

3. Appraiser's Report, 11–16, "Arizona 13 Navajo," Records of Economic Analysis, Applications and Loans Division, RG 221, NARA-CP.

4. Also see note 8. "Snowflake Project," Report, 5–10, Davis Dam Project Histories, Records of the Office of the Solicitor, Records of the United States Bureau of Reclamation, RG 48, NARA-LN; Elzer Des Jardines Tetreau, "Unemployed Relief in Arizona, 1932–1936: With a Special Analysis of Rural and Town Relief Households," Agricultural Extension Service, Experiment Station Bulletin no. 156 (Tucson: University of Arizona, 1937), 85; U.S. Bureau of the Census, *Census of Population and Housing, Arizona, 1940* (Washington DC: Government Printing Office, 1943); U.S. Bureau of the Census, *Census of Population and Housing, Arizona, 1950* (Washington DC: Government Printing Office, 1953).

5. Dobyns, *The Apache People*, 3.

6. Workers of the Writers' Program of the Work Projects Administration

in the State of Arizona, *The WPA Guide to 1930s Arizona* (Tucson: University of Arizona Press, 1989), 442; Sheridan, *Arizona*, 85–86.

7. Sam Lowe, "Apaches Restore Own History with Fort," *Arizona Republic*, June 18, 2000; Fort Apache Information Sheet, Fort Apache Historic Park, Fort Apache, Arizona; Dobyns, *The Apache People*, 29, 44, 74.

8. Conversations with Spanish-heritage families in the area reveal that most prefer to identify as Spanish rather than Mexican, since they do not consider themselves or their ancestors to have emigrated from Mexico. I use the term "Mexican American" to describe communities with ancestors who emigrated from Mexico to New Mexico after the latter became part of the United States under the Treaty of Guadalupe-Hidalgo (1848). Applewhite, *On the Road to Nowhere*, 16–20.

9. Sheridan, *Arizona*, 196; Peterson, *Take Up Your Mission*.

10. Polk, "Economic Electric Power Survey," 134.

11. Applewhite, *On the Road to Nowhere*, 37; H. V. Clotts, "Report on the Cost of Proposed Power and Irrigation Development at Whiteriver AZ," Records of the Irrigation Division, 1891–1946 (Entry 657), RG 75, NARA-W; W. C. Cose, Chief Engineer, to J. R. Garfield, July 23, 1908, Central Classified Files 757, General Files, 1902–1919, RG 75, NARA-W.

12. Flammer, *Mormon Pioneering Community*, 29–31, 134–41.

13. Lee, interview.

14. "Snowflake Project," Davis Dam Project Histories, RG 48, NARA-LN.

15. Clotts to Olberg, October 31, 1915, Plans and Estimates, and Crouse to Jones, October 28, 1902, "Snowflake Project," Davis Dam Project Histories, RG 48, NARA-LN.

16. H. V. Clotts to C. R. Olberg, Superintendent of Irrigation, October 31, 1915, Plans and Estimates, White River Power and Irrigation Project, Records of the Irrigation Division, 1891–1946, RG 75, NARA-LN; C. W. Crouse, Indian Agent, to William Jones, Commissioner of Indian Affairs, October 28, 1902, Letters Sent, Fort Apache Agency, C. R. Olberg, Superintendent of Irrigation, to W. M. Reed, Chief Engineer, Indian Services, "Application for Power Site," April 10, 1913, Olberg to Reed, July 30, 1910, Report and Letters Relative to Application for Permit by Apache Power Company: San Carlos and Fort Apache Indian Reservation, Records of the Irrigation Division, RG 75, NARA-LN.

17. Prior to 1947, the Bureau of Indian Affairs was called the Office of Indian Affairs. I will use the historically accurate term throughout.

18. Embshoff to Olberg, May 12, 1915, Correspondence, 1907–56, Charles

L. Davis to Cato Sells, Commissioner of Indian Affairs, October 18, 1920, July 15, 1921, Central Classified Files 341, 1907–56, Fort Apache Agency, Olberg to Sells, November 27, 1914, Fort Apache Agency, and C. A. Engle, Assistant Engineer, "Power and Irrigation, White Mountain Reservation," November 1914, Irrigation Division, Reports and Related Records, Arizona, RG 75, NARA-W.

19. "Treaty between the United States of America and the Navajo Tribe of Indians, August 12, 1868," in Kappler, *Indian Treaties, 1778–1883*, 1015–20. Also see Olberg to Sells, November 27, 1914, and C. A. Engle, "Power and Irrigation, White Mountain Reservation," November 1914, Irrigation Division, Reports and Related Records, Arizona, RG 75, NARA-w; Davis, "Indians of the United States," 929–33.

20. Schnauk to Reed, March 31, 1914, Central Classified Files 341, 1907–56, Fort Apache Agency, RG 75, NARA-w; Engle, Irrigation and Power Investigations, Fort Apache Indian Reservation, March 1914, Irrigation Division: Reports and Related Records, Arizona, RG 75, NARA-w; W. M. Reed, Chief Engineer Irrigation to Cato Sells, Commissioner of Indian Affairs, Correspondence, 1907–56, Fort Apache Agency, and W. M. Peterson to Sells, August 15, 1914, Central Classified Files 341, 1907–39, RG 75, NARA-w.

21. Ernest Nelson in *Stories of Traditional Navajo Life and Culture*, 232–39; Fort Apache Information Sheet, Fort Apache Historic Park, Fort Apache, Arizona; W. V. Clotts and R. G. Brady, February 28, 1923, Description of Whiteriver Power and Irrigation Project, Fort Apache Reservation as completed January 19, 1923, and Charles Burke, Commissioner, to William Reed, Central Classified Files 341, 1924, RG 75, NARA-w; Davis, "Indians of the United States," 929–32.

22. "Authorizing Federal Power Commission to Issue Certain Permits and Licenses," House of Representatives, 70th Cong., 2nd sess., Report no. 2313, January 31, 1929, Central Classified Files 341, 1907–56, Fort Apache Agency, RG 75, NARA-w.

23. Olberg to Sells, November 27, 1914, Correspondence, 1907–56, Fort Apache Agency, and C. A. Engle, Assistant Engineer, "Power and Irrigation, White Mountain Reservation," November 1914, Irrigation Division, Reports and Related Records, Arizona, RG 75, NARA-w; Hayden to James Girand, January 29, 1929, C. C. Craigin to Carl Hayden, March 23, 1929, box 616, folder 7, Hayden Papers, ACASU.

24. "Six-Year Construction Plan, Circular No. 2943," and "Schedule of Re-

pairs and Improvements," Central Classified Files 403, Fort Apache Agency, RG 75, NARA-LN; Donner to Burke, February 14, 1929, "Field Matron Work—Domestic Employment," Central Classified Files 970, RG 75, NARA-LN.

25. WPA *Guide to 1930s Arizona*, 443; Davis, "Indians of the United States," 929–33.

26. Janet Lynn Wilson, interview questionnaire conducted by author, September 3, 2000, Lakeside, Arizona; Donner to Bradley, October 3, 1938, and Donner to Collier, March 18, 1941, Central Classified Files 413.1, RG 75, NARA-LN.

27. Donner to Bradley, October 3, 1938, and Donner to Collier, March 18, 1941.

28. Matheney, "Lumbering in the White Mountains."

29. "100 People Who Left Their Mark on the White Mountains: James McNary," *Navapache Independent*, July 18, 1985, 18, 19; Harry R. Kallender, Forester, BIA, "McNary Town and the White Mountain Apache Forest on the Fort Apache Indian Reservation, Arizona," in *Reflections of McNary* (McNary AZ: McNary Reunion Committee, 1989), 17; Mona Campbell, "McNary: Company Town," manuscript, May 6, 1960, 2–6, AHF; Sheridan, *Arizona*, 311–13; *Remembering McNary* (Mountain Video Productions, c. 1989); Blake, interview.

30. Rafe Sweet, "My Memories of McNary," in *Reflections of McNary*, 26; Blake, interview; Vennie White, "Blakes Found Better Life in McNary," *Navapache Independent*, July 25, 1985, 4, 13.

31. Campbell, "McNary: Company Town," 3; Edgar Perry, "I Went to McNary School," in *Reflections of McNary*, 55; *Remembering McNary*; survey of "McNary Day" participants, interviews by author, September 3, 2000, Lakeside, Arizona.

32. Galbreath Development Company Papers, AHF.

33. Arizona Corporation Commission, Case Files, box 2, folder 7, RG 29, Utilities Division, ASA; Lloyd Henning to G. A. Trotter, December 19, 1936, box 6, folder 18, Henning Papers, ACASU.

34. Rhoten, interview.

35. Arizona State Planning Board, "Report of the Power Survey Committee of Arizona Section, American Society of Civil Engineers" (Phoenix, November 20, 1934), 24; Field Appraiser's Report, Agricultural Statistics, "Arizona 6 Navajo," Project Case Files (Entry 3), microfilm, RG 221, NARA-CP.

36. James B. Girand to N. L. Harfield, August 20, 1935, L. A. Sear, Agricultural Statistics, March 12, 1936, May 21, 1937, Project Case Files (Entry 3), microfilm, RG 221, NARA-CP.

37. "Arizona 3 Apache," Lewis to Falkenwald, March 26, 1939, "Arizona 13 Navajo," "Arizona 3 Apache," Project Case Files (Entry 3), RG 221, NARA-CP; "Snowflake Project," Davis Dam Project Histories, RG 48, NARA-LN; Polk, "Economic Electric Power Survey," 142.

38. G. J. Long to Boyd Fisher, May 8, 1937, "Arizona 3 Apache," Correspondence and Agricultural Statistics, REA, May 21, 1937, "Arizona 13 Navajo," Project Case Files (Entry 3), RG 221, NARA-CP; Fullerton, "Gardner Traces Navopache Electric's Development," 1, 4; John McLernon, County Agent Reports, Agricultural Extension Service, 1937, 15A, AZ 301, SCUA.

39. "Arizona 13 Navajo," Project Files Concerning Loans (Entry 6), box 2, March 26, 1939, RG 221, NARA-CP.

40. De Luna, *Public versus Private Power*, 10–11, 14; Sheridan, *Arizona*, 271. Also see Nelson, "Rural Life and Social Change," 38–57.

41. "Snowflake Project," Davis Dam Project Histories, RG 48, NARA-LN.

42. Dysart, Wagnen, and Bennett to Osborn, August 19, 1943, Dougherty to Nixon, REA, October 19, 1943, Osborn to Nixon, October 20, 1943, and Neal to Osborn, December 1, 1943, RG 1, subgroup 14, ASA; "Vast REA Construction Planned for State," *Arizona Republic*, November 15, 1947.

43. Appraiser's Report, 14–16, "Arizona 13 Navajo," Records of Economic Analysis, Applications and Loans Division, RG 221, NARA-CP).

44. G. J. Long to Boyd Fisher, May 8, 1937, "Arizona 3 Apache," Project Case Files (Entry 3), RG 221, NARA-CP; Appraiser's Report, "Arizona 13 Navajo," 9, 11, 13, 16, 19, 27, Addenda, Records of Economic Analysis, Applications and Loans Division, RG 221, NARA-CP.

45. Appraiser's Report, "Arizona 13 Navajo," Addenda, 1, 2, Records of Economic Analysis, Applications and Loans Division, RG 221, NARA-CP; Tribal Relations, Acts of Tribal Councils, Fort Apache, July 1946– December 1946, Holtz to Collier, December 31, 1946, and Colbert to Holtz, December 15, 1947, Central Classified Files 54, Fort Apache Agency, RG 75, NARA-LN.

46. Minutes, 1950–51, "Arizona 13 Navajo," Minutes of Meetings of Borrower Cooperatives 1943–51, Cooperatives' Operations and Management Divisions, Divisional Records, RG 221, NARA-CP.

47. Fort Apache Indian Reservation, Tribal Minutes, October 14, 1946, Central Classified Files 54, Fort Apache Agency, RG 75, NARA-LN.

48. Max Colbert to R. D. Holtz, December 15, 1947, Addenda: Indians, Appraiser's Report, Economic Analysis, "Arizona 13 Navajo," RG 221, NARA-CP.

49. Colbert to Holtz, December 15, 1947.

50. Minutes, October 14, 1946, "Arizona 13 Navajo," RG 221, NARA-CP; Tribal Relations, Acts of Tribal Councils, Fort Apache, July 1946–December 1946, Central Classified Files 54, Fort Apache Agency, RG 75, NARA-LN; Resolutions 162, 173, Fort Apache Indian Reservation Tribal Minutes, December 2, 1946, Central Classified Files 54, Fort Apache Agency, RG 75, NARA-LN.

51. C. J. Warren, Vice President, to Max Colbert, December 26, 1947, Appraiser's Report, Economic Analysis, "Arizona 13 Navajo," 1947, 9, 11, 126, RG 221, NARA-CP; Fullerton, "Gardner Traces Navopache Electric's Development," 1.

52. Minutes, March 3, 1948, "Arizona 13 Navajo," 1948–49, 1950–51, RG 221, NARA-CP.

53. "Arizona 13 Navajo," Field Activities Reports, 1946–1951, Applications and Loans Division, Divisional Records, April 3, 1948, December 6–9, 1948, RG 221, NARA-CP.

54. R. D. Holtz to W. A. Brophy, Commissioner of Indian Affairs, July 22, 1946, and December 31, 1946, Tribal Relations, Acts of Tribal Councils, Fort Apache, July 1946–December 1946, Central Classified Files 54, 1940–1956, and Annual Report, 1952, Central Classified Files 31, RG 75, NARA-W.

55. Harold Patten to Carl Hayden, March 8, 1957, Hayden to Patten, April 11, 1957, Dewey Farr, Navopache General Manager, to Hayden, June 14, 1957, Patten to Hayden, May 8, 1958, and Patten to Hayden, April 29, 1959, box 398, folder 8, Hayden Papers, ACASU.

56. Patten to Hayden, April 12, 1961, S. D. Gordom to Guy McCafferty, April 4, 1961, and Darrell W. Crawford to S. D. Gordom, March 3, 1961, box 398, folder 8, Hayden Papers, ACASU; Rhoten, interview; R. E. McNelly to Clyde Ellis, February 5, 1949, "Arizona 13 Navajo," Field Activities Reports, Applications and Loans Division, Divisional Records, RG 221, NARA-CP.

57. Rhoten, interview; Richer, Field Activities Report, April 2, 1952, Applications and Loans Division, Divisional Records, RG 221, NARA-CP; "Are Your Records Safe?" *Rural Lines*, May 1959, 16.

58. Field Activities Reports, "Arizona 13 Navajo," May 1–5, 1951, Field Activities Reports, Applications and Loans Division, Divisional Records, RG 221, NARA-CP.

59. Grace Ketchum to Carl Hayden, January 25, 1955, Robert Bell to Hayden, February 4, 1955, Arthur Wright to Hayden, August 5, 1957, Fred Strong to Hayden, August 26, 1957, and Ira F. Walker to Carl Hayden, July 19, 1960, box 338, folder 7, Hayden Papers, ACASU; Eddy, interview; "Navopache on the Move," *Fort Apache Scout*, October 1975; Rhoten, interview; Dewey Farr to Juanita Jones, August 2, 1960, and Juanita Jones to Carl Hayden, January 12, 1961, box 398, folder 8, Hayden Papers, ACASU.

60. "Are Your Records Safe?" 15; Project Case Files, Entry 10, 1946, "Arizona 13 Legal," RG 221, NARA-CP.

61. "Ellis Warns of Master Plan to Destroy Rural Electrification," *Trico Livewire*, November 1958; Minutes, Annual Meeting, Sulphur Springs Valley Electric Cooperative, Inc., February 8, 1949, Minutes of Meetings of Borrower Cooperatives, 1943–51, Cooperatives' Operations and Management Divisions, RG 221, NARA-CP; De Luna, *Public versus Private Power*, 109; Childs, *The Farmer Takes a Hand*, 17, 23.

62. "Will You Leave These Freedoms to Your Children?" *Saturday Review* article included in Clyde T. Ellis, General Manager, National Rural Electrification Association, to Carl Hayden, October 18, 1957, Ellis to Hayden, December 22, 1958, and Ellis to Hayden, May 8, 1959, box 338, folder 7, Hayden Papers, ACASU.

63. Dewey Farr to Carl Hayden, June 14, 1957, box 398, folder 8, Mildred F. A. Saacke to Hayden, June 25, 1963, and A. L. Meyer to Carl Hayden, April 1, 1963, box 338, folder 6, Hayden Papers, ACASU.

64. See chapter 1 for an explanation of the phrase "skim the cream." "Policy Service Directors Confirm Top Executives," *Arizona Republic*, March 4, 1952; A. L. Meyer to Barry Goldwater, May 8, 1962, Richard A. Dell, REA, to Carl Hayden, May 3, 1963, Clyde Ellis to Carl Hayden, December 22, 1958, and R. J. McMullin to Carl Hayden, July 1, 1963, box 338, folder 6, Hayden Papers, ACASU; Clapp, "Crisis in Rural Electrification."

65. Eddy, interview.

66. R. F. Richter, Traveler's Report, March 11, 1948, Field Activities Reports, Applications and Loans Division, Divisional Records, RG 221, NARA-CP.

67. McNulty, interview; Edward F. Crawford to Richard F. Richter, "Arizona

13 Navajo," April 3, 1948, "Arizona 13 Navajo," Field Activities Report, June 14, 1948, April 23–28, 1949, September 13, 14, 1950, Field Activities Reports, Applications and Loans Division, Minutes, "Arizona 13 Navajo," October 24, 1952, RG 221, NARA-CP; William H. Grove to Norman Clarks, Verde Electric, March 21, 1955, GCSEC.

68. Samuel Schurgin to Hayden, February 4, 1964, Harvey Rice to Hayden, April 1, 1964, Norman Clapp to Hayden, March 19, 1964, and S. D. Gordom to Hayden, July 23, 1965, Correspondence, 1957–69, box 300, folder 6, Hayden Papers ACASU.

69. Pence, *The Next Greatest Thing*, 191–93; Articles of Incorporation, GCSEC; Arthur J. Paul, "Arizona Currents 1965–1977," GCSEC; "All Right, What Is Wrong about an Electric Co-op?" *Tucson Daily Citizen*, September 24, 1963.

70. McNulty, interview; John Glatz to A. O. Bicknell, November 3, 1961, GCSEC; "ACC to Set Boundaries," *Arizona Daily Star*, August 8, 1962.

71. Correspondence between S. D. Gordom and Paul Fannin, 1966–67, 90th Congress, box 32, folder 12, Fannin Papers, AHF.

72. President's National Advisory Commission on Rural Poverty, *The People Left Behind*.

73. Richard Greenwood, Press Secretary to Carl Hayden, to Sanford Gordom, July 19, 1967, 90th Congress, box 32, folder 12, Fannin Papers, AHF; Gordom to Goldwater, April 18, 1969, 91st Congress, box 32, folder 24, Howard Bethel to Goldwater, November 17, 1971, 92nd Congress, box 25, Goldwater Papers, AHF.

74. Grace Ketchum to Carl Hayden, January 25, 1955, and Stella Hughes to Public Relations Department, TRICO, January 24, 1967, box 313, folder 89, Hayden Papers, ACASU.

75. "Helping Farmers Use Irrigation: Short Courses Spurs Interest," *Rural Electrification News*, July 1952, 16–18.

76. Field Activities Report, November 16 and 17, 1948, April 2, 1952, July 7–11, 1952, April 27–30, 1953, Lena Mae Anlauf to Dewey Farr, April 1953, D. E. Jones, Traveler's Report, November 17, 1948, Applications and Loans Division, Field Activities Reports, "Arizona 13 Navajo," RG 221, NARA-CP; Rhoten, interview.

77. *Navopache Transmitter*, 1951–55, copies in Henning Papers, ACASU.

78. Blake, interview.

79. Annual Report of the Home Demonstration Agent, Apache County, 1953–1965, Annual Report of the Home Demonstration Agent, Navajo County, 1953, 3–7, 24–25, and 1954, 5–10, AZ 302, SCUA.

80. Home Demonstration Agent Annual Report, Apache County, 1953, 8, AZ 302, SCUA.

81. Florence D. McKnight, Home Extension Agent, Fort Apache Agency, Narrative Report for the Year of 1938, 1939, 1938–47, and Home Demonstration Agent Annual Report, Apache County, 1953, 8, AZ 302, SCUA.

82. Annual Report of the Home Demonstration Agent, Navajo County, 1953, 3–7, 24–25, and 1954, 5–10, AZ 302, SCUA.

83. Narrative Section, Annual Report, 1946, Reports of the Agricultural Extension Service, 352, 353, Central Classified Files 919, Fort Apache Agency, 1938–47, RG 75, NARA-LN.

84. Capps, "Social Change among the White Mountain Apache," 28–32; Bernstein, *American Indians and World War II*, 131–58.

85. John Chissey to BIA, August 25, 1959, file 10591, box 75, Fort Apache Agency 1959, Central Classified Files 620, RG 75, NARA-W.

86. Capps, "Social Change among the White Mountain Apache," 32; Bernstein, *American Indians and World War II*, 142–44.

87. Annual Extension Report, 1951, Fort Apache Agency, RG 75, NARA-LN; Division of Extension and Industry, 1938–47, Central Classified Files 919, Fort Apache Agency, RG 75, NARA-LN.

88. Jerry E. Hutchison, principal investigator, National American Research Associates, Health, Education and Welfare Committee, White Mountain Apache Office of Education, "Apache: Comprehensive Educational Plan, White Mountain Apache Tribe" (Lawrence KS: Native American Research Associates, 1978), 10.

89. Marion P. Royer, Social Worker, Report, January 1963, Central Classified Files 54, RG 75, NARA-W.

90. *Fort Apache Scout*, September 1962.

91. Campbell, "McNary: Company Town," 4; Dewey Farr to Carl Hayden, August 23, 1955, box 179, folder 19, Hayden Papers, ACASU.

92. "Lupe Named to Phone Advisory Board," *Fort Apache Scout*, June 15, 1975, 4; "Raymond Endfield, Jr., Named to Navopache Board," *Fort Apache Scout*, May 1975, 10; Reddy, *Statistical Record of Native North America*, 890; Endfield, interview.

93. Kallender, "McNary Town and the White Mountain Apache Forest," 18; "Energetic Apaches Give Up Warlike Roles," *Timberline*, April 1961; "Are Your Records Safe?" 16.

94. National Advisory Commission, *Rural Poverty*.

95. "Are Your Records Safe?" 16; Tribal Minutes, September 5, 6, 1962,

folder 3991, Central Classified Files 54, Fort Apache Agency, RG 75, NARA-W.

96. "Are Your Records Safe?" 16.
97. Brigham, "Lighting the Reservation," 85.

3. "A Light in Every Hogan"

1. Ration quoted in B. Johnson, *Traditional Navajo Life and Culture*, 334.
2. Paul Jones, Inaugural Address, Chairman, Navajo Tribal Council, Series 84–88, box 3, folder 8, Goldwater Papers, AHF.
3. H. W. Johnson, "Rural Indian Americans in Poverty," i.
4. Navajo-Hopi Rehabilitation Hearings quoted in Needham, "'A Piece of the Action.'"
5. L. A. Robbins, *Navajo Energy Politics*, 1; Chamberlain, *Under Sacred Ground*, x; For more information on Native Americans' efforts to control this development, see Needham, "A Piece of the Action"; and Ambler, *Breaking the Iron Bonds*.
6. For an in-depth discussion of the relationship between energy development on the Navajo Reservation and southwestern cities, see Needham, *Power Lines*.
7. Peterson, "Headgates and Conquest," 270; Iverson, *Navajo Nation*, 6; Everett Ross and Ted J. Adamczyk, "Power Requirements Study," Navajo Tribal Utility Authority (February 1995), 16, copy in Research Library, NTUA-HQ.
8. McPherson, *Sacred Land, Sacred View*, 81–82, 90–91; Iverson, *Diné*, 7–21.
9. David M. Brugge, "Navajo Prehistory and History to 1850," in *Handbook of Native North American Indians*, vol. 10, *Southwest*, ed. Alfonso Ortiz (Washington DC: Smithsonian Institution, 1979), 489–96; Leeper, "Impact of Water Control," 78–79; Boman, *Consumptive Use*, 2.
10. Iverson, *Diné*, 35–65; Robert A. Roessel Jr., "Navajo History, 1850–1923," *Handbook of Native North American Indians*, 10:506–14.
11. "Report of Work" in *Teaching and Training in Home Economics*, June 2, 1924, box 104, Central Classified Files 812, RG 75, NARA-LN.
12. Polk, "Economic Electric Power Survey," 128.
13. "Treaty between the United States of America and the Navajo Tribe of Indians, June 1, 1868," reprinted in Iverson, *Diné*, 325–34; Simmons, *New Mexico*, 150–51; Roessel, "Navajo History, 1850–1923," 513, 517; Leeper, "Impact of Water Control," 81.

14. Iverson, *Navajo Nation*, 17; Polk, "Economic Electric Power Survey," 59; Wolf, interview; Brigham, "Lighting the Reservation," 87.

15. "Organization of Home Economics Classes," Navajo Agency, "The Unit Kitchen as a Factor in Home Economics Education," Fort Apache Agency, "Teaching and Training Home Economics," c. 1924, box 104, San Carlos Agency, Central Classified Files 812, RG 75, NARA-LN; Max M. Drefkoff, "An Industrial Program for the Navajo Reservation," January 1948, Phoenix Area Office, Subject Files, box 56, RG 75, NARA-LN; for more on this program see Trennert, *The Phoenix Indian School*.

16. Meriam et al., *The Problem of Indian Administration*, 11–15, 348–448.

17. Quoted in Brigham, "Lighting the Reservation," 87; Abstracts and Official Reports Concerning School Plants, Entry 739, RG 75, NARA-W.

18. John Collier to Fairbanks, Morse and Company, April 28, 1934, "Diesels, Power Plants for Day Schools," Construction Subject Files, Phoenix Area Office, box 63, RG 75, NARA-LN; "Report on Navajo Situation," July 40, 1947, p. 70, Central Classified Files 64, Navajo Area Office, box 39, RG 75, NARA-LN; Iverson, *Diné*, 174.

19. Federal Administration Division of Investigations, Public Works Administration, Construction, Subject Files, 1833–37, box 62, Phoenix Area Office, May 21, 1936, RG 75, NARA-LN; Kluckhohn and Leighton, *The Navaho*, 94; "Contracts: Heat Light Power Gas and Water," Central Classified Files 284, 1945–52, Navajo Agency, RG 75, NARA-LN; Zah, interview.

20. Iverson, *Navajo Nation*, 35 (Collier quote), 36–37; also see Iverson, *Diné*, 133–36, 155–57.

21. Edward Poynton to Roy H. Bradley, December 7, 1938, Correspondence of Superintendent of Construction, 1933–1940, Phoenix Area Office, box 61, RG 75, NARA-LN.

22. R. L. Tolson, building superintendent, to Edward C. Green, November 10, 1947, Green to J. T. Lefler, October 20, 1947, and John Hedquist, purchasing officer, to Mr. Ed Cata, February 20, 1947, Central Classified Files 284, Heat, Light, Power, Gas and Water, 1946–1950, box 114, Navajo Area Office, RG 75, NARA-LN; Zah, interview.

23. J. M. Stewart to Daisy Albert, January 14, 1946, and J. M. Stewart to Paul D. Merrill, Fort Wingate Trading Post, April 9, 1945, Central Classified Files 284, Heat, Light, Power, Gas and Water 1946–1950, box 114, Navajo Area Office, RG 75, NARA-LN.

24. Kluckhohn, "Navahos in the Machine Age," 196–97; Drefkoff, "An Industrial Program for the Navajo Reservation."

25. Iverson, *Diné*, 181, 188–90; Bernstein, *American Indians and World War II*, 131–58; Kluckhohn and Leighton, *The Navaho*, 19; White quoted in Chamberlain, *Under Sacred Ground*, 83.

26. "Summary of Conditions and Outline of Reservation, Navajo Indian Reservation, 1947," 2, Socio-economic Conditions, Phoenix Area Office, Division of Extension and Industry, General Correspondence, 1931–1952, 1947, RG 75, NARA-LN.

27. O'Neill, "The 'Making' of the Navajo Worker," 379.

28. Iverson, *Navajo Nation*, 31, 51, 56; Iverson, *Diné*, 188–90; Iverson, *"For Our Navajo People"*; Bruce Gjeltema, Gallup NM, conversation with Leah S. Glaser, May 5, 2001; Zah, interview.

29. Proceedings of the Meeting of the Navajo Tribal Council, November 20–21, 1939, folder 9, box 3, Dodge Papers, ACASU.

30. Iverson, *Navajo Nation*, 53; Iverson, *Diné*, 209; Drefkoff, "An Industrial Program for the Navajo Reservation."

31. Iverson, *Navajo Nation*, 56–57; Wolf, interview.

32. Krug and Warne quoted in Needham, "A Piece of the Action"; see Cohen, *Consumers' Republic*, for a discussion of how Americans equated consumerism with democracy.

33. "Power and Light Plant, Sale to J. Taylor," July 24, 1951, and "Utilities, Manager of Tribal Enterprises Authorized to Negotiate Sale of," September 21, 1951, Advisory Committee Meeting in Navajo Tribal Council Resolutions (1922–1951), 381, 619, Navajo Tribal Council, Navajo Agency, Central Classified Files 53, RG 75, NARA-W; Bernstein, *American Indians and World War II*, 159–75.

34. See Needham, *Power Lines*, for more information on how energy development on reservations contributes to urban expansion in the Southwest.

35. Wilkinson, *Fire on the Plateau*, xiv.

36. Navajo Council Tribal Minutes, "Radio," February 10, 1954, 96, Central Classified Files 54, Navajo Agency, RG 75, NARA-W; Cronemeyer quoted in Iverson, *"For Our Navajo People,"* 106–8.

37. Navajo Council Tribal Minutes, January 5, 1953, Central Classified Files 54, Navajo Agency, RG 75, NARA-W.

38. D. V. Vann, "Tribal Council Sets Television Survey," *Navajo Times*, December 1959, 11–12; "Ganado Group Holds Television Drive," *Navajo Times*, November 1960, 3; "My Opinion," *Navajo Times*, January 31, 1962, 7.

39. Navajo Tribal Council Minutes, July 10, July 20, 1956, Central Classified Files 54, Navajo Agency, NARA-W; *Navajo Parade of Progress: Eleventh Annual Navajo Tribal Fair* (Window Rock AZ, August 1957); Nagata,
Modern Transformations of Moenkopi Pueblo, 76–80.

40. Navajo Tribal Council Minutes, July 10, July 20, 1956.

41. *Navajo Parade of Progress*.

42. Paul Jones, Inaugural Address, Chairman, Navajo Tribal Council, Series 84-88, box 3, folder 8, Goldwater Papers, AHF; "Navajo Tribe Requests Extension of Ten Year Program," *Navajo Times*, November 1958,
8; "$5 Million for Public Works Program," *Navajo Times*, November
1959, 12; "New Road Construction on the Navajo Reservation," *Navajo
Times*, December 1959, 9; "Low-Cost Housing for Navajos," *Navajo
Times*, February 1960, 4.

43. B. H. Critchfield to Assistant to the Commissioner of Indian Affairs,
March 8, 1950, District Director Classified Files, box 1, Phoenix Area
Office, 1947–1949, RG 75, NARA-LN; Navajo Tribal Council Minutes,
November 29–December 2, 1949, Central Classified Files 64, Navajo
Area Office, RG 75, NARA-LN.

44. Wolf, interview; Files 6825-49, 11083, 19440, 20025, Application and
Loan Division, Field Activities Reports, 1948–49, "New Mexico 22
McKinley," RG 221, NARA-CP; File no. 6825-49, Central Classified Files
377, Navajo Agency, 1949, RG 75, NARA-W; "NTUA Is Negotiating for
More Facilities," *Navajo Times*, July 30, 1964.

45. Heyer, "Progress through Power," 50; "Journal of the Navajo Tribal
Council," January 22, 1959, Central Classified Files 54, RG 75, NARA-W.

46. Accomplishment Report, Navajo Tribal Utility Authority, 1963, and
Annual Report of the Navajo Tribal Utility Authority, 1984, 7, Research
Library, NTUA-HQ; Eddy, interview.

47. "New Power System for Shiprock Area," *Navajo Times*, August 4, 1960,
12; Heyer, "Progress through Power," 50; "Journal of the Navajo Tribal
Council," January 22, 1959, RG 75, NARA-W; Wolf, interview.

48. Maurice McCabe, "Status Report on Power Distribution Reservation
Wide," August, 18, 1960, p. 87, box 101, file no. 00-1960, Central Classified Files 54, RG 75, NARA-W.

49. NTUA file 8699, 1960, RG 75, NARA-W; "Navajo Tribal Utility Report,"
Navajo Times, January 1961, 2; "New Power System for Shiprock Area."

50. Navajo Tribal Council Minutes, August 18, 1960, 89, Navajo Agency,
Central Classified Files 54, RG 75, NARA-W.

51. Navajo Tribal Council Minutes, August 18, 1960, 89.

52. Bruce Kipp, "Navajos Block Utility from Bringing Electricity to Hopis," *Phoenix Gazette*, April 15, 1960, 20.

53. See Farmer, *Glen Canyon Dammed*; Bureau of Reclamation, U.S. Department of the Interior, Operation of Glen Canyon Dam, Final Environmental Impact Statement, March 1995 (PDF version of document).

54. Young, *Political History of the Navajo Tribe*, 158–62; "New Power System for Shiprock Area"; Heyer, "Progress through Power," 51–53; "Power Facilities to Become Reality," *Navajo Times*, December 1960; "Electric Power Soon in Town of Navajo," *Navajo Times*, June 7, 1961; Leland Gardner, Walter J. Wolf Retirement Banquet, Gallup, New Mexico, May 4, 2001.

55. Pearson, "'We Have Almost Forgotten How to Hope.'"

56. Navajo Tribal Council Minutes, August 19, 1960, Navajo Agency Office, Central Classified Files 54, RG 75, NARA-W.

57. *The Fifteenth Annual Tribal Fair: The Era of Resource Development* (Window Rock AZ, September 7–10, 1961), 104.

58. Young, "A Decade of Progress"; Navajo Tribal Council Minutes, December 6, 1961, Navajo Agency Office, Central Classified Files 54, RG 75, NARA-W; Wolf, interview.

59. File 8699, box 103, Central Classified Files 259, Navajo Agency, RG 75, NARA-W.

60. Telegram, Thomas G. Morris and Joseph M. Montoya, Members of Congress to Paul Jones, Chairman, Navajo Tribal Council, September 7, 1961, box 313, folder 88, Hayden Papers, ACASU; "REA Power to Be Considered," *Navajo Times*, February 28, 1962.

61. Eddy, interview; Wolf, interview.

62. Navajo Agency and Tribal Minutes, November 1961, Navajo Agency, NTUA file, Central Classified Files 54, RG 75, NARA-W.

63. Tribal Minutes, November 1961, Navajo Agency, Central Classified Files 54, Navajo Agency, RG 75, NARA-W; Iverson, "Peter McDonald," 223; Iverson, *Diné*, 246.

64. Navajo Tribal Council Minutes, November 30, 1961, December 1, 1961, Navajo Agency Office, Central Classified Files 54, RG 75, NARA-W.

65. "Arizona Power Line Finished Months Ahead of Schedule," *Navajo Times*, September 19, 1962, 16; "Electric Power Soon in Town of Navajo"; "Tribal Utilities Builds New Line," *Navajo Times*, August 23, 1961, 4; Wolf, interview.

66. "Electric Power Comes to Tribe, Tribal Utility Authority Energizes Line System," *Navajo Times*, May 30, 1962; "Tribal Utility Authority Energizes Power Line System," "A Switch Is Pulled," "A Light Goes On," and "Backbone Transmission Project Brings Light to Hogan," *Navajo Times*, June 13, 1962; "NTUA: 'A Light in Every Hogan,'" *Navajo Times*, September 5, 1962, 1.

67. "Accomplishment Report for the Navajo Tribal Utility Authority," 1963, 7, NTUA-HQ; Annual Report of the Navajo Tribal Utility Authority, 1969, 1–2, 1970, 1971, NTUA-HQ; C. Mac Eddy to Management Board, June 8, 1969, General Manager's Files, 1960–1990, Records Management, NTUA-HQ; Sheridan, *Arizona*, 301.

68. D. G. Callaway, J. E. Levy, and E. B. Henderson, *The Effects of Power Production and Strip Mining on Local Navajo Populations*, Lake Powell Research Project Bulletin no. 22 (Los Angeles: Institute of Geophysics and Planetary Physics, University of California, June 1976), 13; John D. Grahame and Thomas D. Sisk, eds., "Power Generation on the Colorado Plateau," at *Canyons, Cultures, and Environmental Change: An Introduction to the Land Use History on the Colorado Plateau*, http://www.cpluhna.nau.edu; Lewis, "Native Americans and the Environment."

69. Navajo Tribal Council Minutes, 1963–1966, Central Classified Files 54, Navajo Agency, RG 75, NARA-W; Accomplishment Report, Navajo Tribal Utility Authority, 1963, and Annual Report of the Navajo Tribal Utility Authority, 1999, NTUA-HQ; Wolf, interview.

70. Wolf, interview; Eddy, interview; Mac Eddy, General Manager, NTUA, to Richard Wood, Assistant Administrator, REA, March 16, 1966, box 313, folder 88, Hayden Papers, ACASU; E. R. Brown, REA, to Eddy, February 20, 1968, General Manager's File, Records Management, NTUA-HQ.

71. Eddy, interview; Wolf, interview; Dalton, interview; Annual Report of the Navajo Tribal Utility Authority, 1984, 13–14, NTUA-HQ.

72. Revised Plan of Operation, October 12, 1965, NTUA-HQ.

73. Eddy, interview; Annual Report of the Navajo Tribal Utility Authority, 1967, 3, NTUA-HQ.

74. Annual Report of the Navajo Tribal Utility Authority, 1966, 1984, NTUA-HQ; Eddy, interview.

75. Mac Eddy to Management Board, March 9, 1970, General Manager's Files, Records Management, NTUA-HQ; Niethammer, *I'll Go and Do More*, 177; Dalton, interview; Eddy, interview.

76. "Power Supply Study," October 23, 1967, and Roy Cleveland to Malcolm

Dalton, September 11, 1987, General Manager's Files, Records Management, NTUA-HQ; Benally, interview.

77. Wolf, interview; Eddy, interview; Mac Eddy, General Manager, NTUA, to Richard Wood, Assistant Administrator, REA, March 16, 1966, box 313, folder 88, Hayden Papers, ACASU; E. R. Brown, REA, to Eddy, February 20, 1968, General Manager's File, Records Management, NTUA-HQ.

78. Kipp, "Navajos Block Utility," 20; Jim Cook, "Oldest Town Finally Gets Electricity," *Arizona Republican*, November 28, 1961, 16; Annual Reports of the Navajo Tribal Utility Authority, Records Management, NTUA-HQ; Brugge, *Navajo-Hopi Land Dispute*, 155–58.

79. Mac Eddy to Management Board, July 18, 1969, and Annual Report, 1984, 34, General Manager's Files, Records Management, NTUA-HQ; Betty Begay to Barry Goldwater, June 16, 1975, and Val McBrown to Barry Goldwater, November 7, 1975, Goldwater Papers, AHF.

80. For more information on these laws see King, *Cultural Resource Laws and Practice*, 51–190, 276–77.

81. Navajo Tribal Council Minutes, 1965, Central Classified Files 54, RG 75, NARA-W; "A Few of the Many Chapter Houses for Community Use," *Navajo Times*, November 25, 1965, 10–11; Benally, interview.

82. Annual Report of the Navajo Tribal Utility Authority, 1984, 33, NTUA-HQ; Dalton, interview.

83. Robert Autobee, "A Piece of Gold: The Struggle to Build the Navajo Power Plant" (paper presented at the Thirty-ninth Annual Conference of the Western History Association, Portland, October 8, 1999), copy in author's possession.

84. Wolf, interview.

85. "NTUA: 'A Light in Every Hogan,'" 1.

86. "Total Power and Energy Requirements, Navajo Tribal Utility Authority," in R. W. Beck and Associates, "Electrical System Study, NTUA" (October 1969), II-5, Records Management, NTUA-HQ; Iverson, *Diné*, 188–89; Zah, interview; Benally, interview.

87. "A Century of Progress," *Navajo Times*, June 18, 1968; Link, interview.

88. Advertisements, *Navajo Times*, 1960–1968; "Tribal Utility Authority Energizes Power Line System," *Navajo Times*, April 25, 1962, 9.

89. "House Wiring for the People," Annual Report of the Navajo Tribal Utility Authority, 1966, 31, 32, NTUA-HQ; "Tribal Utilities Builds New Line," 4–5.

90. Laverne Bartos, "The NTUA Story" (Window Rock AZ: Navajo Tribal

Utility Authority, 1968), copy in Department of the Interior Library, Washington DC; "NTUA Holds Safety Session," *Navajo Times*, October 5, 1967, 12; Eddy, interview.

91. Kipp, "Navajos Block Utility," 20; Cook, "Oldest Town Finally Gets Electricity," 16.

92. Eddy, interview; "Up, Up, and Away?" *Navajo Times*, May 2, 1968, 18; Heyer, "Progress through Power," 51; Annual Report of the Navajo Tribal Utility Authority, 1999, NTUA-HQ.

93. Kluckhohn and Leighton, *The Navaho*, 45; Al Harvey, "Navajos Making Better Homes in District 16," *Navajo Times*, June 3, 1965; see Niethammer, *I'll Go and Do More*, for more on Annie Dodge Wauneka.

94. Division of Extension and Industry Annual Reports, Central Classified Files box 350, RG 75, NARA-LN; Home Demonstration Agent Report, 1953, Apache and Navajo Counties, AZ 302, SCUA; Annual Report of the Navajo Tribal Utility Authority, 1976, NTUA-HQ; Benally, interview.

95. Navajo Tribal Council Minutes, December 6, 1961, Central Classified Files 54, RG 75, NARA-W; Eddy, interview; Benally, interview; Zah, interview.

96. Deesheeny Nez Tracy in B. Johnson, *Traditional Navajo Life and Culture*, 157.

97. "Housing Plans on the Navajo Reservation," *Navajo Times*, January 3, 1962; Record of Advisory Committee, p. 173, April 6, 1964, Navajo Area Office, Central Classified Files 54, RG 75, NARA-W.

98. "Membership of Hopi Clubs Growing Fast" and "Hopi 4-H Clubs Do Things," *Arizona Farmer Ranchman*, March 17, 1956.

99. Mills, *Hopi Survival Kit*, 12; "Ralph Selina, Hopi," translated by Thomas Ban Yacya, folder 18, AZ 374, SCUA; Brugge, *Navajo-Hopi Land Dispute*, 165–66; Clemens, *Roads in the Sky*, 194.

100. Terez Jolan, "Hotevilla Wins," AZ 374, SCUA.

101. Mills, *Hopi Survival Kit*, 12; "Construction of Road and Utility Line Causes Rift at Hotevilla," *Hopi Action News*, May 23, 1968; Nagata, *Modern Transformations of Moenkopi Pueblo*, 80; Clemens, *Roads in the Sky*, 194.

102. Editorial, *Hopi Action News*, August 5, 1966; "Problems of My Community," *Hopi Action News*, November 18, 1966; "A Student's Viewpoint of Hotevilla," *Hopi Action News*, July 12, 1968.

103. Benedek, *The Wind Don't Know Me*, 25; Lewis, "Reservation Leadership."

104. Nagata, *Modern Transformations of Moenkopi Pueblo*, 209–11.

105. *Hopi Action News*, September 9, 1966, 4.

106. Nagata, *Modern Transformations of Moenkopi Pueblo*, 80; Clemens, *Roads in the Sky*, 194; Winona La Duke, "Traditionalists Get Electricity without Objectionable Power Lines: Hopi Woman Is Solar Electrician for the Hopi Foundation," *News from Indian Country*, November 15, 1994, 8.

107. Benally, interview; Benedek, *The Wind Don't Know Me*, 14.

108. Quoted in Amerman, "Newcomers to the Urban West," 35.

109. "New TV Business Is Opened Here," *Navajo Times*, March 28, 1963; "TV-Radio Service Opened by Navajo," *Navajo Times*, April 11, 1963; Kaibeto School to Goldwater, Congressional Papers, 92nd Congress, box 52, folder 5, Goldwater Papers, AHF; Annual Report of the Navajo Tribal Utility Authority, 1965, 1–2, Research Library, NTUA-HQ.

110. Navajo Tribal Council Minutes, 1964, Central Classified Files 54, RG 75, NARA-W.

111. Deescheeny Nez Tracy in B. Johnson, *Traditional Navajo Life and Culture*, 164, 165.

112. Rada, "Rameh Navajo Radio," 365; B. L. Smith and Brigham, "Native Radio Broadcasting in North America"; Kent, "The Effects of Television Viewing."

113. Benally, interview; Bartos, "The NTUA Story"; Deescheeny Nez Tracy in B. Johnson, *Traditional Navajo Life and Culture*, 165; Nagata, *Modern Transformations of Moenkopi Pueblo*, 208–11.

114. National Advisory Commission, *Rural Poverty*; Bechtel Corporation, "Electric System Planning and NTUA Organizational Study" (March 1964), in Records Management, NTUA-HQ; Janelle Goatson, "HUD and NTUA Provide Electricity for Kaibeto Homes," *Navajo Times*, August 10, 1995, A11; Annual Report of the Navajo Tribal Utility Authority, 1971, NTUA-HQ; "Trailer Utility Charges by NTUA," *Navajo Times*, January 6, 1969, 4.

115. Benedek, *The Wind Don't Know Me*, 227, 230–31.

116. Betty Begay to Barry Goldwater, 1975, 94th Congress, box 84, folder 43, Goldwater Papers.

117. Navajo Tribal Council Minutes, December 6, 1961, Central Classified Files 54, RG 75, NARA-W; Bartos, "The NTUA Story"; Benally, interview.

118. "NTUA Has Lowest Rates in Area," *Network*, September 1993, 1; "A Summary Presentation to the Navajo Tribal Council of the Overall

Structure, Purpose, and Growth of the Navajo Tribal Utility Authority" (January 1983), table II, NTUA-HQ; Energy Information Administration, "Energy Consumption and Renewable Energy Development Potential on Indian Lands" (Washington DC: U.S. Department of Energy, March 2000), ix; Zah, interview.

119. Bailey and Bailey, *History of the Navajos*, 281; U.S. Bureau of the Census, *Census of Housing: 1970, Volume 1, Housing Characteristics for States, Cities, and Counties. Arizona* (Washington DC: Government Printing Office, 1972); U.S. Bureau of the Census, "American Indians," *Census of the Population: 1970, Subject Report* (Washington DC: Government Printing Office, 1973), table 10; Tobey, *Technology as Freedom.*

120. Clemens, *Roads in the Sky*, 277; Bailey and Bailey, *History of the Navajos*, 283–85; "Who Are NTUA's Customers and What Are Their Utility Needs?" *Network*, March 1993, 3; National Rural Electrification Cooperative Association Market Research, "Navajo Tribal Utility Authority Consumer Attitude Survey Results" (Lincoln NE: National Rural Electrification Cooperative Association Market Research, May 1988), NTUA-HQ.

121. "Grand Prize," *Navajo Times*, October 10, 1963, 3; photograph caption, *Navajo Times*, April 8, 1965, 11; Maggie Wilson, "Opposing Cultures of Navajos Meet Head On," *Navajo Times*, August 1, 1962.

122. Benally, interview; Dockstader, "Tradition Updated," 40; Andrew Nagen, "A Personal Look at Navajo Weavings," *The Wingspread Collector's Guide to Santa Fe, Taos and Albuquerque* 15 (2001).

123. Kluckhohn, "Navahos in the Machine Age," 197.

124. H. W. Johnson, "Rural Indian Americans in Poverty," i–ii, 2.

125. Quoted in Trimble, *The People*, 122, 126.

126. Reisner, *Cadillac Desert*; White, *The Organic Machine*; Worster, *Rivers of Empire*; O'Neill, *Working the Navajo Way*.

127. Wolf, interview.

128. Iverson, *Navajo Nation*, xxiii–xxiv; Iverson, *Diné*, 188–89; Zah, interview.

129. Zah, interview; Earl and Sorrell quoted in Annual Report of the Navajo Tribal Utility Authority, 1999, 20, NTUA-HQ.

130. "NTUA and Tucson Electric Power Enter Power Supply Agreement," *Network*, February 1993, 1, 4.

131. Ambler, *Breaking the Iron Bonds.*

Conclusion

1. Harold Roberts, "He Was There When It All Began," *Arizona Currents*, December 1977, 4.
2. Arizona State Planning Board, "Report of the Power Survey Committee of Arizona Section, American Society of Civil Engineers" (Phoenix, November 20, 1934), 32.
3. Lowitt, *The New Deal and the West*, 227–28.
4. See Cannon, "Power Relations," for another study which concludes that the REA challenged individualism.
5. Sheridan, *Arizona*, 304, 306.
6. These included Sulphur Springs Valley Electric Cooperative at Willcox, Littlefield Electric Cooperative at Littlefield, Graham County Electric Cooperative at Pima, Trico Electric Cooperative near Marana, Verde Electric Cooperative in Cottonwood, Mohave Electric Cooperative at Kingman, Duncan Valley Electric Cooperative at Duncan, and Navopache Electric Cooperative at Lakeside.
7. Ross, "Every Home a Laboratory," 22.
8. Nye, *Electrifying America*, 384.
9. Spence, "Early Uses of Electricity," 147.
10. "San Bernardino Valley Residents to Get Electric Service," *Currents*, Summer 1991, 1, 11; "Electricity at Last!" *Currents*, Fall 1991, 1–2; Twila Shelton, interview.
11. *The HiLiner*, February 1965, 6, 7, 9, copy at SSVEC.
12. Gaskell, interview.
13. Underground Water Commission, "The Underground Water Resources of Arizona" (20th Legislature of the State of Arizona, January 1, 1953), 121–25, ACASU; Bliss, County Agent Report, 1940, AZ 301, SCUA; Schultz, *Southwestern Town*, 96; V. W. Lee, "Economic Factors," 91; Sloan, interview; Frank and Twila Shelton, interview.
14. "Grapes in the Desert: Could Willcox Be Wine Country?" *Arizona Range News*, February 22, 2006; A. O. Kime, "Kansas Settlement, Arizona: A Farming Community," at *Matrix of Mnemosyne*, http://www.matrixbookstore.biz/kansas_settlement.htm.
15. See Tobey, *Technology as Freedom*, for a discussion of how segregation affected electrification patterns in an urban setting.
16. For more on controversies in energy development on Native American reservations, see Farmer, *Glen Canyon Dammed*; Chamberlain, *Under Sacred Ground*; Lewis, "Native Americans and the Environment"; S. L. Smith and Frehner, *Indians and Energy*.

17. L. A. Robbins, *Navajo Energy Politics*, 1; D. G. Callaway, J. E. Levy, and E. B. Henderson, *The Effects of Power Production and Strip Mining on Local Navajo Populations*, Lake Powell Research Project Bulletin no. 22 (Los Angeles: Institute of Geophysics and Planetary Physics, University of California, June 1976).

18. Mander, *In the Absence of the Sacred*.

19. Deloria, "Traditional Technology."

20. James, "Conclusions," 166.

21. For discussions of Native American responses to capitalism and technology, see Ambler, *Breaking the Iron Bonds*; Catton, *Inhabited Wilderness*; Fixico, *Invasion of Indian Country*; Hosmer, *American Indians in the Marketplace*; Colleen O' Neill, *Working the Navajo Way*, 142–59; Lewis, "Reservation Leadership."

22. Paul Chaat Smith, exhibit text for *Our People* (National Museum of the American Indian, 2003). Throughout the museum the exhibit text references the term "survivance," coined by Gerald Vizenor in *Manifest Manners* to mean, according to Smith's exhibit text, "more than survival . . . holding on to ancient principles while eagerly embracing change. It means doing what is necessary to keep cultures alive."

23. Cohen, *Consumers' Republic*, 404.

24. Robert Kuttner, "An Industry Trapped by Theory," *New York Times*, August 16, 2003.

25. Jamie Reno, "The Blackout of 2000: Why the Power Industry Can't Meet Surging Demand," *Newsweek*, August 14, 2000, 33; Max Jarman, "Electric Deregulation Hits Poor Arizona Areas Hard," *Arizona Republic*, August 16, 2000, A1.

26. Annual Report of the Navajo Tribal Utility Authority, 40th Anniversary Edition, 1999, 17, NTUA-HQ; Declan McCullagh, "Clinton Tackles Digital Divide," *Wired News*, February 22, 2000, http://www.wired.com/news/politics/0,1283,33002,00.html; Kathleen Ingley, "Rural Arizona Poverty Persists," *Arizona Republic*, November 22, 2000, B1–2; "Students in Tribe Go Online," *Tempe Tribune*, April 26, 1999, B3.

27. Energy Information Administration, "Energy Consumption and Renewable Energy Development on Indian Lands" (Washington DC: U.S. Department of Energy, March 2000); Lisa Nurnberger, "Native American Phones," *All Things Considered*, National Public Radio, aired October 20, 1999.

28. "Arizona Accelerates Solar Electricity Access for Tribes," *U.S. States*

News, August 28, 2007; Michelle Rushlo, "Sun Powers Navajo Homes through New Program," *Associated Press State and Local Wire*, March 5, 2000.

29. Felicity Barringer, "Navajos Hope for Millions a Year from Power Plant," *New York Times*, July 27, 2007, A14; Powell and Long, "Landscapes of Power."

30. Richardson, "Role and Performance of Public Power," 14; Munson, *From Edison to Enron*, 186–87.

Bibliography

Manuscript Collections

Arizona Collection, Archives and Special Collections, Hayden Library, Arizona State University, Tempe
    Thomas Chee Dodge Papers
    Carl T. Hayden Papers
    Lloyd Henning Papers
Arizona Electric Power Cooperative, Benson, Arizona
Arizona Historical Foundation, Hayden Library, Arizona State University, Tempe
    Paul Fannin Papers
    Galbreath Development Company Papers
    Barry Goldwater Papers
Arizona Historical Society, Tucson
    Isabella Greenway Papers
Arizona State Archives, Arizona State Library, Archives and Public Records, Phoenix
    Record Group 1, Governor's Office, Subgroups 10, 12, 14, 16, 17, 18, 20 (Governors Phillips, Stanford, Osborn, Pyle, Fannin, McFarland, Williams)
    Record Group 26, Arizona Commission on Indian Affairs
    Record Group 29, Arizona Corporation Commission
    Record Group 75, Records of the Arizona Power Authority
    Record Group 91, Works Progress Administration
Frank Norris Library, National Rural Electrification Cooperative Association Building, Arlington, Virginia
Grand Canyon State Electric Cooperative, Phoenix, Arizona
National Archives and Records Administration, College Park, Maryland
    Record Group 83, Bureau of Agricultural Economics

Record Group 207, Department of Housing and Urban Development
Record Group 221, Rural Electrification Administration
National Archives and Records Administration, Pacific Region, Laguna
Niguel, California
Record Group 48, Office of the Secretary of the Interior
Record Group 75, Bureau of Indian Affairs
National Archives Building, Washington DC
Record Group 75, Bureau of Indian Affairs
Navajo Tribal Utility Authority Corporate Headquarters, Ft. Defiance,
Arizona
Records Management
Research Library
Navopache Electric Cooperative, Lakeside, Arizona
Salt River Project Research Archives, Salt River Project, Tempe, Arizona
Special Collections, Main Library, University of Arizona, Tucson
AZ 302, Reports of Home Demonstration Agents, 1918–1958
AZ 304, Reports of the University of Arizona Agricultural Extension
Service, 1918–1958
AZ 374, Hopi Traditionalist Movement Papers
Sulphur Springs Valley Electric Cooperative, Willcox, Arizona

Interviews

*All interviews were conducted by the author, and the tapes are in the
author's possession, unless otherwise noted.*

Benally, Ancita. Tempe, Arizona. March 29, 2001.

Bethel, Howard. Willcox, Arizona. April 2, 1998.

Blake, Vera. McNary, Arizona. July 28, 2000.

Dalton, Malcolm. Chandler, Arizona. May 19, 2001.

Eddy, C. Mac. Phoenix, Arizona. April 8, 1998.

Endfield, Raymond. Flagstaff, Arizona. July 23, 2001.

Gaskell, William. Willcox, Arizona. August 6, 2000.

Hill, Bill. Benson, Arizona. August 6, 2000.

Irving, Violet. Interview by Pamela Hronek, September 30, 1981. Tran-
script. Arizona State Women's Studies Department, Women's
Studies Oral History Project, the Lives of Arizona Women, Private
Conversations and Public Issues, Arizona Collections, University
Libraries, Department of Archives and Manuscripts, Arizona State
University, Tempe.

Layton, Erdine. Thatcher, Arizona. August 7, 2000.

Lee, Esther. Lakeside, Arizona. July 27, 2000.

Link, Martin. Gallup, New Mexico. May 5, 2001.

"McNary Day" participants. Lakeside, Arizona. September 3, 2000. Survey sheets in the possession of the author.

McNulty, James. Tucson, Arizona. June 14, 2000.

Peck, Nelson. Pima, Arizona. August 7, 2000.

Rhoten, Kent. Lakeside, Arizona. July 26, 2000.

Shelton, Frank and Twila. Willcox, Arizona. August 6, 2000

Sloan, Gordon. Willcox, Arizona. August 6, 2000.

Weech, Cherrel. Pima, Arizona. August 7, 2000.

Wolf, Walter J., Jr. Gallup, New Mexico. April 23, 1998.

Zah, Peterson. Tempe, Arizona. March 26, 2001.

Published Sources

Abbott, Carl. *The Metropolitan Frontier: Cities in the Modern American West.* Tucson: University of Arizona Press, 1993.

Ambler, Marjane. *Breaking the Iron Bonds: Indian Control of Energy Development.* Lawrence: University Press of Kansas, 1990.

Amerman, Stephen Kent. "Newcomers to the Urban West: Navajos and Samoans in Salt Lake City, Utah, 1945–95." Master's thesis, Utah State University, 1996.

Andrews, Dean Tim. "Rural Electrification in the United States, 1954–1964," a list of selected references. Copy in Washington DC, National Agricultural Library, 1966.

Applewhite, Karen Miller. *On the Road to Nowhere: A History of Greer, Arizona, 1879–1979.* Phoenix: Karen Miller Applewhite, 1979.

Bailey, Garrick, and Robert Glenn Bailey. *A History of the Navajos: The Reservation Years.* Santa Fe NM: School of American Research Press, 1986.

Barron, Hal S. *Mixed Harvest: The Second Transformation of the Rural North, 1870–1930.* Chapel Hill: University of North Carolina Press, 1997.

Barry, Tom. "Appropriate Technology as Indian Technology." *American Indian Journal* 5 (October 1979): 2–9.

Benedek, Emily. *The Wind Don't Know Me: A History of the Navajo-Hopi Land Dispute.* New York: Vintage Books, 1993.

Benton, Katherine Alexa. "What about Women in the White Man's Camp? Gender, Nation, and the Redefinition of Race in Cochise County, Arizona, 1853–1941." PhD diss., University of Wisconsin–Madison, 2002.

Benton-Cohen, Katherine. "Common Purposes, Worlds Apart: Mexican-American, Mormon, and Midwestern Women Homesteaders in Cochise County, Arizona." *Western Historical Quarterly* 26 (Winter 2005): 429–52.

Bernstein, Alison R. *American Indians and World War II: Toward a New Era in Indian Affairs.* Norman: University of Oklahoma Press, 1991.

Boman, Brian J. *Consumptive Use on the Navajo Indian Irrigation Project.* Farmington NM: Bureau of Reclamation, 1984.

Brigham, Jay L. *Empowering the West: Electrical Politics before FDR.* Lawrence: University Press of Kansas, 1998.

———. "Lighting the Reservation: The Impact of the Rural Electrification Administration on Native Lands." *Journal of the West* 40 (Winter 2001): 81–88.

Brown, D. Clayton. *Electricity for Rural America: The Fight for the REA.* Westport CT: Greenwood Press, 1980.

Brugge, David M. *The Navajo-Hopi Land Dispute: An American Tragedy.* Albuquerque: University of New Mexico Press, 1994.

Cannon, Brian Q. "Power Relations: Western Rural Electric Cooperatives and the New Deal." *Western Historical Quarterly* 31 (Summer 2000): 133–60.

Capeheart, Loretta, and Dragan Milovanivic. *Social Justice: Theories, Issues, and Movements.* New Brunswick NJ: Rutgers University Press, 2007.

Capps, Inez H. "Social Change among the White Mountain Apache Indians from 1800s to the Present." Master's thesis, Montana State University, 1952.

Castaneda, Christopher J. "Energy in the West." *Journal of the West* 44 (Winter 2005): 5–7.

Catton, Theodore. *Inhabited Wilderness: Indians, Eskimos, and National Parks in Alaska.* Albuquerque: University of New Mexico Press, 1997.

Chamberlain, Kathleen P. *Under Sacred Ground: A History of Navajo Oil, 1922–1982.* Albuquerque: University of New Mexico Press, 2000.

Childs, Marquis. *The Farmer Takes a Hand: The Electric Power Revolution in Rural America.* New York: Doubleday, 1952.

Clapp, Norman M. "Crisis in Rural Electrification." Washington DC: Government Printing Office, October 1961.

———. "Re-energizing Rural Electrification." Washington DC: Government Printing Office, August 1962.

Clemens, Richard. *Roads in the Sky: The Hopi Indian in a Century of Change.* Boulder: Westview Press, 1995.

Cohen, Lizabeth. *A Consumers' Republic: The Politics of Mass Consumption in Postwar America*. New York: Knopf, 2003.

Collins, William S. *The New Deal in Arizona*. Phoenix: Arizona State Parks Board, 1999.

Cowan, Ruth Schwartz. *More Work for Mother: The Ironies of Household Technology from the Open Hearth to the Microwave*. New York: Basic Books, 1983.

Coyle, David Cushman. *Electric Power on the Farm*. Washington DC: Government Printing Office, 1936.

Cronon, William. *Nature's Metropolis: Chicago and the Great West*. New York: Norton, 1991.

Davis, Charles. "Indians of the United States: Investigations of the Field Service." In *Hearings by a Subcommittee of the Commission on Indian Affairs*, 3:929–33. Washington DC: Government Printing Office, 1920.

DeGraaf, Leonard. "Corporate Liberalism and Electric Power System Planning in the 1920s." *Business History Review* 64 (Spring 1990): 1–31.

Deloria, Vine, Jr. "Traditional Technology." *Winds of Change* 5 (Spring 1990): 12–17.

De Luna, Phyllis Komarek. *Public versus Private Power during the Truman Administration*. New York: Peter Lang, 1997.

Deutsch, Sarah. *No Separate Refuge: Culture, Class, and Gender on an Anglo-Hispanic Frontier in the American Southwest, 1880–1940*. Oxford: Oxford University Press, 1987.

Dobyns, Henry. *The Apache People*. Phoenix: Indian Tribal Series, 1971.

Dockstader, Frederick J. "Tradition Updated: Contemporary Navajo Weavers Have Experimented Boldly, Developing New Forms and Even New Techniques." *American Craft* 47 (August–September 1987): 39–44.

Ellis, Clyde. *A Giant Step*. New York: Random House, 1966.

Etulain, Richard, ed. *Does the Frontier Experience Make America Exceptional?* Boston: Bedford St. Martin's, 1999.

Farris, N. T. "The Demand for Electric Power in Arizona, 1959–1966." *Arizona Business Bulletin*, March 1967, 62–72.

Farmer, Jared. *Glen Canyon Dammed: Inventing Lake Powell and the Canyon Country*. Tucson: University of Arizona Press, 1999.

Fixico, Donald Lee. *The Invasion of Indian Country: American Capitalism and Tribal Natural Resources*. Boulder: University of Colorado Press, 1998.

Flammer, Gordon H. *Stories of a Mormon Pioneering Community: Linden, Arizona of the Little Colorado Arizona Mission, 1878–1945*. Sandy UT: Excel Graphic, 1995.

Funigiello, Philip. *Toward a National Power Policy: The New Deal and the Electric Utility Industry, 1933–1941.* Pittsburgh: University of Pittsburgh Press, 1973.

Glaser, Leah S. "'An Absolute Paragon of Paradoxes': Native American Power and the Electrification of Arizona's Indian Reservations." In *Indians and Energy: Exploitation and Opportunity in the Southwest,* ed. Sherry L. Smith and Brian Frehner. Santa Fe NM: School for Advanced Research Press, forthcoming.

———. "Rural Electrification in Multiethnic Arizona: A Study of Power, Urbanization, and Change." PhD diss., Arizona State University, 2002.

Gray, Lawrence Roderick. "A Survey of Public Utility Regulation in Arizona with Special Reference to Electric Utilities." PhD diss., University of Virginia, 1938.

Groth, Paul, and Todd W. Bressi, eds. *Understanding Ordinary Landscapes.* New Haven: Yale University Press, 1997.

Hargreaves, Mary W. M. *Dry Farming in the Great Northern Plains: Years of Readjustment, 1920–1990.* Lawrence: University Press of Kansas, 1993.

Hathaway, Dale E., J. Allan Beegle, and W. Keith Bryant. *People of Rural America.* Washington DC: U.S. Department of Commerce, 1960.

Hay, Duncan. *Hydroelectric Development in the United States, 1880–1940.* Washington DC: Edison Electric Institute, 1991.

Heyer, Jo. "Progress through Power: Electrical Training for the Navajo Tribe." Santa Fe: Reynolds Electrical & Engineering Co., 1962.

Hinton, Leanne. "Oral Traditions and the Advent of Electric Power." In *Technology and Women's Voices: Keeping in Touch,* ed. Cheris Kramarae, 180–86. New York: Routledge and Kegan Paul, 1988.

Hirsh, Richard. *Power Loss: The Origins of Deregulation and Restructuring in the American Electric Utility System.* Boston: MIT Press, 1999.

Hodge, C. "Electrifying Arizona: A Short History." *Arizona Highways,* August 1988, 14–19.

Hosmer, Brian. *American Indians in the Marketplace: Persistence and Innovation among the Menominees and Metlakatlans, 1870–1920.* Lawrence: University Press of Kansas, 1999.

Houghton, N. D. "Problems in Public Power Administration in the Southwest—Some Arizona Application." *Western Political Quarterly* 4 (March 1951): 116–29.

Hoy, Suellen M., Michael C. Robinson, and Ellis L. Armstrong. *History of Public Works in the United States, 1776–1976.* Chicago: American Public Works Association, 1976.

Hughes, Thomas Parke. *American Genesis: A Century of Invention and Technological Enthusiasm, 1870–1970*. New York: Viking University Press, 1989.

———. *Networks of Power: Electrification in Western Society, 1880–1930*. Baltimore: Johns Hopkins University Press, 1983.

Hurt, Douglas. "REA: A New Deal for Farmers." *Timeline* 2 (December 1985/January 1986): 32–47.

———, ed. *The Rural West since World War II*. Lawrence: University Press of Kansas, 1998.

Iverson, Peter. *Diné: A History of the Navajos*. Albuquerque: University of New Mexico Press, 2002.

———, ed. *"For Our Navajo People": Diné Letters, Speeches, and Petitions, 1900–1960*. Albuquerque: University of New Mexico Press, 2002.

———. *The Navajo Nation*. Westport CT: Greenwood Press, 1981.

———. "Peter McDonald." In *American Indian Leaders: Studies in Diversity*, ed. R. David Edmunds, 222–43. Lincoln: University of Nebraska Press, 1980.

James, Keith. "Conclusions: Closing the Circuit." In *Science and Native American Communities: Legacies of Pain, Visions of Promise*, ed. Keith James, 165–66. Lincoln: University of Nebraska Press, 2001.

Jellison, Katherine *Entitled to Power: Farm Women and Technology, 1913–1963*. Chapel Hill: University of North Carolina Press, 1993.

Jensen, Joan. "Crossing Ethnic Barriers in the Southwest: Women's Agricultural Extension Education." In *Promise to the Land: Essays on Rural Women*, 220–30. Albuquerque: University of New Mexico Press, 1991.

———. *Promise to the Land: Essays on Rural Women*. Albuquerque: University of New Mexico Press, 1991.

Johnson, Broderick, ed. *Stories of Traditional Navajo Life and Culture*. Tsaile AZ: Navajo Community College Press, 1977.

Johnson, Helen W. "Rural Indian Americans in Poverty." Washington DC: Economic Research Service, U.S. Department of Agriculture, 1969.

Jones, P. "Report on Navajo Progress." *American Indian* 7 (Winter 1956): 21–26.

Kappler, Charles J., ed. *Indian Treaties, 1778–1883*. New York: Interland, 1972.

Keating, Ann Durkin. *Invisible Networks: Exploring the History of Local Utilities and Public Works*. Malabar FL: Krieger, 1994.

Kent, Susan. "The Effects of Television Viewing: A Cross-Cultural Perspective." *Current Anthropology* 26 (February 1985): 121–26.

King, Thomas. *Cultural Resource Laws and Practice: An Introductory Guide.* 2nd ed. New York: AltaMira Press, 2004.

Kline, Ronald R. *Consumers in the Country: Technology and Social Change in Rural America.* Baltimore: Johns Hopkins University Press, 2000.

Kluckhohn, Clyde. "The Navahos in the Machine Age: How a Primitive People through Unusual Capacity for Adaptation Have Prospered in Technological Times." *Technology Review* 44, no. 4 (1942): 178–80, 194–97.

Kluckhohn, Clyde, and Dorothea Leighton. *The Navaho.* Cambridge: Harvard University Press, 1958.

Knox, K. L. "Public Utility Regulation in Arizona." *Arizona Business Bulletin* 17 (March 1970): 3–13.

Kolstad, Charles, B. Grimmer, P. Reno, and J. Tutt. *Appropriate Technology and Navajo Economic Development.* Los Alamos NM: Los Alamos Scientific Laboratory of the University of California, 1976.

Kroeber, Karl. *Technology and Tribal Narrative.* Albuquerque: University of New Mexico Press, 1989.

Lee, Carol Anne. "Wired Help for the Farm: Individual Electric Generating Sets for Farms, 1880–1930." PhD diss., Pennsylvania State University, 1989.

Lee, Verren Wilson. "Economic Factors Affecting the Long Term Outlook for Irrigated Farming in Sulphur Springs Valley, Arizona." Master's thesis, University of Arizona, 1967.

Leeper, John. "The Impact of Water Control on Small Scale Navajo Irrigation Systems." PhD diss., Colorado State University, 1989.

Lewis, David Rich. "Native Americans and the Environment: A Survey of Twentieth Century Issues." *American Indian Quarterly* 19 (Summer 1995): 423–50.

———. "Native Americans: The Original Rural Westerners." In *The Rural West since World War II*, ed. Douglas Hurt, 12–37. Lawrence: University Press of Kansas, 1998.

———. "Reservation Leadership and the Progressive-Traditional Dichotomy: William Wash and the Northern Utes, 1865–1928." *Ethnohistory* 38 (Spring 1991): 124–48.

Limerick, Patricia Nelson, Clyde A. Milner II, and Charles E. Rankin, eds. *Trails: Toward a New Western History.* Lawrence: University Press of Kansas, 1991.

Lindstrom, David Edgar. *Farmers and Rural Organizations.* Champaign IL: Garrard Press, 1948.

Lipsitz, George. *The Possessive Investment in Whiteness: How White People Profit from Identity Politics.* Philadelphia: Temple University Press, 1998.

Long, Richard F. "The Big Hunt: Indians Seek Industry." *Opportunity* 2 (March 1972): 29–30.

Lowitt, Richard. *The New Deal and the West.* Norman: University of Oklahoma Press, 1984,

Mails, Thomas E. *The Hopi Survival Kit.* New York: Stewart, Tabori, and Chang, 1997.

Mander, Jerry. *In the Absence of the Sacred: The Failure of Technology and the Survival of the Indian Nations.* San Francisco: Sierra Club Books, 1991.

Martin, Patricia Preciado. *Songs My Mother Sang to Me: An Oral History of Mexican-American Women.* Tucson: University of Arizona, 1996.

Marvin, Carolyn. *When Old Technologies Were New: Thinking about Communications in the Late Nineteenth Century.* New York: Oxford University Press, 1988.

Marx, Leo. *The Machine in the Garden: Technology and the Pastoral Idea in America.* New York: Oxford University Press, 1964.

Matheney, Robert L. "Lumbering in the White Mountains of Arizona, 1919–1942." *Arizona and the West* 33 (1976): 237–56.

Matsumoto, Valerie. *Farming the Home Place: A Japanese Community in California, 1919–1982.* Ithaca NY: Cornell University Press, 1993.

May, Catherine L. "The Arizona Power Authority." Master's thesis, Arizona State University, 1999.

McPherson, R. S. *Sacred Land, Sacred View: Navajo Perceptions of the Four Corners Region.* Provo UT: Brigham Young University, 1992.

"Meeting the Utility Needs of the Navajo Nation." *Winds of Change* 3 (Spring 1988): 25–26.

Melcher, Mary. "Tending Children, Chickens, and Cattle: Southern Arizona Ranch and Farm Women, 1910–1949." PhD diss., Arizona State University, 1994.

Melosi, Martin V. *Coping with Abundance: Energy and the Environment in Industrial America.* New York: Knopf, 1985.

———. *The Sanitary City: Urban Infrastructure in America from Colonial Times to the Present.* Baltimore: Johns Hopkins University Press, 2000.

Meriam, Lewis, et al. *The Problem of Indian Administration: Summary of Findings and Recommendations.* Washington DC: Institute of Government Research, 1928.

Mills, Thomas E. *The Hopi Survival Kit.* New York: Stewart, Tabori, and Chang, 1997.

"Modern Technology in a Native Environment." *American Vocational Journal* 50 (1975): 15–53.

Munson, Richard. *From Edison to Enron: The Business of Power and What It Means for the Future of Electricity.* Westport CT: Praeger, 2005.

Myers, William Alan. "Electricity in Orange County, California, 1890–1940: A Case Study of the Socio-economic Impact of Technology." Master's thesis, California State University, Fullerton, 1991.

———. "Rejecting the Regulatory Compact: California Slides into Utility Restructuring." *Journal of the West* 44 (Winter 2005): 38–44.

Nagata, Shuichi. *Modern Transformations of Moenkopi Pueblo.* Urbana: University of Illinois Press, 1970.

Napier, Archk, and Tom Sasaki. "The Navajo in the Machine Age: Human Resources are Important, Too." *New Mexico Business* 11 (July 1958): 2–5.

Nash, Gerald D. "Science in the Wartime West." In *The American West Transformed: The Impact of the Second World War,* 1253–77. Lincoln: University of Nebraska Press, 1985.

National Advisory Commission. *Rural Poverty: Hearings before the National Advisory Commission on Rural Poverty—Tucson, Arizona, January 26 and 27, 1967.* Washington DC: Government Printing Office, September 1967.

Needham, T. Andrew. "'A Piece of the Action': Navajo Nationalism, Energy Development, and Metropolitan Inequality." In *Indians and Energy: Exploitation and Opportunity in the American Southwest,* ed. Sherry L. Smith and Brian Frehner. Santa Fe NM: School of Advanced Research Press, forthcoming.

———. *Power Lines: Urban Space, Energy Development, and the Making of the Modern Southwest, 1945–1975.* Princeton NJ: Princeton University Press, forthcoming.

Nelson, Paula M. "Rural Life and Social Change in the Rural West." In *The Rural West since World War II,* ed. Douglas Hurt, 38–57. Lawrence: University Press of Kansas, 1998.

Niethammer, Carolyn. *I'll Go and Do More: Annie Dodge Wauneka, Navajo Leader and Activist.* Lincoln: University of Nebraska Press, 2001.

Nye, David E. *American Technological Sublime.* Cambridge: MIT Press, 1994.

———. *Consuming Power: A Social History of American Energies.* Cambridge: MIT Press, 1998.

———. *Electrifying America: Social Meanings of a New Technology. 1880–1940*. Cambridge: MIT Press, 1990.

———. "Electrifying the West." In *The American West, as Seen by Europeans and Americans*, ed. Rob Kroes, 183–203. Amsterdam: Free University Press, 1989.

O'Neill, Colleen. "The 'Making' of the Navajo Worker: Navajo Households, The Bureau of Indian Affairs, and Off Reservation Wage Work, 1948–1960." *New Mexico Historical Review* 74 (October 1999): 375–405.

———. *Working the Navajo Way: Labor and Culture in the Twentieth Century*. Lawrence: University Press of Kansas, 2005.

Parman, Donald L. *The Navajos and the New Deal*. New Haven: Yale University Press, 1976.

Pascoe, Peggy. "Western Woman at the Cultural Crossroads." In *Trails: Toward a New Western History*, ed. Patricia Nelson Limerick, Clyde A. Milner II, and Charles E. Rankin, 40–58. Lawrence: University Press of Kansas, 1991.

Pearson, Byron E. "'We Have Almost Forgotten How to Hope:' The Hualupai, the Navajo, and the Fight for the Central Arizona Project, 1944–1968." *Western Historical Quarterly* 31 (Autumn 2000): 297–316.

Pence, Richard A., ed. *The Next Greatest Thing*. Washington DC: National Rural Electric Cooperative Association, 1984.

Peterson, Charles S. "Headgates and Conquest: The Limits of Irrigation on the Navajo Reservation, 1880–1950." *New Mexico Historical Review* 68 (July 1993): 269–90.

———. *Take Up Your Mission: Mormon Colonizing along the Little Colorado River, 1870–1900*. Tucson: University of Arizona Press, 1973.

Polk, Orval H. "An Economic Electric Power Survey of Arizona." PhD diss., University of Colorado, 1940.

Pomeroy, Earl. *The Pacific Slope: A History of California, Oregon, Washington, Idaho, Utah, and Nevada*. New York: Knopf, 1965.

Powell, Dana, and Dailan J. Long. "Landscapes of Power: Environmental Activism and Renewable Energy in Indian Country." In *Indians and Energy: Exploitation and Opportunity in the Southwest*, ed. Sherry L. Smith and Brian Frehner. Santa Fe NM: School for Advanced Research Press, forthcoming.

Pratt, Wayne Truman. "A Study of Changing Conditions among the White Mountain Apache Indians." Master's thesis, Texas A&M University, 1938.

President's National Advisory Commission on Rural Poverty. *The People Left Behind*. Washington DC: Government Printing Office, 1967.

Rada, Stephen E. "Rameh Navajo Radio and Cultural Preservation." *Journal of Broadcasting* 22, no. 3 (1978): 361–71.

Reddy, Marlita A., ed. *Statistical Record of Native North America*. Detroit: Gale Research, 1995.

Reisner, Marc. *Cadillac Desert: The American West and Its Disappearing Water*. New York: Penguin Books, 1993.

Reno, Philip. *Mother Earth, Father Sky, and Economic Development: Navajo Resources and their Use*. Albuquerque: University of New Mexico Press, 1981.

Richardson, Alan H. "The Role and Performance of Public Power: Separating Fact from Ideology." *Electricity Journal* 12 (June 1999): 14.

Robbins, L. A. *Navajo Energy Politics*. National Science Foundation, Lake Powell Research Project, Bulletin no. 54. Los Angeles: Institute of Geophysics and Planetary Physics, University of California, August 1977.

———. "The Navajo Nation and Industrial Development." *Southwestern Economics and Society* 2 (Spring 1977): 47–70.

Robbins, William G. *Colony and Empire: The Capitalist Transformation of the American West*. Lawrence: University Press of Kansas, 1994.

Rose, Mark. *Cities of Light and Heat: Domesticating Gas and Electricity in Urban America*. University Park: Pennsylvania State University Press, 1995.

Ross, Amy Elisa. "Every Home a Laboratory: Arizona Farm Women, the Extension Service, and Rural Modernization, 1932–1952." PhD diss., Arizona State University, 1998.

Rudolph, Richard, and Scott Ridley. *Power Struggle: The Hundred-Year War over Electricity*. New York: Harper and Row, 1986.

Ruiz, Vicki. *From Out of the Shadows: Mexican American Women in the Twentieth Century*. New York: Oxford University Press, 1998.

Rural Electrification Administration. *Annual Reports*. Washington DC: Government Printing Office, 1938–70.

———. *Annual Statistical Reports*. Washington DC: Government Printing Office, 1938–70.

Sasaki, Tom T. "Sociocultural Problems in Introducing New Technology on a Navaho Irrigation Project." *Rural Sociology* 21 (1956): 307–10.

Schackel, Sandra. "Ranch and Farm Women in the Contemporary American West." In *The Rural West since World War II*, ed. Douglas Hurt, 99–118. Lawrence: University Press of Kansas, 1998.

Schultz, Vernon B. *Southwestern Town: The Story of Willcox, Arizona.* Tucson: University of Arizona Press, 1964.

Sheridan, Thomas. *Arizona: A History.* Tucson: University of Arizona, 1995.

Smith, Bruce L., and Jerry C. Brigham, "Native Radio Broadcasting in North America: An overview of Systems in the United States and Canada." *Journal of Broadcasting and Electronic Media* 36, no. 2 (1992): 183–93.

Smith, Merritt Roe, and Leo Marx, eds. *Does Technology Drive History? The Dilemma of Technological Determinism.* Cambridge: MIT Press, 1994.

Smith, Roger Vernon. "The Operation of the Farmers Home Administration in Selected Areas of Arizona." Master's thesis, University of Arizona, 1958.

Smith, Sherry L., and Brian Frehner, eds. *Indians and Energy: Exploitation and Opportunity in the American Southwest.* Santa Fe NM: School of Advanced Research Press, forthcoming.

Simmons, Marc. *New Mexico: A Bicentennial History.* New York: Norton, 1977.

Sorensen, Barbara. "Sovereignty in the Utility Infrastructure—Recognizing Tribal Choices." *Winds of Change* 15 (Winter 2000): 26–31.

Spence, Clark C. "Early Uses of Electricity in American Agriculture." *Technology and Culture* 3, no. 2 (1962): 142–60.

Sternberg, Arnold C., and Catherine M. Bishop. *Indian Housing: 1961–1971, A Decade of Continuing Crisis in the United States.* Report prepared for the Committee on Interior and Insular Affairs, 94th Cong., 1st sess., February 1975, Committee Print.

Stubblefield, Thomas M. "Economic Survey of Navajo County." Tucson: Agricultural Extension Service, April 1953.

Sulphur Springs Valley Electric Cooperative. *The Power of Cooperation: A History of Sulphur Springs Valley Electric Cooperative, 1938–2003.* Willcox AZ: Sulphur Springs Valley Electric Cooperative, 2003.

Tobey, Ronald. *Technology as Freedom: The New Deal and the Electrical Modernization of the American Home.* Berkeley: University of California Press, 1995.

Trennert, Robert A., Jr. *The Phoenix Indian School: Forced Assimilation in Arizona, 1891–1935.* Norman: University of Oklahoma Press, 1988.

Trimble, Stephen. *The People: Indians of the American Southwest.* Santa Fe NM: School of American Research Press, 1993.

U.S. Congress, House, Committee on Interstate and Foreign Commerce.

A Bill to Provide for Rural Electrification and for Other Purposes. 74th Cong., 2nd sess. Washington DC: Government Printing Office, 1936.

U.S. Congress, House, Conference Report no. 2219, *Rural Electrification Act of 1936.* 74th Cong., 2nd sess. Washington DC: Government Printing Office, 1936.

U.S. Department of Agriculture. *Economic Needs of Farm Women.* Washington DC: Government Printing Office, 1915.

U.S. Federal Power Commission. *Arizona Power Survey.* Washington DC: Federal Power Commission, 1942.

Uth, Robert. *The Spirit of Cooperation.* Washington DC: Nat'l-Tele Productions, 1994.

Vizenor, Gerald. *Manifest Manners: Postindian Warriors of Survivance.* Middletown CT: Wesleyan University Press, 1994.

Von Hoffman, Alexander. *Local Attachments: The Making of an American Urban Neighborhood, 1850–1920.* Baltimore: Johns Hopkins University Press, 1994.

West, Elliot. "Walter Prescott Webb and the Search for the West." In *Writing Western History: Essays on Major Western Historians,* ed. Richard W. Etulain, 167–91. Albuquerque: University of New Mexico Press, 1991.

Westrum, Ron. *Technologies and Society: The Shaping of People and Things.* Belmont CA: Wadsworth, 1991.

White, Richard. *The Organic Machine: The Remaking of the Columbia River.* New York: Hill and Wang, 1995.

Wilkinson, Charles. *Fire on the Plateau: Conflict and Endurance in the American Southwest.* Washington DC: Island Press, 1999.

Williams, James. *Energy and the Making of Modern California.* Akron: University of Ohio Press, 1997.

Worster, Donald. *Rivers of Empire: Water, Aridity, and the Growth of the American West.* New York: Oxford University Press, 1985.

Wright, Forest Blythe. *Electricity in the Home and on the Farm.* 3rd ed. New York: Wiley, 1950.

Young, Robert W. "A Decade of Progress: The Navajo Yearbook Report." No. 8, 1951–1961. Window Rock AZ: Navajo Agency, 1961.

———. *A Political History of the Navajo Tribe.* Tsaile AZ: Navajo Community College Press, 1978.

Zucker, Ross. *Democratic Distributive Justice.* New York: Cambridge University Press, 2001.

Index

agriculture (cont.)
improvements, 57–61, 72, 87, 214; in White Mountain region, 78–83, 85, 98, 101. *See also* farmers; farms; irrigation; irrigation pumping; ranchers; ranching
Ahkeah, Sam, 146
Akimel O'odham (Pima) community, 25
Albert, Daisy, 143
alfalfa, 31, 54, 58
Alpine AZ, 81, 99, 102, 121
alternative energy, 7, 191, 223
Ambler, Marjane, 207
American Indian Science and Engineering Society, 219
American Legion Hall (Pinetop), 103, 105
American West: Arizona as representative of, 14, 18, 224; community power in, 210–15; effect of electrification on, 220; history of electricity in, 6–13; migrations to, 6; Native Americans and electricity in, 4; notions of progress in, 7–10, 11; political progress in, 8, 10–12; settlement patterns, 5; study of electrification of, 5, 8–13, 19–20. *See also* Arizona
America's Independent Electric Light and Power Companies, 110
Anasazi, 135
Apache County, 78, 79, 97, 101, 121, 127. *See also* Navopache Electric Cooperative
Apache County Board of Supervisors, 98

Apache Indians: and access to electricity, 216, 217; benefits of electrical cooperatives for, 115; labor camps of, 60; as victims or consumers, 204. *See also* Fort Apache Indian Agency; Fort Apache Indian Reservation; *specific bands*; White Mountain Apache Indians
Apache National Forest, 96, 101, 107
Apache Power Company, 85–86
Apaches de Nabajó. *See* Navajo Indians
Apache-Sitgreaves National Forest, 79, 102, 125
appliances: demonstrations of, 62, 63, 186–87; expense of, 198; gas- and kerosene-powered, 22; in labor camps, 60; loans for, 61; marketing of, 61–68, 181; Moenkopi villagers' purchase of, 191; Native Americans' purchase of, 204; and Navajos and Hopis, 132, 139, 140, 176, 193–95, 198, 200, 203; NTUA instructions on use of, 182–83, *184*; power provision for small, 98; REA encouragement of, 44–45, 49; school instruction on, 122; and Southwest Forest Industries employees, 95; and White Mountain Apaches, 90, 91, 104, 122; in White Mountain region, 102, 118–19. *See also* lighting; *specific appliances*
Aravaipa Canyon, 26, 53
Aravaipa Creek, 27

archeological sites, 159, 176. *See also* sacred sites

area coverage, 38–40, *42*

Arizona: areas of study, *15*; community control of electricity in, 211–15; energy sources in, 130; environmental consequences in, 215–16; legislation on cooperative service areas in, 114; Native American population in, 132; Native American tribes' access to electricity in, 4; overview of electrification in, 13–20; power distribution in, 221–24; pre–World War II electrical requirements, 51–52; regulatory activity in, 158; rights on Colorado River, 160; statehood of, 86; types of rural communities in, 20, 23–24; urbanization of, 14–16; utility interests during Cold War, 110; wartime electrical demands in, 99–100. *See also* American West; climate; landscape; *specific places*

Arizona Corporation Commission, 14–16, 96, 98, 110, 112, 114, 222

Arizona Currents, 113, 118

Arizona Edison Electric Company, 36, 112, 118

Arizona Electric Power Cooperative Association, 56–61. *See also* Sulphur Springs Valley Electric Cooperative (SSVEC)

Arizona Farmer Ranchman, 188

Arizona Farm Production Power Use Program, 118

Arizona General Utilities Company, 35, 41, 54

Arizona Power Authority (APA), 52–53, 56, 100

Arizona Producer, 61

Arizona Public Service (APS): advertisement in *Navajo Times*, 168; expiration of agreement with NTUA, 206; formation of, 112; on Hopi lands, 189, 190; instruction by, 183, 187; management of Tombstone, 56; and Navajo-Hopi land dispute, 174, 175; in Old Oraibi, 175; as part of conglomeration, 178; power line design, 200; as power source for Navajos, 157–62; rates of, 221; and recreational enterprises, 127; and sacred sites, 189; and Tuba City, 131, 152, 154, 176

Arizona Range News, 57

Arizona Republic, 223

Arizona State Fair, 186

Arizona State Planning Board, 210

Arizona Territory, 14, 18, 25–26, 28, 31

artesian wells, 28

Arthur, Chester, 137

arts and crafts, 138, 153

assimilation: curbing of policies, 141; of Navajos, 139, 150, 205; through technology, 3, 87, 88, 130, 138–39, 192; and termination, 148

barley, 54, 58

Barron, Hal, 9

Bartos, Laverne, 182–83, *184*

Basin Light and Power Company, 154–55

28, 83; and power demands in
   Shiprock, 154
Bush, George W., 2
butane, 33, 142, 196
Bylas AZ, 54, 69
Byrd, Mrs. C. M., 49, 50

Cady, M. W., 93
Cady Lumber Company, 93. *See also*
   Southwest Forest Industries
California, 1–2, 4, 5, 57, 60, 169,
   170, 221, 222
Calva AZ, 69
Camp Apache, 80. *See also* Fort
   Apache Indian Agency; Fort
   Apache Indian Reservation
Canada, 135
Canyon Creek Apache Indians, 79
Canyon Day AZ, 103, 106
Canyon de Chelly, 181
Capps, Inez, 122
Carmody, John, 22–23
Carson, Christopher "Kit," 137
Carson, H. L. "Kit," 173
Carter, Jimmy, 178
Catron County NM, 116
Cedar Creek AZ, 109
Central Arizona Light and Power
   Company, 106, 112
Central Arizona Project, 160
Central AZ, 35
Chambers AZ, 121
chapter houses, 169, 177, 183
Chicago World's Fair (1893), 7
Chihuahua, Mexico, 26
chilies, 58
children, 49, 64, 66, 121–22,
   190–93

Chimopavy 4-H club, 188
Chinese, 80
Chinle AZ, 151, 167–68, 187, 199
Chipsulavi homemaker club, 186
Chiricahua Apache Indians, 24–26,
   79–80
Chiricahua Cattle Company, 28
Chiricahua Mountains, 24, 26, 29
Christianity, 122
Church of Jesus Christ of Latter-
   Day Saints. *See* Mormons
Cibecue Apache Indians, 79, 80
Cibecue AZ, 106, 108, 109, 123, 125,
   129
Citizens Utilities, 221
civil rights, 115, 134, 148, 211, 222
Clapp, Norman, 111
Clifton AZ, 23, 37
climate: effect on appliance market,
   63; and food preservation, 21;
   of northeastern Arizona, 135;
   and role in development, 12;
   and role in electrification, 212;
   of southeastern Arizona, 27–28;
   of White Mountain region, 78,
   94, 107–8, 119. *See also* drought;
   landscape
Clinton, Bill, 222
clubs. *See* electrification clubs; 4-H
   programs; homemaker clubs
clustered housing, 195, 197
coal: APS's purchase of, 157; deposits on Native lands, 4, 133, 134,
   154, 160; heating and lighting
   with, 140; Navajo interest in,
   151, 162, 169, 173; Peabody Coal
   Company mining of, 175; pollution from, 170

Cochise (Chiricahua Apache), 24
Cochise AZ, 43
Cochise County: communal cooperation in, 39, 40, 42; economy of, 32; effect of electricity in, 56–61; electrification clubs in, 66, 68; environmental consequences in, 215; extension workers in, 121; federal land in, 30; homes using electric heat in, 65; landscape and climate of, 27; Mexican American land in, 26; population of, 24, 44, 57–58, 79; REA application of, 23, 43–48. See also Sulphur Springs Valley Electric Cooperative (SSVEC)
Cochise County Farm Bureau, 42–43
Cochise County Stock Growers' Association, 30
Cochise-Graham Cattle Growers' Association, 30
coffee makers, 63, 119
Cohen, Lizabeth, 11, 220
Colbert, Max, 104
Cold War, 78, 109–16, 147, 211
Collier, John, 140, 142
Colorado, 134
Colorado Plateau, 81, 135, 148, 149
Colorado River, 47, 52–53, 97, 100, 127, 148, 159, 160, 169
Colorado River Storage Project (CRSP), 159
Committee to Get REA on Eagle Creek, 116
communal cooperation: of agrarian communities, 14, 29, 30, 35–36, 39–41, 46, 61, 70–71; and Arizona "power war," 39–40; of Navajos, 153; for REA loan application, 18; in White Mountain region, 81, 82, 84–85. See also electrical cooperatives; localism

communications technology, 36, 127, 144, 147, 148, 194, 202. See also Internet access; radios; telephone service; televisions
community action program, 190
consumer demand, 85, 92–93, 99–100, 102, 109, 141, 153, 163, 174. See also electrical load; power consumption
Continental Divide Electric Cooperative, 154, 158, 159, 165, 168
Cooke, Morris, 38–39, 44
Cooley AZ. See McNary AZ
Coolidge Dam, 47
copper, 16, 37, 51, 59–60
corn, 31, 85, 136, 216
Coronado Trail, 107
Corrizo Apache Indians, 79
cotton, 16, 54, 58, 59, 60, 214
Cottonwood-Pinon section of joint-use area, 176
Council of Energy Resource Tribes (CERT), 219
Country Life Commission, 30
Country Life Movement, 11, 22, 30, 44, 61, 115, 147. See also reformers
Cowbelles (Blue River), 109
Croasdale, Terry, 61
Cronemeyer, Hoskie, 150–51, 161
Crook, George, 80
Crouse, C. W., 92–93
Crownpoint NM, 131, 139, 199

domestic work, 21–23, 34, 57, 139–40
Dominy, Floyd, 160
Donner, William, 90–92, 120
Dos Cabezas community, 33
Dos Cabezas Mining District, 33
Dos Cabezas mountain range, 29
Double Adobe AZ, 49, 55
Douglas AZ, 23–25, 33, 59, 62
drought, 27–30, 37, 54, 82. *See also* climate
dry farming, 27, 31. *See also* agriculture
Duncan Valley Electric Cooperative, 54, 213, 256n6

Eagar AZ, 81, 106, 121
Eagle Creek AZ, 109, 114, 115, 116
easements, 48, 49, 107, 152, 189. *See also* rights-of-way
East Fork AZ, 106
economy: alternative energy sources and, 223; American ideal of, 2, 5, 225n2; American West's wartime, 99–100; of Cochise County, 23, 32; development of in American West, 10–13, 16, 20, 211; electrical cooperatives' role in, 116; and electricity's effect on southeastern Arizona, 57–61; electrification's effects on Native Americans', 217–19; of Navajos and Hopis, 136, 138, 145–49, 170, 179, 181, 191; and power distribution, 219–20; REA's role in transformation of, 23, 38, 40, 45–46, 73; and regulation debate, 221, 222; role of in electrification, 19, 20, 132, 133,

209, 210; self-supporting on reservations, 204; of southeastern Arizona, 25, 39, 45; transformation to industrial, 6; transformation to tourist, 126–27; of White Mountain region, 78, 79, 82, 102, 127, 128–29
Eddy, C. Mac, 111, 163, 165, 171–74
education, electrical: of Apaches through electrical cooperatives, 115; assimilation through, 139–40, 192; of domestic consumers, 61–69, 118–24, 181–83; on electrical safety, 118–19, 182–83, 184; government programs for, 70, 72, 210, 212, 217; lack of in Native populations, 133; lack of in southeastern Arizona, 44; of Navajos and Hopis, 137–44, 151–53, 161, 162, 168, 179, 181–85; through television, 192–93; of White Mountain residents, 118–23. *See also* demonstration meetings; vocational training
electrical cooperatives: appeal to domestic market, 61–69; and Colorado River project, 52, 53; competition of, 109–16, 222; concerns about power supply, 56; effect of World War II on, 51; Navajos and Hopis as members of, 165, 177; NTUA's resemblance to, 163, 182; organizational structure of, 178; REA funding for, 41, 213; transformation of rural West, 23, 72; women's work with, 67. *See also* communal cooperation; *specific electrical cooperatives*

electrical engineers (Navajo),
166–67
electrical load: through domestic
market, 61–69; at Fort Apache
Reservation, 90–92; gaining by
crossing reservations, 129, 156;
of Navopache cooperative, 104,
117, 118; of NTUA, 169; as REA re-
quirement, 44, 73; in southeastern Arizona, 33–34, 40, 60, 71,
72; of SSVEC, 41, 43–46, 49, 52,
53, 56; in White Mountain region, 102, 103. *See also* consumer demand; power consumption
electrical terminology manuals, 64
electrical wire, 60
electric bills, 62, 198
The Electric Company (television
program), 192
Electric Farm and Home Authority, 61
electricity: changes in American
views of, 4; as commodity, 221;
role in communities, 2. *See also*
entries beginning with "power"
electrification: and community
pride, 209–10; consequences of,
215–18; definition of, 4–5; overview of in Arizona, 13–20
electrification advisers, 118
electrification clubs, 66, 68, 188.
See also demonstration meetings; homemaker clubs
Eleventh Annual Navajo Tribal Fair
(1957), 152
Elfrida AZ, 32, 43, 58, 66
Elk Mountain AZ, 108
Ellis, Clyde, 110

El Paso TX, 169
employment: electrification's effects
on, 204, 205, 215, 217–18; with
NTUA, 172–74, 177, 182–85; opportunities for Navajos and Hopis, 133, 144–45, 150, 152–53, 161,
165, 167, 169, 170, 197, 199;
opportunities for White Mountain Apaches, 124, 126; with
SSVEC, 71
Endangered Species Act, 176
Endfield, Raymond, Jr., 125
energy conservation, 2, 51, 91, 92,
97, 183. *See also* environmental
responsibility; recycling
Energy Information Administration, 4–5
energy shortages, 174, 177
English, Glenn, 5
English-language instruction, 150
Enlarged Homestead Act (1909), 29
Enron, 2, 3–4, 224
environmental consequences, 133,
149, 159, 160, 170, 175, 215–18.
See also natural resources
environmental laws, 176
environmental responsibility, 7.
See also energy conservation;
recycling
equity: in access to technology, 147,
221–24; during Cold War, 111;
in electrification, 2–5, 8, 11, 132,
210, 220–21, 226n4
erosion, 31, 37, 159. *See also* soil
conservation
ethnic groups: and diversity in
American West, 13, 18, 20, 212;
and electrical distribution, 210,

Graham County Electric Cooperative (GCEC), 54, 62, 68–70, 213, 256n6. *See also* Arizona Electric Power Cooperative Association; electrical cooperatives

Grand Canyon, 160

Grand Canyon State Electrical Cooperative (GCSEC), 113, 178, 213

gravity irrigation, 31, 54, 82, 101. *See also* irrigation

Great Depression. *See* New Deal

Great Plains, 8, 31

The Great Plains (Webb), 12

Great Society, 116

Greer AZ, 81, 102

grid system, 25–26, 219–21

groundwater. *See* water supply

"Guideposts in Buying Household Equipment" pamphlet, 65

Handy Watts, 118, *119*, 182

Hannagan Meadows AZ, 106–9, 115

Harrington, Lillie, 22

Hawley Lake, 126

Hayden, Carl, 109, 113, 114

Healing v. Jones, 175

health issues, 185, 186, 195, 205, 218. *See also* hospitals

heat: electric, 65; gas, 36, 83, 84, 140; in Indian schools, 140; in Mormon homes, 83; in Navajo homes, 196, 197; in White Mountain Apache homes, 95

Heber AZ, 81, 102, 103

Helmers, Howard, 55

Henning, Lloyd, 96

HiLiner newsletter, 49

Hill, Bill, 71

Hispanics: impact of television on, 194; in northeastern Arizona, 135–36; in southeastern Arizona, 24–25, 228n4; at Southwest Forest Industries, 93, 95; in White Mountain region, 79, 81, 108, 211, 238n8. *See also* Mexican Americans; Mexicans; Spanish Americans

Hogan, William, 4

hogans: constructing for religious purposes, 185; continued use of, 145, 192; declining use of, 199–200; electrification of, 132, 161, 168, 181, 200; pre-electrification, *196*; security lights for, 198; stone construction of, 154. *See also* housing

Holbrook AZ, 83, 97, 100, 102, 112, 175

Holtz, R. D., 77, 104

home demonstration meetings. *See* demonstration meetings

home economics curriculum, 65, 69, 139, 185

home economists, 186–87

Home Extension Service, 66

homemaker clubs, 120, 121, 185–86. *See also* electrification clubs

home ownership, 70, 73

homesite leases, 177

Homestead Act (1862), 26, 29, 81, 87

homesteading, 23, 25, 27, 28, 37, 44, 73, 81. *See also* settlement patterns

Hon-Dah Resort Casino, 126

Hooker, Henry Clay, 26

Hoover Dam, 169

Hopi Action News, 190, 191

Hopi Foundation, 191

Hopi Indian agencies, 139, 175

Hopi Indians: and access to electricity, 206, 216, 217; children of and electricity, 188, 190–93; and education on electrical use, 186; effect of Indian Reorganization Act on, 141; as electrical suppliers and consumers, 179–81; electrification and, 133, 134, 178, 179, 183, 200; energy sources on land of, 130; on environmental consequences, 170; history of, 135–36; introduction to electricity, 137–40; isolation from industrialization, 143, 147; land dispute with Navajos, 174–75; lease agreement with Peabody Coal, 169; maintenance of traditional life, 181, 188–91, 200, 219; negotiating with Arizona Public Service Company, 159; population of, 79; as victims or consumers, 203–7

Hopi Reservation: barriers to electrification on, 196–99; description of, 135; energy development on, 149; establishment of, 137; service on, 174–76; wiring of sacred kiva at, 183

Hopi traditionalist movement, 188–91

Hopi Tribal Council, 175, 189

hospitals, 91, 151, 204. *See also* health issues

Hotevilla AZ, 189, 200

Hotevilla 4-H club, 188

housing: for agricultural laborers, 60; construction and remodeling of, 65, 90–91, 116, 123; Native Americans' exposure to modern, 122–23; on Navajo and Hopi reservations, 137, 142, 145, 153–54, 161, 169, 174, 185, 188, 195–200, 205; postwar types and locations of, 69; programs for, 123–24, 134, 195–97, 204; role of in electrification, 19; shortage in southeastern Arizona, 57; for Southwest Forest Industries employees, 94; wiring of framed, 91. *See also* domestic market; hogans; wickiups

Hualapai tribe, 160

Hubbell, John Lorenzo, 138, 141

Hughes, Stella, 116

Hughes, Thomas, 10

Hurt, Douglas, 20

hydroelectric power production: in Arizona, 16, 18; on Colorado River, 131, 148, 159–61; and electrification of Native communities, 134; environmental consequences of, 217; federal money for, 38; role in electrification of rural West, 4, 5, 7, 211; and SSVEC, 47, 52–53; in White Mountain region, 84–87, 89–90, 97–98. *See also* power production

Indian agency employees, 84, 138, 143, 206

Indian Extension Service, 182, 185–86. *See also* Agricultural Extension Service (AES)

Indian Health Service Hospital, 154, 155
Indian Irrigation Service, 85–86, 91
Indian Reorganization Act (IRA), 141–43
Indian Wells AZ, 160, 167–68
industrialization: in American West, 5, 6, 8–12, 130, 210–15; of Apaches, 115, 124–27; in Arizona, 14–16, 19, 72, 220–21; effect of on reservation life, 204–6, 219; through electrification, 2–3; encouragement of at Fort Apache, 120; government programs for, 134; Mormons' experience with, 83; and Native American assimilation, 87–89; Native American response to, 13, 187; on Navajo Reservation, 132, 133, 137–41, 143–55, 157, 161, 168, 170, 179, 181–82, 195; NTUA employees' adaptation to, 185; in southeastern Arizona, 32–34, 57; in White Mountain region, 80, 102, 128; World War II–era, 51, 53. *See also* technology; urbanization
infrastructure: and alternative power sources, 223–24; community control of, 213; construction by NTUA, 167; effect of on reservation life, 204; in northeastern Arizona, 134, 147, 149; and regional economies, 210; and securing of REA loan, 41; in White Mountain region, 83
Intermountain High School, 185
Internet access, 222
irons: advantages of electric, 67; Apaches' use of, 123; on Navajo Reservation, 132, 168; NTUA instructions on use of, 183; in Navopache service area, 118, 119; popularity of, 198; pre-electrification, 21–22, 95; White Mountain region's use of, 102
irrigation: by Apaches, 87–88, 90, 91; in Arizona, 16; Bureau of Reclamation project for, 83; and electrical load, 34; and electrification of West, 7, 210; encouragement of settlement with, 10; information sources about, 117; by Navajos, 138, 145; at Rainbow Lake, 127; in southeastern Arizona, 25, 27, 29, 30; in White Mountain region, 78, 82–86. *See also* agriculture; gravity irrigation; water supply
irrigation districts, 38, 40, 41, 43, 47, 70, 97–98, 112
irrigation pumping, 51; economic effect of, 57–59, 214; environmental consequences of, 215–16; funding of, 61, 129; and Lyman Water Company, 97; possibility in southeastern Arizona, 28, 31; project in Cochise County, 23; REA studies on, 44, 54, 58–59, 72; and SSVEC, 42, 43, 45–46, 49, 50, 53, 55, 73; systems on federal land, 37–38. *See also* agriculture; water supply
Irving, Violet, 45
Iverson, Peter, 144, 146, 204

James, Keith, 218
Jefferson, Thomas, 7, 8, 138

land values, 57, 73, 214
Largo, Jimmie, 151
laundry, 21–22, 44
laundry appliances: advantages of
    electric, 67; advertisements for,
    181; encouraging use of, 182; at
    Fort Apache Reservation, 90;
    Native Americans' desire for,
    69; in Navajo homes, 132, 198,
    200; in Navopache service area,
    118; NTUA instructions on use
    of, 183; as priority of domestic
    consumers, 62, 65; and White
    Mountain region electrical load,
    102
Lay, Ken, 3, 224
lead mining, 53
Lechee chapter house, 169
Lee, Esther, 84
Lee, Lawrence, 77, 84, 127
lettuce, 58, 60
Leupp Indian agency, 139
Leupp AZ, 157
Lewis, David Rich, 13
lightbulbs, 34, 62, 84, 182, 196,
    198, 202. See also lighting
lighting: and Apaches, 90, 95, 104;
    and appliance market, 65; elec-
    trical in southeastern Arizona,
    36; in Indian schools, 140; Mor-
    mons' pre-electrification, 83; Na-
    tive Americans' desire for, 69,
    104; and Navajos, 140, 142–43,
    198; in Navopache service area,
    118, 120; REA customer surveys
    on, 44; for Southwest Forest In-
    dustries employees, 95. See also
    lightbulbs

Link, Martin, 181
Lipan Apache Indians, 79–80
Littell, Norman, 146, 150, 164–66
Little Colorado River valley, 81, 82
Littlefield Electric Cooperative, 213,
    256n6
livestock raising. See ranching
localism: and alternative energy
    sources, 223; role of in electri-
    fication, 7, 12–13, 19, 20, 35–36,
    209–21, 224; in southeast-
    ern Arizona, 35–36, 69–74. See
    also communal cooperation;
    demographics
"The Long Walk," 137
Louisiana, 93
Lowitt, Richard, 5
lumbering: effect of electricity on,
    16, 53, 214; introduction at Fort
    Apache Reservation of, 92–93;
    in White Mountain region, 77,
    79, 93–97, 102, 105, 124, 125,
    127. See also sawmills; wood
Luna NM, 99, 103
Lupe, Ronnie, 126
Lyman Dam, 82
Lyman Water Company, 97

The Machine in the Garden (Marx), 8
maize, 58
Mander, Jerry, 218
manganese mine, 102
Manifest Destiny, 7, 10
Manifest Manners (Vizenor), 257n22
Marble Canyon, 160
Marshall Plan model, 147
Marx, Karl, 6
Marx, Leo, 8

Mascot settlement, 33
Maverick AZ, 105, 108
McCabe, Edward, Jr., 171, 174
McCabe, Maurice, 156–58, 168
McCarthyism, 110, 211
McDonald, Peter, 167, 173
McKnight, Florence D., 120–21
McNary AZ, 77, 93–96, 100, 102,
    104–6, 120, 124, 129. *See also*
    Southwest Lumber Company
McNary General Store, 119
McNary, James G., 93
McNeal AZ, 32, 43, 47, 49, 62
McNulty, James, 114
McPherson, Joseph, 166–67
Meriam Report, 140
Meritt, E. B., 89–90
Mesa Verde, 135
Mescalero Apache Indians, 79–80
meters, 91, 143
The Metropolitan Frontier (Abbott), 8
Mexican Americans: on appliances,
    64, 67–68; definition of, 238n8;
    homes of, 60; Homestead Act
    on, 26; and Navopache Electric
    Cooperative, 103, 118; popula-
    tion in Arizona, 18, 24–25; pre-
    electrification chores of, 21–22;
    settlement in southeastern Ari-
    zona, 24–25, 33–34; settlement
    on Navajo lands, 136. *See also*
    Hispanics
Mexican-American War (1846–48),
    24, 26, 136
Mexicans, 33, 60, 80. *See also*
    Hispanics
Mexico, 33, 136
Miami AZ, 37

Midwest, 7, 25, 28, 108
military bases, 24, 37, 51, 52, 56, 80
military service, 69, 122–23, 181
milo (sorghum grain), 58
mineral resources, 80, 102, 136,
    138, 148, 149. *See also* mining
    operations
miners, 9
mining operations: in Arizona, 16–
    18; and Arizona Electric Power
    Cooperative Association, 59–60;
    and development of electric
    power, 210–11; environmental
    consequences of, 217, 218; gov-
    ernment programs for, 70; in
    southeastern Arizona, 23, 25,
    26, 32, 33, 36–37, 39, 49, 53. *See
    also* mineral resources
Mishongnavi homemaker club, 186
missions, 91, 92, 139, 206
mission schools, 146
modernization. *See*
    industrialization
Moenkopi AZ (Hopi village), 175
Moenkopi Pueblos, 190, 191
mohair, 138
Mohave County, 221
Mohave Electric Cooperative, 213,
    256n6
Mohave Power Plant, 169
monopolies, 7, 36, 38
Montana, 132
Montoya, Esperanza, 21
Moquis. *See* Hopi Indians
Morenci AZ, 37
Morgan, Jacob, 146
Mormons: as consumers, 63; elec-
    tricity used by, 183; extension

Mormons (*cont.*)
work with, 121; and hydroelectric power production, 97; introduction of utility service by, 35;
and REA loan request, 98–99;
in southeastern Arizona, 25, 29,
37; in White Mountain region,
78, 79, 81–84, 101, 107, 128, 211
Mountain States Telephone and
Telegraph Company, 146
Mount Baldy, 78
Mount Graham, 27, 53
municipalities, 41
Musket, James, 152
mutual water companies, 30

Nagen, Andrew, 203
Napolitano, Janet, 223
National Advisory Committee on
Rural Poverty, 115
National Electrical Code, 143
National Environmental Protection
Act, 176
National Historic Preservation Act,
176
National Park Service lands, 176
National Rural Electric Cooperative
Association (NRECA), 5, 113, 118
National Rural Electrification Con-
test, 66
Native Americans: and access to
electricity, 212, 216–18; and ac-
cess to technology, 9, 222; AES's
work with, 120–21; as agricultur-
al laborers, 60; attitudes toward
electricity of, 13, 68–69, 104,
187; benefits of electrical cooperatives for, 115; and control of en-

ergy resources, 206–7; effects of
electrification on, 122, 218–19,
257n22; environmental consequences on lands of, 217–18; establishment of forts and reservations for, 80; farming in Navajo
County, 101; legal status of, 13,
122, 123, 133, 150, 164, 206, 216;
percentage electrified, 4, 206;
population in Arizona, 18, 132;
rural traditions of, 132–33; segregation of, 216; in southeastern Arizona, 24; termination of,
148; as victims or consumers,
203–7; in White Mountain region, 79, 82, 211. *See also* reservations; *specific tribes*
Natoni, Morris, 150
natural resources, 20, 128–29, 133,
138, 144, 148–49, 159, 179, 212.
See also environmental consequences; *specific resources*
Navajo Central Indian Agency, 144
Navajo Community College, 203
Navajo cotton camps, 60
Navajo County, 78, 79, 97, 101, 112,
121, 127, 186. *See also* Navopache
Electric Cooperative
Navajo County Fair, 186
Navajo Dam, 177
"Navajo Electric Blanket," 182
Navajo Farm Training Program, 153
Navajo Forest Products Industries,
173–74
Navajo Generating Station, 169,
218
Navajo-Hopi joint-use area, 174,
176, 177

Navajo-Hopi Long Range Rehabilitation Act, 147, 153–54, 164, 172
Navajo Housing Authority, 174, 199
Navajo Indian agencies, 139, 140, 142
Navajo Indian Agency, 142–44, 154, 155, 176, 213
Navajo Indian Irrigation Project, 177, 179
Navajo Indians, 202; and access to electricity, 196–99, 216, 217; achieving area coverage, 134; electrification's effects on, 179–81; energy sources on land of, 130, 206; government funding for business enterprises of, 147; history of, 135–44; introduction to electricity, 137–40; maintaining traditional life, 145–46, 148, 183–88, 191–95, 200–203, 219; negotiating with outside corporations, 148, 156, 157, 161; notions of progress by, 150, 151, 162, 181, 193, 203, 205; percentage electrified, 4, 206; population of, 79; on termination threat, 148; at Theodore Roosevelt Boarding School, 88; as victims or consumers, 203–7. *See also* Navajo Reservation; Navajo Tribal Council; Navajo Tribal Utility Authority (NTUA)
Navajo Mountain, 177
Navajo NM, 197
"Navajo Parade of Progress," 152
Navajo Power Plant, 177
Navajo Reservation: advocating for electrification of, 144; agricul-ture on, 137–38; barriers to electrification on, 176–77, 196–99; Bill Clinton at, 222; delinquent accounts on, 96; description of, 134–35; electrification's effects on, 181; environmental consequences of energy development on, 217–18; expansion of, 137; firewood stockpiling on, 153; nationalism on, 204; postwar power development on, 144–55; power to, 131–34; promotion of energy development on, 178; settlement patterns on, 136. *See also* Navajo Indians; Navajo Tribal Utility Authority (NTUA)
Navajo Times, 168, 180–83, 200, 201
Navajo Tribal Council: on affordability of electricity, 198; on APS right-of-way, 159; and consumer demand, 174; and environmental consequences, 218, 223; on housing, 195–96; and industrialization of reservation, 147–51, 155, 157; issuing utility franchises, 152; leasing property, 175, 178; and NTUA, 156, 165, 170–73; opposition to dams, 160–61; postwar leadership of, 146; on REA loan stipulations, 164; reorganization of (1930s), 141–42; on reservation living conditions, 188; on television reception, 192–93. *See also* Navajo Indians
Navajo Tribal Fair (1957), 152
Navajo Tribal Utility Authority (NTUA): attitudes toward, 182; consequences of, 218; costs of

Navajo Tribal Utility Authority (*cont.*)
power line extensions, 197; creation and goals of, 155–57, 213; distribution network, *180*; expansion of, 167–70, 172–74, 176–79, 195–96; hiring of home economist, 186–87; housing assistance from, 199, 200; as independent enterprise, 170–79; instruction on appliance use, 182–83, *184*; on Internet access, 222; motto of, 193; organizational structure of, 166–67, 178; "Plan of Operation," 164; power sources of, 157–62, 168–69; rates of, 198; and REA loan, 165; rejection of Navajos and Hopis, 203–6; service area and customers, 168; and system construction, 177; uniqueness of, 162–67. *See also* Navajo Indians; Navajo Reservation

Navajo-U.S. treaty (1868). *See* Treaty of 1868

Navajo Vocational Training Program, 153

Navopache Electric Cooperative: C. Mac Eddy with, 174; during Cold War, 109; competition of, 112–14; educational programs of, 118, 123; groundsmen of, 124; history and development of, 97–103, 213, 256n6; incorporation of, 100; integration of, 103–6, 128; meeting of, *117*; multicultural marketing of, 116–27; regional difficulties of, 106–9; representative of REA cooperatives, 129; service area of, 77–79, 116–17;

transforming Apache traditional life, 124–26; and White Mountain Apaches, 124–27. *See also* Apache County; Navajo County

Navopache Transmitter, 118

Neal, William, 100

Needham, Andrew, 147

Networks of Power (Hughes), 10

Nevada, 169

New Deal, 4, 5, 18, 36–40, 95, 110, 141, 143, 167, 220. *See also* Rural Electrification Administration (REA)

New Mexico: AES activities in, 67; electrical cooperatives in, 117; military attacks on Navajos, 136–37; mineworkers' demands in, 68; Navajo Power Plant construction in, 177; Navajos forced into, 137; Navopache Electric Cooperative in, 78–79, 103, 106, 116; as part of Navajo Reservation, 134, 167; REA borrowers in, 154; regulatory activity in, 158; request for White Mountain Electric Cooperative extension in, 99

New Mexico Territory, 136

New Oraibi AZ, 175

Norris, George, 38–39

Northern Arizona Utilities Company, 106, 112

Northwest Ordinance, 26

Nutrioso AZ, 81, 99, 121

Nye, David, 5, 214

Office of Indian Affairs (OIA): attitudes toward technology, 87;

power distribution (*cont.*)
debate on, 3, 4, 220–24; Navajos' loan request for, 165; by Navopache cooperative, 103–9; under New Deal, 18; REA's goal of, 38, 214; REA systems for, 75–76; and relationship to consumption, 180–81; in Sulphur Springs valley, 40, 52; in White Mountain region, 77–78, 94, 101, 108–9, 128. *See also* distributive justice; power transmission

power lines: costs of, 197; grant to repair, 91; and integration of Navopache cooperative, 104; materials for, 100; on Navajo Reservation, 153; of Navopache cooperative, 107–8; photographs and cartoons of, 200, 201; REA funding for, 41, 43; of SSVEC, 47–50, 53; to Whiteriver from Fort Apache, 90. *See also* power transmission

power market, 2–4

power outages, 1–2, 62, 221

power plants: in Graham County, 53; in Lakeside, 77, 127; on Native lands, 133; on Navajo Reservation, 142–43; Navopache acquisition and integration of, 103–6; in New Mexico, 154; REA construction loan for, 56; scarcity of in Arizona and New Mexico, 144; in southeastern Arizona, 32, 36; in Sulphur Springs valley, 40; in White Mountain region, 84, 86, 101, 107, 117, 124

power production: Arizona legislature on, 100; at Fort Apache Reservation, 92; through industrial waste recycling, 94; nationwide debate on, 3–5, 220–24; on Native lands, 4, 206–7; of Navopache cooperative, 124; and relationship to consumption, 34; in White Mountain region, 97, 98. *See also* hydroelectric power production

power rates, 4, 41, 85, 221–22

power sources: of Fort Apache Indian Reservation, 77, 86, 128–30; of NTUA, 157–62, 173; and REA loan, 41, 46; and settlement of southeastern Arizona, 69; of SSVEC, 52, 55, 56; in White Mountain region, 85

power systems, 3, 12–13, 47–50, 83–85

power transmission: and Colorado River project, 52, 100; between Farmington and Shiprock, 156; nationwide debate on, 4; on Navajo Reservation, 139, 152, 154, 157, 160, 167–70, 189; Navajos' loan request for, 165, 174–75; to Phoenix, 157; REA loan for, 56; in southeastern Arizona, 36; to Theodore Roosevelt Boarding School, 90; in White Mountain region, 97–99, 101, 105, 108–9, 128. *See also* power distribution; power lines

"power wars," 6, 39–40

Printup, Bessie, 120

private companies: and community

control of electrification, 211–12, 214; and competition with cooperatives, 110–12, 117; and control of technology, 6; and electrical load in southeastern Arizona, 34–36, 41; at Fort Apache Reservation, 93; and hydroelectric power, 52, 85; and integration of Navopache cooperative, 106; nationwide debate on, 38, 211, 224; and Navajos and Hopis, 134, 152, 157, 204; number of in Arizona, 16; and power distribution, 220; REA as foil to, 72, 99; in southeastern Arizona, 32, 39, 40; in White Mountain region, 96
Progressivism, 6, 115, 116, 213
property leases, 153, 155, 157, 164, 177, 178. *See also* land ownership
Protestants, 25
public companies, 38, 39, 220
public housing programs, 195–97. *See also* housing
Public Utility Holding Company Act (PUHCA) (1935), 7, 38, 39
Public Utility Regulatory Policies Act (1978), 7
Public Works Administration (PWA), 37–38, 91
Pueblo Indian societies, 79, 135, 136
Pueblo Viejo community, 26

"The Quarters," 94–95

race, 10, 12, 67, 73. *See also* ethnic groups
radio broadcasting transmitters, 144

radio communication systems, 147
radio programs, 66, 186
radios: marketing of, 63–64; Native Americans' desire for, 69; and Navajos, 144, 149–51, 168, 194, 196, 198; in Navopache service area, 118; White Mountain Apaches' use of, 123; in White Mountain region, 102
railroad, 5, 8, 16, 26, 83, 101, 102, 138, 185. *See also* transportation
railroad towns, 32
Rainbow Bridge, 159, 170, 217
Rainbow Lake, 84, 127
ranchers, 9, 20, 29–31, 42–50, 64, 71, 213. *See also* agrarian nation; agriculture; farmers
ranching: in Apache-Sitgreaves National Forest, 125; benefits of electrification in, 116; energy development's effects on, 133; and environmental consequences, 216, 218; government programs for, 70; by Navajos, 135–38, 145, 153; role of in electrification, 212; in southeastern Arizona, 25–32, 37, 57, 69; as supplemental source of income, 71; techniques in southeastern Arizona, 73; by White Mountain Apaches, 87; in White Mountain region, 79–81, 83, 85, 93, 101, 107, 109. *See also* agrarian nation; agriculture
ranges, electric, 44, 45, 72, 139, 182, 186, 198, 200. *See also* appliances
Ration, Tom, 131
REA. *See* Rural Electrification Administration (REA)

reclamation projects, 41. *See also* Bureau of Reclamation

recreational enterprises, 53, 102, 107, 111, 126. *See also* tourism industry

recycling, 94. *See also* energy conservation; environmental responsibility

Red Mesa AZ, 158

reformers, 20, 87, 209. *See also* Country Life Movement

refrigerators: marketing of, 63–64, 181; Native Americans' desire for, 69; and Navajos and Hopis, 194–95, 198, 200; in Navopache service area, 118–19; NTUA instructions on use of, 183; REA customer surveys on, 44, 45, 72; wattage used by, 34; White Mountain Apaches' use of, 123. *See also* appliances; food freezers; food preservation

regional networks: Apaches in, 204; created through electrification, 19, 20, 56, 70, 214; Fort Apache Indian Reservation in, 86; on Hopi and Navajo land, 134; monopolies of, 36; Navopache building of, 103; NTUA's intent to build, 176; and REA loan, 40; transformation of rural West, 211; in White Mountain region, 84–85, 96, 100–101, 127–30

regulation/deregulation, 3–7, 14–16, 38–39, 219–24

relocations, 69, 122, 137, 188, 196

renewable energy sources, 223

reservations: electrification's effects on, 204–5, 211, 217–18; federal money for, 37, 38; as first power recipients, 212–13; gaining electrical load by crossing, 129; lack of power on, 115, 216; natural resources on, 133; as rural West concept, 20. *See also* Native Americans; *specific reservations*

reservation schools, 91. *See also* boarding schools; day schools

Reserve NM, 103, 108, 118

residency, permanent, 104, 108

Returned Indian Students Association, 146

Reynolds Electric and Engineering Company, 167, 185

Riggs family, 26

rights-of-way: on contested Navajo-Hopi land, 174–77; on Navajo Reservation, 146, 152, 154, 156–60, 189; securing across reservations, 96, 124; of SSVEC, 48; in White Mountain region, 102, 105, 107–8, 126

Rivers of Empire (Worster), 10, 69

roads: on Navajo and Hopi lands, 189, 195; Navajo-Hopi Long Range Rehabilitation Act on, 164; in northeastern Arizona, 147; in southeastern Arizona, 24, 57; in White Mountain region, 83, 90, 101, 102, 124. *See also* transportation

Roberts, Harold, 209

Roosevelt, Franklin D., 2, 39, 141

Roosevelt, Theodore, 30

Roosevelt Dam, 16

Rose, Mark, 7, 11

Round Valley, 81

Round Valley Light and Power Company, 106
Round Valley Water and Storage Ditch Company, 82
rugs, Navajo, 145, 202–3
Ruiz, Vicki, 67–68
rural America: Arizona as representative of, 14; federal programs for electrification of, 3; significance of energy to, 2; skepticism of technology in, 44; traditions of, 33–34, 71; types of communities in Arizona, 20; U.S. Census Bureau identification of, 9, 79, 132; use of technology in, 8–10, 12; young people in, 65–66
Rural Electric Bank, 114–15
The Rural Electric Minuteman, 113
Rural Electrification Act, 38–39
Rural Electrification Administration (REA): and Apaches, 104, 125, 204; areas targeted by, 70, 71; creation and goals of, 37, 213; distribution systems, 75–76; on economic benefits of electricity, 38; evaluation system, 73–74; expansion of, 195; on Graham County cooperative, 54; and irrigation pumping, 50, 58–59; loan application process and requirements, 18, 40, 61, 98, 100–101, 108, 128, 214; loan for plant and transmission system, 56; marketing to domestic consumers, 61, 63; mascot of, 118, *119*, 182; Mormon women's response to, 121; on Native American power use, 69; and Navajos, 141, 159; and Navopache Electric Cooperative, 97–103, 105, 108, 109, 118; in New Mexico, 154; NTUA loans from, 163–66, 171–72, 174–75, 178; opposition to, 109–17; and "power war" in southeastern Arizona, 39–40; pre–World War II applicants to, 73; report on electrical use (1937), 72; role in economic transformation, 211; role in electrification, 7; and San Carlos Apaches, 69; in southeastern Arizona, 57, 72; Sulphur Springs valley loan application to, 40–48; surveys by, 43–44, 54, 72, 100, 102, 103, 118; threat to loan program of, 115–16; and transformation of rural West, 22–23; in White Mountain region, 77–78, 127–30; during World War II, 50–55
Rural Electrification News, 44, 64, 66
Rural Lines, 57

sacred sites, 133, 170, 183, 189, 205, 217. *See also* archeological sites
Safford AZ, 35, 41, 53, 54, 60, 183
sage, 58, *58*
Saint David AZ, 52
Sakiestewa, Willard S., Sr., 176
Salazar, Epimenio, 21
Salazar, Rosalia, 21
Salazar family, 21–22, 26
Salt of the Earth, 68
Salt River Project, 16, 83, 85, 86, 89, 90, 178. *See also* Salt River Valley Water Users Association (SRVWUA)

Salt River valley, 16, 23, 90
Salt River Valley Water Users Association (SRVWUA), 40. *See also* Salt River Project
San Bernardino CA, 215
San Carlos Apache Indian Agency, 68–69
San Carlos Apache Indian Reservation, 24, 47, 54, 80, 86
San Carlos Apache Indians, 68–69, 133
San Carlos Irrigation and Drainage District, 40
Sanders homemaker club, 120
Sanderson, W. H., 28
San Francisco River, 82
sanitation, 120, 140
San Juan County, 155
San Pedro River, 25
San Pedro valley, 23, 28, 52
San Simon Creek, 27
San Simon Electric Light and Power Company, 35
San Simon valley, 23, 28, 42
Santa Cruz County, 113–14, 221
Santa Cruz River, 25
sawmills, 80, 92–94, 102, 107, 108, 116, 127, 153–54. *See also* lumbering
"Sawmill Valley." *See* Lakeside AZ
Schad, J. L., 58
school curriculum, 65–66, 69, 122, 139–40, 185. *See also* education
schools: construction of, 147, 195; delivery of power to, 91, 154, 155, 167, 206; and effect on reservation life, 204; and power generation at Pinon, 176. *See also* boarding schools; day schools

self-determination: of Native Americans, 204, 206; of Navajos, 146, 158, 164, 165, 172, 178, 179; through rural electrification, 214; and termination, 148
Sells, Cato, 92
Sesame Street, 192
settlement patterns: of American West, 8, 10, 12; in Arizona, 14, 18; of Navajos and Hopis, 153, 199; in southeastern Arizona, 23–32, 37, 57–58, 60–61; in White Mountain region, 78–81, 101, 125–26. *See also* homesteading
sewage service, 125, 140, 155, 165, 185, 189–91
sewing machines, 95, 121, 123, 132, 181, 186
Shelton, Frank, 62–63
Shelton, Twila, 71–72
Sheridan, Thomas, 82, 212
Sherman Indian Boarding School, 120
Shiprock NM, 139, 143, 154–56, 158, 160, 168, 174, 199
Show Low and Taylor Irrigation Company, 84
Show Low AZ, 81, 98, 102, 103, 112, 121
Show Low Creek, 84–85
Show Low–Silver Creek Water Conservation and Power District, 84
Shumway AZ, 81, 83, 98
Shungopavi homemaker club, 186
Sierra Bonita Ranch, 26
Sierra Vista AZ, 56
Silver Creek, 82–85, 98

Sulphur Springs Valley Electric
Cooperative (*cont.*)
Cold War, 110; consequences
of, 215; construction of electrical system, 47–50, *48, 50, 51*;
creation of, 40–50, 213, 256n6;
customer surveys by, 43–44; employees of, 47, 49, 71; encouraging electrical use, 49, 118; expanding customer base, 53–56;
incorporation of, 43; and local
community, 70–71,
73; opting out of, 44; power
plant, *55*; and San Carlos Apache
Indian Agency, 69; service area
and customers of, 215; World
War II's effects on, 50–56. *See
also* Arizona Electric Power Cooperative Association; Cochise
County; electrical cooperatives;
Graham County
Sumatzkuku, Sarah Jane, 190
Sunrise Ski Resort, 126
"survivance" concept, 257n22
sweathouses, 191
Sweet, Rafe, 95

Talawejei, Charlie, 143
Tate, Harvey, *58*
Taylor AZ, 81, 83, 103
Taylor Grazing Act (1934), 37
technological determinism, 10, 212
technology: access to in American
West, 5–11; and cultural bias,
209, 210; effect on Native American life, 205, 206, 216–19; and
environmental consequences,
216; equality of access to, 147,
221–24; and Graham County
farmers, 54; historiography of,
9–11; Hopis' attitudes toward,
191; Mormons' experience with,
83; Native American resistance
to, 188–89; Navajos' attitudes toward, 150, 192; Native American
attitudes toward, 218–19; in New
Mexico, 68; school curriculum
on, 65–66; in southeastern Arizona, 25, 27, 73; transformation
of West through, 5, 6; and wom-
en's work opportunities, 67. *See
also* industrialization; urbanization; urban life
Teec Nos Pos AZ, 167
telecommunications services.
See Internet access; telephone
service
telephone service: on Hopi lands,
189; on Navajo Reservation, 142,
146, 149; and Navopache line
extensions, 108; in northeastern Arizona, 147; provided by
REA cooperatives, 213; scarcity
of in Arizona and New Mexico,
144; in White Mountain region,
96, 101
television sets: advertisements for,
181; in Apache homes, 125; in
Navajo and Hopi homes, 149,
151–52, 162, 176, 192–94, 198,
199, 200; NTUA instructions on
use of, 183; popularity of, 65
Tenakhongva, Cheryl, 190
Tenakhongva, Ted, 185
Tennessee Valley Authority (TVA),
37, 38, 143, 166, 178
termination, 148

Texas, 57–58, 108, 117
Thatcher AZ, 35, 54, 183
Theodore Roosevelt Boarding
    School, 88–90, 89, 139
Timber and Stone Act, 81
Timber Culture Act, 81
The Timberline, 125
Tobey, Ronald, 11
Tohatchi community, 192
Tohono O'odham community, 25
Tohono O'odham Tribal Utility Au-
    thority, 221
Tolson, R. J., 143
Tombstone AZ, 24, 33, 56
Toreva 4-H club, 188
Toreva homemaker club, 186
tourism industry, 53, 100, 116, 126–
    28, 176, 195, 210, 214–15. *See
    also* recreational enterprises
Tracy, Deesheeny Nez, 187, 193–94
trading posts, 138, 139, 141, 151, 154,
    206
trailer parks, 195, 196, 197
transmission. *See* power
    transmission
transportation, 101–2, 127, 132, 150.
    See also railroad; roads
Treaty of 1868, 137–38, 179
Treaty of Guadalupe-Hidalgo
    (1848), 18
treaty rights, dismissal of, 148
tribal constitutions, 141–42
tribal enterprises, 164–65, 167, 172,
    204, 213
Tribal Resource Institute in Busi-
    ness, Engineering, and Science,
    219
Tribal Rural Electrification Pro-
    gram, 223

tribal trust lands, 123, 165
Trico Electric Cooperative, 113–14,
    213, 256n6
Truman, Harry, 99, 110
Tuba City Indian agency, 139, 143
Tuba City AZ, 131, 143, 152, 154, 157,
    169, 175, 176
Tucson AZ, 14, 18, 27, 30, 65, 115,
    126, 162
Tucson Electric Power, 113–14, 206
Turner, Frederick Jackson, 7–8, 10

Udall, Stewart, 169
United Order, 82
University of Arizona, 30, 46
University of Oklahoma, 167
uranium, 4, 133, 134, 149, 152, 155
urban customers, 34, 51, 111–13
urbanization: of American West, 6,
    8–12, 212; in Arizona, 14–16, 72;
    through cooperative rural orga-
    nization, 73; through electrifica-
    tion, 20; of Native Americans,
    133; U.S. government promotion
    of, 3, 64–65; in White Mountain
    region, 94. *See also* industrial-
    ization; technology
urban life: effect of rural electrifica-
    tion on, 214–15; Native Ameri-
    cans' exposure to, 69, 104, 153,
    181, 188, 190, 199, 217
U.S. Army, 136–37. *See also* military
    bases
U.S. Census Bureau, 9, 24–25, 79,
    132, 228n4
U.S. Congress: and competition of
    power providers, 111, 113–16; and
    decommissioning of Fort Apache,

U.S. Congress (*cont.*)
88; and demarcation of Apache
reservations, 80; on deregulation, 5; on farming, 29; on hydroelectric power, 52, 131; land
distribution acts of, 81; and
Navajos, 137, 147, 164; and par-
titioning of Navajo and Hopi
land, 176; on private utilities, 38;
termination of Native American
tribes, 148; World War II–era
legislation by, 51. *See also* U.S.
government
U.S. Department of Agriculture, 61,
64–65, 203. *See also* Agricultural
Extension Service (AES)
U.S. Department of Energy, 4–5
U.S. Department of the Interior, 96
U.S. Forest Service, 53, 96, 102, 107
U.S. Geological Service, 117
U.S. government: and access to
technology in West, 11, 12; agricultural programs of, 69–70;
and control of Arizona, 18; and
control of hydroelectric power,
16; educational programs of, 67;
and electrification of northeastern Arizona, 134, 179; electrification programs of, 3, 72; encouraging power consumption,
61; and environmental consequences, 216; land distribution
of, 25; and loans during Cold
War, 109, 110; on modernization of Native Americans, 206;
on Navajo and Hopi land status,
174; Navajos employed with,
145; power transmission system
to Shiprock, 160; promotion of

modernization, 64–65, 134, 217;
on quality of life, 20; on race
and class, 68; regulation/dereg-
ulation by, 5–7, 38–39, 219–21,
224; relationship with Navajos
and Hopis, 136–44, 146–47; role
in electrification, 4–5, 209, 210,
212; in White Mountain region,
79, 128, 129. *See also* Agricultural Extension Service (AES);
land, federal; Rural Electrification Administration (REA); U.S.
Congress
U.S. Indian Service projects, 16
U.S. Soil Conservation Services, 117
U.S. War Department, 80
Utah, 81, 83, 135
Utah Construction Company, 154,
157, 169
Utah Mining and Construction
Company, 162
Utah Power and Light Company, 158
utilities: education in operation of,
183; in Kansas Settlement, 71–
72; on Navajo Reservation, 142–
43, 148, 152, 155; regulation in
Arizona, 14–16; in southeastern
Arizona, 33, 35–36, 38; in Tomb-
stone, 56. *See also* Navajo Tribal
Utility Authority (NTUA)
utopian societies, 82

vacuum cleaners, 181, 198, 200
Valle Redondo. *See* Round Valley
Vanderhoof, Philip W. "Vance," 156,
161, 163, 165, 168, 170, 171
Verde Electric Cooperative, 112, 213,
256n6

Verde River, 83
Vernon AZ, 121
Veterans Administration, 123
Vietnam War, 115
villages, 153
Vizenor, Gerald, 257n22
vocational training, 88, 123, 152–53,
  167, 169, 182–85. *See also* education

Walters, Harry, 203
Warne, William, 147
War on Poverty, 116, 124, 190, 195,
  211. *See also* poverty
water conservation, 82–85
water programs, 14. *See also* hydroelectric power production
water pumping, domestic, 62–63,
  103, 127. *See also* irrigation
  pumping
water service, 56, 125, 132, 140,
  142–43, 155, 182, 185, 191
water storage, 16, 82–83
water supply: and dry-farm movement, 31; effect of electrification
  on, 215–16, 218; on Navajo Reservation, 170; in northeastern
  Arizona, 135, 137, 138; in southeastern Arizona, 27–31, 39, 45–
  46, 57–58; in White Mountain
  region, 78. *See also* irrigation; irrigation pumping
"Watts with the Women" newsletter, 62
Wauneka, Annie Dodge, 166, 173,
  185
Webb, Walter Prescott, 12
Weech, Cherrel Batty, 22

Weech, David, 35
welfare programs, 121, 133
Wesley, Clarence, 69
Western Energy Supply and Transmission Associates (WEST), 178
Westinghouse Company, 66
wheat, 31, 54, 58
Wheeler-Rayburn Bill. *See* Public
  Utility Holding Company Act
  (1935)
White, Richard, 145
"The White City," 7
White Cone AZ, 176, 196
White Mountain Apache Indians:
  4-H clubs of, 122; and desire for
  electricity, 104, 109; legal status
  of, 122; lifestyle of, 79–81, 122–
  23, 130, 186; and lumber industry, 93–97; on national rural
  electrification legislation, 114;
  and Navopache cooperative,
  124–27; as part of non-Native
  power grid, 133; population of,
  79; power demands of, 85–93,
  104–5; and REA loan, 128; reservation of, 101. *See also* Apache
  Indians; Fort Apache Indian
  Reservation
White Mountain Apache Tribal
  Council, 125, 126
White Mountain Electric Cooperative, 99. *See also* Navopache
  Electric Cooperative
White Mountain Recreational Enterprise, 123
White Mountain region: attitudes
  toward electricity in, 84; benefits
  of electrification in, 115–16;

White Mountain region (*cont.*)
construction projects in, 102–3;
demographics of service area,
116–27; description of, 78–79;
extension workers in, 119–22;
integration of power in, 127–30;
leisure and recreation in, 107,
214–15; local electrical systems
in, 84–85, 97; lumbering in, 77,
79, 93–97, 102, 105, 124, 125,
127; population of, 79–83; postwar improvements in, 101–2,
127; power requirements of,
77–79, 99–100; pursuit of REA
funds in, 211; uniqueness of
electrification in, 116–27
White Mountain Utility Authority,
125
White River, 80, 90
Whiteriver AZ: boarding school at,
88; extension of Navopache lines
from, 123; Fort Apache Indian
Agency in, *88*; housing in, 91;
power sources of, 77, 86–87;
power transmission to, 90, 106,
126; residents of, 80; roads to, 83
Whiteriver Fair, 121
Whiteriver Indian Agency, *92*
Whitewater AZ, 66
wickiups, 91, 95, 104, 120, 122, 125
Wide Ruins AZ, 151
Wilkinson, Charles, 149
Willcox AZ, 26, 28–30, 33–34, 43,
47, 52, 62
Willcox Lighting, Pumping, and Ice
Company, 32–33
Willcox Playa, 28
Willeto, Frank, 188

Williams, Paul, 163
Willie Wiredhand, 118, *119*, 182
Wilson, Janet Lynn, 91
Window Rock AZ, 142, 158, 162,
168, 182, 187, 192
wind power, 28, 32, 62–63, 214, 223
Wingate Indian Village, 153, 188
Winslow AZ, 97
wireless technology, 222, 223
Wolf, Walter, 160
women: as cooperative members,
61; education of Apache, 90;
marketing to, 61–68, 120–21,
152; in Navopache service area,
118–21; pre-electrification chores
of, 21–23; REA and Country Life
reformers' appeal to, 44; role of
in NTUA, 185–87; traditional life
of Navajo, 191; use of radios by
Navajo, 151. *See also* domestic
market; gender
wood, 140, 153. *See also* lumbering
Woodruff AZ, 103
wool, 136, 138, 144
World War I, 214
World War II, 50–56, 69, 99, 123,
133, 144, 179, 211
Worster, Donald, 10, 69

Yazzie, Allen, 163
Young AZ, 108, 109
youth programs, 64. *See also* children; 4-H programs

Zah, Peterson, 142–43, 187, 205
zinc mining, 26, 33, 53. *See also*
mining operations
Zuni Indians, 135